Praise for *The Leader's Window*

"Most of the time people don't retain training concepts beyond ninety days. After five years, there are key managers who refer to and use *The Leader's Window*. Several of our most successful executives use the performance contracting process almost religiously. It is no accident that their divisions produce results and they leave solid teams in place when they advance to higher levels."

 J. Kevin Schmidt, Vice President, Human Resources,
 Saint-Gobain Abrasives-North America

"*The Leader's Window* should be required reading for leaders and team members of any organization that is serious about empowering teams to make a difference. Until the L4 System is mastered, other concepts of sharing leadership are without purpose and lacking discipline. This is the very best book for influencing successful work team design and implementation."

 Jack D. Orsburn, Ph.D., President, Orsburn Team Works, Inc.,
 and author of *Self-Directed Work Teams*

"So many emerging leaders are in hot pursuit of the holy grail—the one perfect way to lead. *The Leader's Window* helps them see that there is no one perfect way and provides them with practical tools and approaches to assess situations and lead effectively."

 Thomas J. Bailer, Vice President, Organization Development & Corporate
 Education, The Hartford Financial Services Group, Inc.

"*The Leader's Window* presents a proven approach to raising the performance levels of individuals and teams. It's a consistently effective way to establish goals and priorities, to create smooth and productive working relationships, and to measure and reward fairly. It is especially useful in helping managers strike the critical style balances necessary to coach people of all levels and capabilities to their full performance potential."

 Howard Deck, Vice President, Super Abrasives Division, Saint-Gobain Abrasives

"In my twenty-six years of experience, I have never found any leadership approach that compares with *The Leader's Window* for simplicity, clarity, proactive application and accountability, or measurable achievement. While sharing this approach with hundreds of organizations, I've gotten rave reviews. *The Leader's Window* works!"

 Robert P. McClendon, Jr., President, McClendon Management, Inc.

"*The Leader's Window* approach has provided our managers the tools they need to improve communications, with the appropriate mix of clear direction and support, to all our field technicians. We've found that constant focus on these basic needs makes leading our team successfully much easier and more profitable."

 Gerald M. Riggs, President, Ampam Riggs Plumbing

"*The Leader's Window* is more than a management theory. It turns on the light for managers to realize that a 'one-size-fits all' leadership style does not work. It gives managers the 'how-to' training they need to manage people effectively."

 Fred Hermann, Vice President of Operations,
 Younger Brothers Construction

"*The Leader's Window* is an incredibly practical book that takes the mystery out of leadership. It speaks to the challenges of leaders at all levels and gives them tools that really work on the job with their people. Can leadership be learned? With this book, the answer is yes!"

Ashley Penney, President, Catalyst Consulting & Training

"*The Leader's Window* and the taxonomy of leadership styles the authors have devised are both insightful and useful. They can help reduce execution risk."

Dick Sabot, Chairman, eZiba.com,
and Professor Emeritus of Economics, Williams College

"The unique insights offered in this book are bound to add value to you and your company. If the authors' concepts are implemented within an organization, it will operate more efficiently by increasing the effectiveness of management, resulting in less rework and much higher profits."

Roy Humphreys, President, Shea Homes

THE
Leader's
Window

MASTERING THE FOUR STYLES

OF LEADERSHIP TO BUILD

HIGH-PERFORMING TEAMS

• Second Edition •

JOHN D. W. BECK
NEIL M. YEAGER

DAVIES-BLACK PUBLISHING
Mountain View, California

Published by Davies-Black Publishing, an imprint of CPP, Inc., 1055 Joaquin Road, 2nd Floor, Mountain View, CA 94043; 800-624-1765.

Special discounts on bulk quantities of Davies-Black books are available to corporations, professional associations, and other organizations. For details, contact the Director of Marketing and Sales at Davies-Black Publishing; 650-691-9123; fax 650-623-9271.

Visit the Davies-Black web site at www.daviesblack.com.

Printed in the United States of America.

Library of Congress Cataloging-in-Publication Data
Beck, John D. W.
     The leader's window: mastering the four styles of leadership to build high-performing teams / John D. W. Beck, Neil M. Yeager.—2nd ed.
          p. cm.
     Includes bibliographical references and index.
     ISBN 978-1-85788-676-4
     1. Leadership. 2. Teams in the workplace. I. Yeager, Neil M. II. Title
     HD57.7 .B428 2001
     658.4'092—dc21

                                                                2001028949

SECOND EDITION
First printing 2001

Contents

Preface

If you are part of any business, at any level, in almost any part of the world, you know that leadership and teamwork are two drivers of organizational success for the twenty-first century. You also know that leaders are continually challenged by the never-ending change and uncertainty of the contemporary workplace.

The global economy is putting unprecedented pressure on every organization to give customers what they want in the most cost-effective ways. The organizations that will thrive in this competitive environment will be the ones that can focus the brainpower of their people—the ones that have leaders who can get teams to deliver results.

Are you that kind of leader? Or do you find yourself struggling to transform individuals in your organization into a high-performing team?

Do you know what kind of leadership works in every situation or would you like to be sure you are using the right leadership approach with the right people at the right times?

Do you know how to turn unmotivated people into highly effective workers? Or are you too busy with your own work to get the people around you to do what needs to be done?

If these are the kinds of questions that prevent you from harnessing the power of the people in your organization, then we'd like to introduce you to a proven, surefire formula for success that we call The Leader's Window^{SM}.

What is The Leader's Window? It's a structure with four small windows of leadership—four equally good but different styles for leading people. Each one has its place, and this book will give you many examples of leaders who use each style with great success. The challenge is knowing where and when to use each one and developing your agility to use all four. That's what The Leader's Window is all about.

In this book, we will show you a new strategy for leading individuals. The best leaders in every organization have been doing this for years. Once you understand it, you will know what to do to help your people perform to the best of their potential.

We will also show you a new strategy for orchestrating the group dynamics that can make or break a team. The best leaders know how to inspire groups to great accomplishments. Once you know what they do, you will know how to take advantage of the power of team spirit.

Finally, we will show you how to put these two strategies together: four simple secrets for building and maintaining the high-performance teamwork that is necessary for guaranteeing your organization's long-term success.

"Isn't being a leader more about good instincts than elaborate techniques?" you may ask. While using your intuition to help you be effective as a leader can prove very valuable, there is a complexity in today's workplace that requires more than just good instincts.

"Aren't real leaders born?" you might ask. Leading is more than a birthright reserved for the lucky few. We know from our work in many organizations for the past twenty-five years that most people can learn how to lead. We also know that learning to lead in today's complex world is a lot more complicated than who you know and where you come from.

Most of the leaders and aspiring leaders we know talk about feeling boxed in by conflicting demands—one set of messages from above pressuring them to lead forcefully, and a different set of messages from below expecting them to lead empathically. Do you feel trapped in this kind of box? The Leader's Window will show you the way out of this trap with a solution that meets the needs of the people you work for and the people who work for you.

By following the secrets of The Leader's Window, you'll learn a step-by-step approach to maximizing the full potential of everyone around you, and you'll learn how to adapt and change your approach as situations change and circumstances shift.

These are demanding times in an increasingly competitive world. The organizations that endure will be able to make the most of their human resource—their people. We know from our experience that The Leader's Window can help you be one of those people—a leader who can give your organization the competitive edge—and we welcome the opportunity to help you develop that edge.

JOHN BECK   NEIL YEAGER

Acknowledgments

The Leader's Window is based on The L4® System for High-Performing Teams, which was designed and developed by coauthor John Beck, one of the founders of the Charter Oak Consulting Group of Berlin, Connecticut. Charter Oak is a team of consultants who specialize in helping organizations strengthen their performance through leadership, teamwork, and organizational effectiveness.

Over the years, significant input to The L4 System has been provided by the members of the Charter Oak team. L4 was initially developed with substantial support from Elizabeth Beck, Jonathan Spiegel, and Tony Daloisio. Over the last ten years, important transformations to the system have been provided by coauthor Neil Yeager. We also appreciate the support of other Charter Oak colleagues past and present who have embraced our ideas and challenged our thinking: Barry Carden, Diane Flaherty, Rene Carew, Cliff Scott, Christine Galske, Carlene Merrill, Jeff Stone, Gisele Garcia, Jean Kim, Roberta McLaughlin, and Jim Hassinger. Special thanks go to Charter Oakers Cathy Crosky and Moira Garvey, whose research assistance was invaluable in helping us update the real-world examples that bring the L4 styles to life. As a team effort, The L4 System is based on more than 100 years of collective experience working with Fortune 500 companies, as well as small and medium-sized businesses, government agencies, universities, and not-for-profit organizations.

Special acknowledgment needs to be given to Ken Blanchard and Paul Hersey (1982), coauthors of Situational Leadership Theory, which was the forerunner of The L4 System, and without which L4 would not exist. When Ken was a professor at the University of Massachusetts, both of us had the honor of learning about leadership at the feet of one of the masters. Feedback from our clients and input from our colleagues has made L4 significantly different from Situational Leadership, but without Ken's guidance and the knowledge base of Situational Leadership, we would never have started down the L4 path.

The Hersey-Blanchard Situational Leadership Theory defined the four leadership styles in terms of task behavior and relationships behavior; and Blanchard's Situational Leadership II described the same styles in terms of directive behavior and supportive behavior. In addition, the designations of S1-S2-S3-S4 were first used by Hersey and Blanchard (1982) as a shorthand way to refer to the four leadership styles in a sequence that progresses from most control to least control. Their theory is the foundation of what we call the development cycle.

The L4 System also has some roots in the earlier leadership models on which Situational Leadership was based. In fact, the four basic leadership styles are based on a long history of leadership theories that we would like to acknowledge. Lewin, Lippitt, and White (1960) used the terms authoritarian and democratic to define leadership styles; Tannenbaum and Schmidt (1958) defined a continuum of boss-centered versus subordinate-centered leadership styles. Stogdill and Coons (1959) used the terms initiating structure and consideration to define the four leadership styles in the Ohio State University Leadership Studies (which laid the groundwork for all situational leadership approaches). Rensis Likert (1961) studied the differences between production-centered and employee-centered leaders. Blake and Mouton's (1964) Managerial Grid defined leadership styles in terms of concern for production versus concern for people. Fred E. Fiedler's (1967) Contingency Theory examined the situations that were best suited for task-directed versus human relations leaders. William J. Reddin's (1967) 3-D Model defined the four styles in terms of task-oriented versus maintenance-oriented leaders, effective versus ineffective. R.F. Bales (1958) used the terms task-oriented versus maintenance-oriented in his research on leadership in groups.

We would also like to acknowledge Victor Vroom for his work on decision making, Joe Litterer and Al Ivey for their thoughts on managerial communication, and B. F. Skinner for his ideas on behavioral reinforcement theory.

In the area of group development, we want to acknowledge the work of many theorists including Will Schutz, Jack and Lorraine Gibb, Warren Bennis and Herb Shepard, and Bruce Tuckman.

We also want to thank Jack Orsburn for his insights on self-directed teams and the ways in which L4 helps them work.

We want to thank our agent, Elizabeth Knappman, who always helps us get our ideas into print. And we are grateful to our colleagues at Davies-Black: Lee Langhammer Law and Alan Shrader for bringing us in, Laura Ackerman-Shaw, Jill Anderson-Wilson and Francie Curtiss for their production and editorial advice and counsel, and Laura Simonds for her support and encouragement in promoting the book.

We also want to say thank you to our clients—the companies who have hired us, the thousands of managers who have attended our training programs, and the hundreds of leaders who have invited us in to bring The Leader's Window to life in their organizations. Without them, our ideas would not have been given a true trial by fire. Their compliments have encouraged our belief that we are onto something new and very valuable. Their criticisms have helped us refine our thinking and make it highly practical. And their war stories from the front lines of management experience have given us the understanding to bring our ideas to life.

Finally, on a more personal note, we are deeply appreciative of our spouses, Elizabeth Beck and Cletha Roney, for their encouragement and support. We also want to thank our children, Laura and Andrew Beck and Ben Roney-Yeager, for sharing us with our computers, modems, and fax machines throughout this endeavor.

About the Authors

JOHN D. W. BECK

John Beck is a founding director of the Charter Oak Consulting Group. Incorporated in 1986, Charter Oak is a management consulting firm that specializes in the people side of business—leadership, teamwork, and organizational effectiveness.

Beck is the creator of *The Leadership 4 System* and coauthor of *The Leader's Window* (first edition, 1994, with Neil Yeager). His consulting focuses on leadership—360-degree feedback and executive coaching based on competency models that are custom-tailored to each client organization's language, culture, opportunities, and challenges. Beck also helps functional and cross-functional teams improve the quality of their teamwork as they confront real-time problems, and he promotes organizational effectiveness by helping leadership teams realign their organizations to produce improved results. Beck conducts training programs on The L4 System, Communication 4 Effective Leadership, Coaching Skills, Teambuilding 4 High Performance, Leadership 4 High-Performing Teams, Consulting Skills, and Organization Alignment.

He has worked with many organizations, including Boise Cascade, BP, Accenture, Carrier, the Connecticut State government, PricewaterhouseCoopers, The Hartford, Heublein, Lotus, Mass Mutual, MCI, Otis, Pratt & Whitney, Saint-Gobain, Shawmut National Bank, and Travelers.

Before starting Charter Oak, Beck spent ten years as a professor in the business school at the University of Hartford. At the university, he served as director of the master of science in organizational behavior program, chairman of the management department, and dean of graduate studies.

He completed his master's and doctoral degrees in organization development at the University of Massachusetts and his bachelor's degree in English at Dartmouth College. He is a founder of the OD Network of Western New England, a past president of the organization, and a former member of its executive committee.

Beck's personal interests include tennis, skiing, windsurfing, movies, plays, books, and complex puzzles. Above all, he loves spending time with his wife, Elizabeth, and two children, Laura and Andrew.

NEIL M. YEAGER

Neil Yeager is a director of the Charter Oak Consulting Group and has twenty years of experience as an organization development consultant. His recent client engagements have focused on executive leadership development through individual and team coaching as well as custom course design and consultation in leadership, change management, and team development. Recent clients include AT Kearney, Bear Stearns, British Petroleum, Carrier, Compaq, Intel, LTV Steel, McKinsey & Company, and Otis Elevator.

He is a frequent speaker at large-scale corporate meetings, specializing in helping organizations create high-impact learning in limited time periods. He has expertise in the development of competency models for the purpose of conducting 360-degree feedback at the executive and managerial levels and in the creation of customized corporate mentoring programs.

Yeager is nationally known in the areas of career and organization development and has written five books in the field: *The Leader's Window* (first edition, 1994, with John Beck), *The Career Doctor* (1991), *Power Interviews* (1990, 1998, with Lee Hough), and *CareerMap* (1988). His book *Power Interviews* was on the 1998 best-seller list of the *Wall Street Journal's National Business Employment Weekly*. He is a frequently quoted expert, and his comments have appeared in the *New York Times, Fortune, Money,* the *Wall Street Journal,* and other national publications.

Yeager is a former senior faculty member in the master's in management program at Cambridge College, where he taught courses in organizational theory and behavior. He was the founding director of the Adult Career Transitions Program at the University of Massachusetts at Amherst.

Yeager holds a doctoral degree in organization development from the University of Massachusetts at Amherst and a master's degree in counseling psychology and a bachelor's degree in English from Central Connecticut State University.

Among his interests are spending time with his family on his farm in western Massachusetts, bicycling, listening to live music, and building his music collection.

Welcome to the World of Leadership

INTRODUCTION

When we first published *The Leader's Window* in 1994, the L4 System for leading high-performing teams had been in existence for seven years. There have been considerable changes in the system as we have adapted it to match the realities of the work world and the increasingly complex demands on leaders. Welcome to the world of leadership.

Seven years after the first edition, much has changed in the marketplace. The transformation of the global economy into a frenetic environment where dot-coms come and go has created a level of economic uncertainty that is unprecedented. Brick and mortar companies are attempting to transform themselves into "click and mortar" entities agile enough to compete in the e-commerce arena. Financial services firms are gobbling each other up at lightning speed, turning them into complex transactional mazes. Industrial giants are consolidating at a dizzying rate, reducing the number of players to a small but powerful few. All of this has created an environment in which effectively leading individuals, teams, and whole organizations can seem like an overwhelmingly daunting task.

Add to this complexity the heightened competition for technologically savvy professionals in a tight labor market. Factor in the arrival of Generation X employees and the free-agent worker mentality they have spawned. Consider the increased preponderance of technology-driven workplace dynamics, resulting in the proliferation of virtual teams and telecommuting. It's easy to see how the ability to attract, develop, and retain talent has become an even more formidable leadership task than it was when the world was simpler and more predictable.

In addition to presenting our latest thinking on how to utilize The Leader's Window to be the best leader you can be, throughout this new edition we will offer advice on how to deal with organizational and cultural changes that impact your leadership effectiveness. We will also offer advice on how to effectively lead people who are fundamentally different from you and how to work with people you will never meet because you are in different parts of the world.

THE LEADER'S DILEMMA: THE PROBLEM

It's easy to be confused about leadership.

First you heard that being a leader means having a vision, pursuing it with passion, and doing whatever it takes to get your people to bring that vision to life. So you got busy driving your people, challenging them to do the right things, pushing them to do everything the right way.

Then you heard a speaker who seemed to make a lot of sense. She said that you won't get the most out of your people over the long run if you keep pushing them relentlessly. You have to support their efforts, this speaker said, help your employees grow and develop, encourage them, and motivate them. So you sat down and talked with the people who work for you, listened to their concerns, and tried coaching them as well as you could.

Then, just when you thought things were moving in the right direction, you read an article claiming that the answer lies in empowerment. Make people feel powerful, it said, and you will be enhancing your own power. Give your people lots of responsibility, and they will learn how to do whatever needs to be done. So you backed off, left your people alone, and waited for them to start feeling empowered. And you really hoped they would because, after the recent downsizing, you didn't have time to spend with them anyway.

The bad news was that your empowered workforce quickly became stretched thin and stressed out from all those responsibilities. The good news was that you had just read a new book that assured you that good leadership is decisive leadership. Take people's suggestions, this author said, but keep hold of the reins. That is the best way to get your employees' buy-in and commitment while ensuring that things get done right. So now you have started spending more time with your people, listening to their ideas and redirecting them whenever they seem to be having problems.

The next wave of inspiration will probably send you back to cracking the whip like you used to do in the first place. If this merry-go-round sounds familiar to you, welcome to the leader's dilemma.

The leader's dilemma is a concern for anyone faced with managerial responsibilities as we head into the twenty-first century. For years, those attempting to explain good leadership have suggested that leadership is a science. From the mechanistic influence of Frederick Taylor's *The Principles of Scientific Management* (1911) to the humanistic, behavioral science approaches of the 1960s to the search for excellence and one-minute solutions of the 1980s, people have been trying to pinpoint the answer to the leadership question.

In Search of Excellence (Peters and Waterman 1982) helped a lot of executives recognize the need to build a strong organizational culture, and *The One-Minute Manager* (Blanchard and Johnson 1981) reminded all managers to set goals and give praise. But most managers are still looking for more complete explanations about how to lead. Unfortunately, what has emerged is more philosophical explanations for leadership. Leaders need to take control, said Warren Bennis and Burt Nanus in their book *Leaders: The Strategies for Taking Charge* (1985). There is an art to leadership, proclaimed Max Depree, chairman of the Herman Miller Furniture Company, in his inspirational book *Leadership Is an Art* (1989).

In the 1990s, the quest to understand what it takes to build and sustain organizations expanded outward. Margaret Wheatley, in her thought-provoking book *Leadership and the New Science* (1992), suggested that we could understand organizations better by looking to the sciences of quantum physics, chaos theory, and molecular biology. In *The Fifth Discipline* (1990), Peter Senge and his colleagues at MIT proposed the notion of the learning organization, a systems approach to managing organizations that urged organizational leaders to conquer their company's learning disabilities. Their "systems approach" continued to have broad appeal throughout the 1990s as they released several volumes on how to create learning organizations, including *The Fifth Discipline Field Book* (1994) and *The Dance of Change* (1999).

At the same time that would-be leaders sought help by looking to other disciplines, they also went inward. Having effective habits and the right principles are the keys, suggested Stephen Covey in his book *Principle-Centered Leadership* (1990). Building on his groundbreaking *7 Habits of Highly Effective People,* he paved the way for looking at leadership from the inside out. The study of emotional intelligence became popular as the notion that understanding self and others gained broad acceptance as a key to corporate success. Daniel Goleman's books *Emotional Intelligence* (1994) and *Working with Emotional Intelligence* (1998) suggested that EQ was a greater factor for leadership success than IQ, and the corporate world embraced the notion of "know thyself" (and each other) like never before. The continued success and increased popularity of personality inventories like the *Myers-Briggs Type Indicator*® (MBTI®) instrument further reinforced the value of psychology in the workplace.

Yet most people who have tried to lead—successfully or otherwise—know that taking charge is easier said than done. Inspiration, good habits, and right principles are absolutely critical but aren't always enough. Broadening your perspective by exploring the universe and the psyche is a worthy pursuit but doesn't in and of itself lead to results. Taking charge can give you credibility, and inspiration may be the catalyst for getting others to take action. Principles are most likely the right foundation for aligning yourself and your organization, and increased awareness of self and others helps you make better choices. But the bottom line is that performance that leads to desired results must be orchestrated carefully if you are going to succeed as a leader.

So what's the answer? All the clients we work with are trying to increase their competitiveness by driving down costs, listening to their customers, empowering their employees, and creating a team-based culture committed to continuous improvement. Some days they find themselves going crazy because they aren't sure if they should be driving or listening, empowering or improving. What they want to know is how to do all of these things at once.

THE LEADER'S WINDOW: THE SOLUTION

We believe there is a solution to this complex question of leadership. It does not come from a debate about art versus science, inspiration versus perspiration, character versus competence, or principles versus power. It comes from understanding the essential behaviors for simultaneously challenging a team of people to reach for a vision while empowering each individual team member to take the actions that are needed to achieve that vision. High-performance leadership exists when everyone, leaders and followers, is performing at his or her highest level—whether alone or in teams—all of the time.

The guide we use for ensuring that your approach to leadership works all the time, every time, is called The Leader's Window. The Leader's Window will not give you a quick fix, because leading people requires a concerted effort and needs to be sustained over time. What it will give you is a methodology for using your actions as a leader in a focused and purposeful way. It is a guide for promoting teamwork that maximizes the potential of every individual while fully utilizing the power that can come from getting a group of people to work together to achieve a shared mission.

To understand the secrets of The Leader's Window, you will need to learn the art and science of what we call The Leadership 4 System. Sometimes we just refer to the system as Leadership 4. And sometimes we simply call it L4. Whatever you decide to call it, Leadership 4 is a highly refined approach to understanding the needs of both individuals and groups in a way that leads to high-performance teamwork. It is about people doing their best because they're skilled, knowledgeable, empowered, interested, confident, willing, and aligned with the goals of your organization.

The L4 System is based on prior research on leadership, communication, decision making, reward systems, individual motivation, and group development. By expanding on those ideas, making them more precise and user friendly, L4 will teach you how to lead others in a way that maximizes results for them, for you, for your team, and for the organization you are a part of.

From your journey through The L4 System and mastery of its simple, yet proven, techniques, you will discover the secrets of The Leader's Window and unravel the mysteries of high-performance leadership. As you read through this book, you will receive practical as well as inspirational advice that will make you a more effective leader.

Here's an overview of what you will find:

- Chapter 1 sets the stage for thinking about leadership by emphasizing that teamwork requires getting each team member to perform to the best of his or her potential and creating group dynamics that foster synergy among those individuals. It also includes a short questionnaire that invites you to say what you would do if you were the leader in ten managerial situations.

- Chapter 2 defines the four leadership styles of The L4 System in terms of decision-making, communication, and recognition strategies and illustrates each style with well-known TV characters.

- Chapters 3 through 6 bring each leadership style to life with profiles of political and business leaders plus real case studies that show the value of each style.

- Chapter 7 shows you your personal Window of Leadership, including the main, backup, and limited styles that you selected on the questionnaire in chapter 1. You will also get feedback about the strengths and weaknesses of your leadership profile.

- Chapter 8 introduces the empowerment cycle for leading individuals — a new strategy based on our research about what the best leaders really do. This strategy totally revamps the way most managers have been taught to work with people, and it is extremely simple to use. Included are real-world examples of how the best leaders make the new paradigm work for them.

- Chapter 9 explains how to match all four styles to a follower's task-specific potential by using a simple method for diagnosing ability and motivation. This chapter also gives you additional feedback about your responses to the ten cases in chapter 1. You will see whether you are using the styles with the right people at the right times.

- Chapter 10 invites you to try out the concepts from chapters 8 and 9 and shows you how to bring them to life with real cases and a question-and-answer format that guides you to create your own applications. It also includes information on how to manage the new reality of the free-agent workforce and how to best use technology when leading individuals.

- Chapter 11 addresses the issue of personality and leading individuals. Using the four preference scales of the *Myers-Briggs Type Indicator* assessment, you will learn how to effectively empower people who operate from each of the eight personality preferences.

- Chapter 12 shifts away from leading individuals to the question of creating effective group dynamics. It introduces the group devlopment cycle for understanding and leading groups and includes cases to illustrate this way of thinking. It also includes advice on how personality can affect group dynamics.

- Chapter 13 puts The Leader's Window together by showing you how to integrate the individual empowerment cycle with the group development cycle. The four secrets in this chapter explain how to use the four leadership styles in a clear sequence that builds and maintains high-performing teams. Real-world cases illustrating this sequence show you how it is done and the consequences of ignoring the secrets. Included are the seven myths of teamwork and tips on how to deal with virtual teams.

Whether you are the CEO of a company, an upper-level manager, a frontline supervisor, or the informal leader of the XYZ task force, *The Leader's Window* will provide you with insights, information, and practical tools for harnessing the potential of each individual and transforming that potential into high-performing teams.

Windows on the World
of Leadership

CHAPTER 1

The only constant is change. As we enter the twenty-first century, it is hard to think of an industry that has not undergone massive transformation in the past ten years. It's impossible to know for certain what the future will bring, but if the trend at the start of the new millennium is any indication, there will be more mergers, acquisitions, divestitures, spin-offs, and start-ups.

Companies are merging at an astounding rate. Exxon and Mobil have joined forces. BP spent the 1990s systematically acquiring its competitors, including Amoco and Arco. Disney owns ABC and ESPN, GE owns NBC, and AOL Time Warner is creating a media empire the likes of which has never been seen before. American Airlines purchased TWA. Upstart Worldcom bought MCI, while Bell Atlantic joined forces with GTE and Vodaphone to create the cellular powerhouse Verizon.

While many corporations are merging to survive and thrive in this volatile global marketplace, others are shrinking as they struggle to hold on to market share. Industry icons like AT&T and Xerox have seen their value drop precipitously. So have Lucent, Intel, and Microsoft. This sort of change has become so commonplace that in late 2000, when insurance giant Aetna sold a significant percentage of its customer base to ING in order to focus exclusively on medical insurance, no one batted an eye.

A little more surprising, because it had existed under a bubble of optimism, was the large-scale reduction of players in the dot-com world. Recent estimates are that 90 percent of the dot-coms existing at the end of 2000 will fail within the next few years unless they are anchored to a more traditional "brick and mortar" company—or are adopted by a more venerable one. For example, e-tailing giant Amazon.com currently has interests in Drugstore.com, Pets.com, HomeGrocer.com, and a host of other struggling ventures.

The volatility has been accelerating for some time. When corporate giants like IBM and General Motors went through several massive white-collar layoffs in the 1990s, it became clear that the corporate landscape was changing irrevocably. By the end of 2000 such actions had become commonplace. If you had been hoping that job security in America was going to make a comeback, or that lifelong employment would be adopted as the way to compete globally, you knew that hope was gone and started digging in for the long fight.

The truth is that the implicit pact between worker and leader has been banished forever. The idea of motivating good performance with job security may have helped the leaders of the industrial age or even the "intrapreneurs" of the first leg of the information age, but it is not enough for the leaders of the emerging age of uncertainty. The new employment model is free agency. Long employed in the sports world, it has replaced the model of the organization man or woman and the careerist model that followed.

Successful leaders of the twenty-first century will be those who give these free agents what they need, when they need it, in a form in which they can use it. The new leaders will be those who provide people with what they need to perform to the best of their potential. This approach is a far cry from either the authoritarian approach or the gentle helper approach espoused in earlier leadership theories. It is an approach based on the belief that volatile organizations require adaptable leaders—people who understand the dynamics of life in the contemporary organization and who are experts at matching their leadership actions to employees' performance needs.

As the business world continues to reinvent and restructure itself, one of the most significant changes is the demise of the professional manager. Since the onset of the industrial revolution, those at the top have depended on these "middle managers" to make sure that those at the bottom do what needs to be done. The wholesale elimination of layers of middle managers whose role was to orchestrate the activities of others means that everyone in an organization is now a potential manager. Add in new employment models resulting in large numbers of contract employees and consultants, plus new organizational models that make reporting relationships ambiguous, and the picture gets even more complicated. What today's managers need most— including everyone from the CEO to the person at the lowest level in the shrunken hierarchy—is to learn how to lead in the fast lane.

Working with other people to do more with fewer resources is the biggest challenge facing organizations as we begin the twenty-first century. Not just big corporations are affected. Small and medium-sized businesses are struggling just to stay alive, and as big corporations continue to reinvent themselves, more small businesses are cropping up on the horizon. Not-for-profits are also squeezed tighter than ever. And government agencies are under incredible scrutiny, not to mention whole governments that are being toppled all over the world.

Leadership is in the headlines every day. George W. Bush versus Al Gore, and the Florida Supreme Court versus the United States Supreme Court, in the 2000 presidential election. Tony Blair in Great Britain. Vladimir Putin in Russia. Zealous leaders perpetuating conflict between Israel and the Palestinians. The clerical leadership of the Mullahs in Iran. The military leadership of Saddam Hussein in Iraq. Tribal leadership in Eastern Europe and in several parts of Africa.

Leadership is what makes business news as well. Ford's Jacques Nasser and his valiant efforts to deal with the Firestone tire crisis. Carly Fiorina's reinvigoration of computer giant Hewlett-Packard. Sam Walton's legacy at Wal-Mart. Jack Welch's tough-minded but people-involving success at General Electric. Andy Grove's ongoing success at Intel. Bill Gates's intellectually confrontational software mecca Microsoft. Oracle's Larry Ellison and his efforts to dethrone Gates as master of the software universe. Michael Dell's direct line to the customer. Herb Kelleher's customer-oriented approach to air travel. Warren Buffet's quiet and consistent stewardship of conglomerate Berkshire Hathaway. The transition at Apple from Steve Jobs's technowizardry to John Sculley's marketing acumen and back to Jobs's creative stewardship. Oprah's burgeoning empire and pervasive influence. Profits and greed on Wall Street. The internationalization of entire industries. Searching for the right partnership between business and government in order to compete in the worldwide marketplace.

Leadership is everywhere—not just at the top, like the world leaders and business leaders mentioned above. Whether you are a CEO or a frontline supervisor, knowing how to lead people is the hardest part of the job. And the underlying questions behind every discussion about leadership are: How do you succeed and how do you avoid failure? How do you breed winners instead of losers? How do you build competitive spirit and avoid complacency? What do you say and do to deliver top-quality results and enhance your reputation as a leader?

Leadership is no picnic. If you are going to learn how to be a good leader, you will have to open your mind to new ideas without discarding all of your old ideas. Moving into the future does not mean letting go of everything you have done in the past. It means getting perpetually smarter about how you integrate the old and the new. It means taking what you know about the science of leadership and blending that with the finesse that comes from the art of leadership.

Learning to lead also means not getting caught up in the unrealistic search for quick-fix solutions to complex problems. If we have learned anything in our years of working with thousands of managers from all kinds of organizations, it is that leadership is one very big challenge. If leadership were easy, a lot more people would be good at it.

Finally, becoming a good leader also means taking a good hard look at yourself because what you think you do may not be what you really do. To help you look at yourself, before you read too far, we want to invite you to play the leadership game with us. This will give you a chance to think about yourself as a leader while you read this book.

WHAT KIND OF LEADER ARE YOU?

On the following pages, you will find ten short cases that will help you think about the ways you lead people. Each case describes a common work situation that is typical of the problems that confront most managers. After each case, you will find four possible actions, each of which is used frequently by a large number of leaders.

As you read each case, don't try to guess the "right" answer. What is right for you may not be right for someone else. Just choose the actions that are typical of you and the ways you interact with people when you are the leader. Here's what to do:

1. Read each case and imagine yourself as the leader in that situation.

2. Read the actions and think about what you typically do in that type of situation.

3. If one action stands out as describing you, give five points to that action by writing the number 5 in the space beside it.

4. If no single action describes how you would handle the situation, you can divide the five points in any combination that adds up to five: $(4 + 1)$, $(3 + 2)$, $(2 + 2 + 1)$.

Be sure that your responses for every case add up to exactly five points, no more and no less. For example:

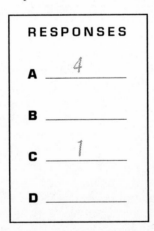

RESPONSES

A _____ 4 _____

B _____

C _____ 1 _____

D _____

Read these cases and have some fun thinking about what you would do in each one. Remember that what you really say and what you really do is where the rubber meets the road in the game of leadership. Later on, in chapters 7, 9, and 12, we will show you how to interpret your responses to these cases so that you can see what your leadership profile looks like.

CASE 1

Tom has recently joined your department and seems nervous about his new work. He is reluctant to take on much responsibility because he is not sure his skills are right for the job. You are confident that he will be fine as soon as he learns the job.

Actions

A. Ask him to identify the skills he brings to the job and then tell him how to use them in productive ways.

B. Give him a full orientation to his new job and tell him what he needs to do to get started.

C. Keep an eye on him from a distance to see what he can figure out on his own.

D. Ask him to identify the skills he brings to the job and help him discover his own ways to apply them.

RESPONSES

A _0_

B _2_

C _1_

D _2_

CASE 2

Susan was assigned to you after a rocky experience in another region. She is talented and confident, but she resists learning the job requirements and wants to work with customers entirely in her own way.

Actions

A. Ask her about her past experience and then tell her how her work here should be done.

B. Ask her about her past experience and then help her think through a plan for getting started.

C. Review the customer list with her and tell her what to do to get started.

D. Give her a chance on her own before saying anything.

RESPONSES

A _0_

B _3_

C _0_

D _2_

CASE 3

Joe has joined your department with great enthusiasm and confidence. He has a proven track record and is in tune with your goals. Mostly, he needs to get oriented to the specifics of his new responsibilities and the ins and outs of how this company works.

Actions

A. Help him to think through the new assignment and develop his own training plan.

B. Let him know that you are confident that he can learn the job on his own.

C. Explain the job requirements and then tell him what he should do and why.

D. Explain the job requirements and then seek his input as you develop a training plan for him.

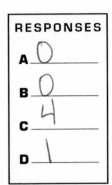

RESPONSES

A __0__

B __0__

C __4__

D __1__

CASE 4

Jane is a great saleswoman who consistently makes you and the company look good. Usually, you just stay out of her way, but lately you have thought that you should let her know that you are still the manager.

Actions

A. Give her recognition for doing so well and remind her that you're there if she needs anything.

B. Ask her to update you on her activities and then tell her which ones you think she should pursue.

C. Ask her what seems to be working best for her and listen to her plans for the near future.

D. Review her customer list and tell her what she should be doing with each one.

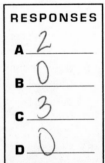

RESPONSES

A __2__

B __0__

C __3__

D __0__

CASE 5

Ted has worked in your department for the past five years. He is technically sound but does not understand the big picture. He has also turned off several people with his aggressive enthusiasm. Since his last performance appraisal, in which you gave him some honest feedback, his confidence seems to be shaken.

Actions

A. Redirect him so that he understands exactly what he needs to do differently.

B. Listen to his concerns and then help him think through the steps he wants to take.

C. Be patient and wait for him to come around on his own.

D. Listen to his concerns and then redirect him so that he understands exactly what he needs to do differently.

RESPONSES

A _0_

B _3_

C _0_

D _2_

CASE 6

You have assigned Martha, one of your best employees, to collect consumer data that will be needed for your department's upcoming strategy meeting. She has been working diligently to get the assignment done on time. Your boss has just requested the data a week early, and you know she will be really upset.

Actions

A. Let her know the boss is looking for the data.

B. Give her a deadline and outline the steps for her to complete the assignment.

C. Ask her what has been done on the assignment and then outline the steps for her to complete it.

D. Ask her what has been done on the assignment and help her create a plan for finishing it.

RESPONSES

A _2_

B _0_

C _0_

D _3_

CASE 7

Barry has been in your area for many years. He is normally a self-starter, and you have always been able to rely on him to get the toughest jobs done. He has deadlines for several major assignments approaching rapidly.

Actions

A. Ask him about his assignments and give him your support on them.

B. Anticipate that he may need support but wait for him to approach you first.

C. Ask him about his assignments and then lay out clear expectations for each one.

D. Lay out clear expectations for each of his assignments and be explicit about what he should be doing.

RESPONSES

A __1__

B __0__

C __4__

D __0__

CASE 8

Jenny is frustrated with her job and actively looking for a transfer. She knows all the required tasks well but has a tendency to be careless even under normal circumstances.

Actions

A. Stay close to the situation and be sure that standards are maintained.

B. Ask her about her concerns and then give her a plan for maintaining standards during the interim.

C. Ask her about her concerns and help her develop her own plan for the interim.

D. Let her know that she is needed to handle the work.

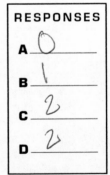

RESPONSES

A __0__

B __1__

C __2__

D __2__

CASE 9

Your organization has embarked on a Quality initiative and you have been assigned to lead a Continuous Improvement Team. The team members represent all of the departments that have a direct interface with yours. The first meeting is today.

Actions

A. Lead group discussions that help the members define the team's mission and their roles.

B. Let the members outline the improvements they are planning to make in their own departments.

C. Clarify the team's mission and explain members' roles and responsibilities.

D. Incorporate members' suggestions as you determine operating principles and procedures.

RESPONSES

A _0_

B _0_

C _2_

D _3_

CASE 10

You are leading a team that has performed well in the past. The team members are experienced and have always handled responsibilities well. Recently, they have seemed burned out and you are afraid their interest will drop off completely.

Actions

A. Leave them on their own for a while before you take any formal action.

B. Redefine their responsibilities clearly and work closely with them until the group is back on track.

C. Ask the group for ideas about changes that are needed and use their input to make improvements.

D. Lead discussions about the current situation and help the group decide what changes are needed.

RESPONSES

A _0_

B _1_

C _2_

D _2_

WHY WERE SOME CASES ABOUT INDIVIDUALS AND OTHERS ABOUT GROUPS?

The cases you just read focused on eight problems about individuals and two that involved group efforts. That is because we believe that to have a high-performing team, you need to lead the individuals on the team in unique ways according to who they are and what they have been asked to do. In addition, you need to lead the group dynamics that emerge as the individual contributors interact with one another and with you. This applies to teams in functional units, departments, and divisions. It also applies to cross-functional teams, project teams, committees, task forces, joint-venture teams, special teams, virtual teams, etc.

WHAT IS A HIGH-PERFORMING TEAM?

In our team-building practice, we work with leaders and their team members to help them develop productive working relationships and overcome self-imposed constraints. We help them clarify where they are going and how they are getting there. We help them eliminate ways in which they are tripping over one another's feet while discovering better ways to take advantage of the full resources available to the group.

This team-building work has given us a unique opportunity for understanding teams. In essence, it has taught us that high-performing teams have

- A clear and unambiguous *mission*
- Clear *goals* with measurable targets for the team as well as for the individuals on the team
- People who have the *skills* necessary to accomplish the mission
- Clear *roles* and responsibilities for each member of the team
- Well-defined *leadership* responsibilities that are shared among team members in ways that maximize openness without sacrificing control
- Clear, timely, and open *communication* down, up, and all the way around, within the team as well as with suppliers and customers
- Effective *decision-making* structures that enable the team to tackle tough problems in a systematic way without getting bogged down in trivia
- Efficient *systems/procedures* that help people get their work done
- Formal or informal *rewards* that value people for their contributions as well as for the team's successes

- An overall *climate* that encourages people to push the edge of the envelope and creates a positive team spirit

Creating and sustaining a high-performing team is no small task. According to Tony Daloisio, the leader of our Charter Oak team that compiled these findings, "Each of these factors represents a key ingredient of a high-performing team. We find that teams can get stuck on any of these issues. What's interesting is that the solutions always come back to the issue of leadership. An ambiguous mission, unclear goals, poor communication, inefficient decision-making procedures, or a lackadaisical climate can be corrected if the leader is committed to working on the problem. If not, it is not likely to get resolved."

So it comes down to you, the leader. You are the driving force. What you say and what you do will determine the success of your team. And what all the leaders throughout your organization say and do will determine the success of your entire organization.

WHY IS TEAMWORK SO IMPORTANT?

Teamwork is essential to the culture of most successful organizations. In our *organization alignment* practice, we have learned that an organization's culture can make or break any change initiative aimed at improvement. All too often, a leader will declare a new vision, develop a new strategy, announce a reorganization, or invest millions of dollars in new systems, only to find that a few years later there is not much difference in the way the company is doing business. That is because the leader has not paid enough attention to the organization's culture. Without confronting old habits and established ways of working together, any major change is likely to fall flat on its face.

Basically, the concept of organization alignment can be likened to the alignment of an automobile or the human skeletal system. When a car is out of alignment it does not function optimally—the tires wear unevenly and more quickly, the gas mileage decreases, and the ride is bumpier than it would be with an aligned vehicle.

Likewise, when a person's body is out of alignment the person is likely to experience back pain, be less flexible, and move far less efficiently and effectively than when the body is aligned. Just as a good mechanic can bring a car back into alignment and a good chiropractor can adjust the body to bring it back into alignment, organizational leaders can do things to bring an organization—or part of an organization—into alignment.

In order to align an organization, there are five dimensions to consider. First, you need to look outside the organization at the *environment* that surrounds it. Who are your customers? Who are your main competitors? What are the technological, economic, or demographic developments that might have a major impact on your organization's future?

Second, you need to identify the core *values* that will align your organization with your environment and simultaneously align your workforce in pursuit of a shared *vision*. Values are at the center of an aligned organization. They are at the core of the vision that drives it forward into the future.

Third, the vision needs to be translated into specific strategies that must be articulated as departmental missions with measurable goals. The *strategy* makes the vision more concrete by turning the core values into an achievable set of targets.

Fourth, the strategy has to be implemented by a *structure* that outlines the roles and responsibilities needed to make the strategy succeed. To bring the structure to life, you also need *systems* in place that can put the strategies into motion.

Finally, the *culture* of the organization must motivate people to act in ways that are consistent with customers' expectations and the core values that drive the organization.

We don't want to minimize any aspect of what it takes to lead a high-performing organization. For an organization to be effective, its leaders have to consider each of the elements of alignment. They need to be aware of the environment, be able to articulate a vision that is shared by followers, know how to focus on the right strategic initiatives, design efficient structures, and put productive systems in place. They also need to create a culture where purposeful, focused teams work smarter and learn faster than the competition.

As Jonathan Spiegel, the head of Charter Oak's alignment practice, says, "Leaders need to recognize that they must create a culture that enables people to achieve their vision. Without integration of individual efforts into productive teamwork, no customer-oriented vision has a chance of succeeding."

Our emphasis in this book is on working with individuals and groups in ways that create the high-performing teams that will give your organization a culture capable of achieving greatness. The Leader's Window can help you create an organizational culture that supports long-term success. This new paradigm for leadership can also enable managers at all levels of your organization to build an organizational culture in which everyone is inspired to perform to the best of his or her potential.

MANAGEMENT BY BUZZWORD

One of the biggest impediments to organizational success is the abundance of buzzwords that wash through corporate hallways in successive waves. While many of these catchphrases reflect worthwhile ideas that have stood the test of time, they cannot, in and of themselves, offer complete solutions. The key is to get beneath the slogans and understand what to do with the meaning they reflect.

Ideas don't become buzzwords unless there is some truth beneath the surface. The problem is that often a leader will latch on to a buzzword and try to align his or her organization behind the particular philosophy it implies.

Figure 1 shows some of the buzzwords we hear most frequently. We suspect that they will sound familiar to you, too. We have grouped them into four small windows held together by a window frame to give you a sneak preview of The 4 Windows of Leadership. You will see later that each set of these buzzwords has its place in a good leader's tool kit.

Window 1 focuses on *vision, passion, drive,* and *results.* Window 2 includes *participation, involvement, synergy,* and *quality.* Window 3 emphasizes *listening, coaching, development,* and *support.* And Window 4 focuses on *trust, empowerment, delegation,* and *letting go.*

Throughout this book we will build on these familiar buzzwords. As we've suggested, behind every buzzword there lies some truth. Our goal is to help you understand what to do with the wisdom of each small window and how to blend all of these truths together into a complete paradigm for effective leadership.

Each of these windows, when used appropriately, can be a powerful force in a leadership relationship. Each can also be a misguided attempt to jump on a buzzword bandwagon.

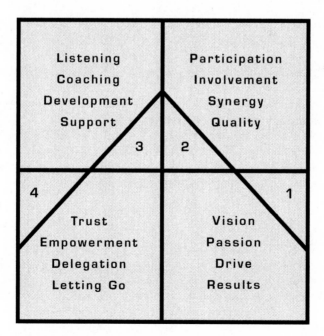

Figure 1 Management by Buzzword

One of the reasons we suspect "management by buzzword" happens so often is that people are seeking simple answers to complex problems. The truth is that effective leaders do a lot of different things under different circumstances—and that all the things they do make sense some of the time. The problem is that the same actions don't make sense at other times.

Articulating a vision for your organization and being impassioned about that vision can be a wonderful thing. Driving your direct reports to achieve results can prove worthwhile. However, forcing your vision on self-motivated people who have a vested stake in their own vision of their work may result in diminished returns.

Preaching the virtues of participation, involvement, and team synergy and continually stressing the importance of quality can lead to cutting-edge problem solving if you're serious about using people's input. It can also result in endless meetings and time-consuming processes.

Using a nurturing approach to managing people by listening to them, coaching them, developing them, and supporting them can lead to high performance. But if the people you're coaching aren't ready, willing, and able to take on the responsibility that comes with this approach, you may be too supportive for your own good.

Finally, finding ways to truly empower people by delegating to them, trusting them, and letting go of control can prove to be beneficial to everyone involved provided you are all positioned to take advantage of this high level of autonomy.

Within each window, there is a set of buzzwords that offers a potential blessing and a possible curse. The blessing emerges when the particular philosophy matches the conditions. The curse rears its ugly head when there is a mismatch between the methodology employed and the leadership needs of the situation. The biggest problems occur when a leader embraces one window for all circumstances and ends up trying to force every situation to fit the strategy instead of the other way around.

Throughout this book, our mission is to help you develop the tools to use the right leadership styles at the right times. We will help you learn to open each window when its messages are needed. Ultimately, that ability will determine whether you are viewed as a fad-following sloganeer or a savvy master of leadership.

USE ALL YOUR GOLF CLUBS

Whether you are supervising an individual, spearheading a team effort, or captaining an entire organization, you need to be open-minded about using a variety of approaches. Every situation will confront you with a new set of circumstances, and each window will give you a set of options. The challenge is to match the right response to each situation.

Instead of thinking of yourself as a professional manager with a set of leadership tools, think of yourself as a professional golfer with a set of very valuable golf clubs.

In golf, there is a reason that you have woods, long irons, short irons, and a putter in the golf bag. You need the woods on the tee and the fairway, the long irons in the rough, the short irons for the sand traps and approach shots, and the putter on the greens.

Imagine how ineffective you would be if you tried to play golf with only one club. If all you had was a putter, you'd be terrible off the tee and in the traps. If you had only woods, you'd be awful in the rough and on the greens. And if all you had was a short iron, you wouldn't get very far off the tee, and you'd tear the greens to shreds. Not only would you be ineffective, but you would look ridiculous.

Many managers try the equivalent at work. They walk around with one approach and try to use it in every situation. They often take pride in being consistent when they are actually being ineffective in most situations—and they often do look ridiculous.

The point is that if you want to be effective as a leader you have to be prepared to use all your clubs. You don't want to use them all at once, but you do want to use each one of them as the circumstances demand.

This may sound easier than it actually is. When you play golf it's easy to know which club to use. On the golf course there is a nice flat spot with little markers to let you know that you are at the tee. The fairway is clearly distinguishable from the rough. You definitely know when your ball is in a sand trap, and the well-groomed grass and the flag serve as clear indicators that you're on the green.

At work it's a lot harder because the clues are never marked that clearly. That's what The Leader's Window is for, to help you see the clues that are there and figure out which clubs to use and when to use them.

The 4 Windows
of Leadership

When you responded to the ten cases in the last chapter, you had four actions from which to choose. Each of those actions is associated with one of the leadership styles of The Leader's Window. In this chapter, we will give you a deeper understanding of these four different approaches to leadership so that you will have a clear picture of what each style looks like.

This is the first step toward mastering the four leadership styles. If you are going to open and close each of the four windows at the right time and apply the wisdom behind the buzzwords in value-added ways, you need to know the words and actions that bring each of these leadership styles to life.

You can't play golf with the pros until you know how to use each golf club.

THE FOUR LEADERSHIP STYLES

The most common way to think about the four leadership styles is in terms of two general types of leader behavior: direction and support.

Being directive means telling people what to do, when to do it, how to do it, and why it should be done. It involves explaining assignments, providing information, and giving people instructions. Direction is associated with downward communication and influence from above. It usually results in close supervision and frequent feedback.

Being supportive is quite different. It is typified by encouraging upward communication, seeking people's ideas, and listening carefully to their responses. Support means respecting people's knowledge and involving them in decision making. It involves building people's confidence, helping them accomplish assignments, and encouraging them to assume responsibility.

Actually, you should think of each type of behavior as a continuum. With direction, you might range from a limited direction, laissez-faire approach to a high-direction, controlling approach. With support, you might range from limited support and minimal interaction to high support and active communication. Between these extremes, there are many points on each continuum.

Figure 2 shows what the four styles look like in terms of direction and support.

These are the basic tools that a leader uses when interacting with other people. Style 1 (S1) is the high direction style. Style 2 (S2) is the high support, high direction style. Style 3 (S3) is the high support style. And Style 4 (S4) is the low support, low direction style.

S1, the High Direction Style

Style 1 refers to taking action without seeking input from others. Leaders who use Style 1 are good at giving assignments and informing team members of the actions they need to take. Their tendency is to tell people what, when, why, and how to proceed while providing close supervision.

S2, the High Support and High Direction Style

Style 2 involves direction from the top based on ideas that are actively solicited from members of the team. Leaders who use Style 2 are good at seeking

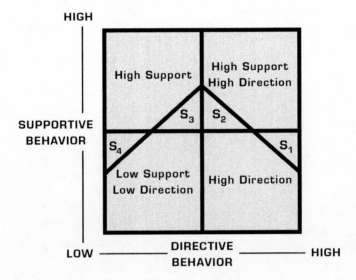

Figure 2 The 4 Basic Leadership Styles

information from key people and asking their opinions on issues. They like to share problems, listen to other people's points of view, and then set a course of action and make assignments.

S3, the High Support Style

Style 3 involves assisting others in areas where they have responsibility. Leaders who use Style 3 are comfortable listening as people discuss problem situations. They ask many questions and provide some input to other people's decisions. They act as a guide and a resource but leave the responsibility with those who are closest to the problem.

S4, the Low Support and Low Direction Style

Style 4 involves leaving people on their own. Leaders who use Style 4 are good at getting out of the way and letting team members make decisions on their own. They don't overwhelm people with information in order to let them work out the details of assignments. They also don't require reams of information about problems or actions that team members have taken.

This is just the beginning. To fully understand these four leadership styles, you have to know more about the key behaviors that put direction and support into action. This means looking at the ways you go about making decisions, your preferred modes of communication, and the types of behavior you tend to recognize and reward in the people you surround yourself with.

WHAT KIND OF DECISION MAKER ARE YOU?

One of the most important aspects of your job as a leader is making timely, high-quality decisions that other people are committed to implementing. This can be done in four different ways. Which method you choose depends in part on the amount of responsibility you like to retain or are willing to give up. It also depends on your preference for interactive participation in the decision-making process.

Responsibility for decision making is a source of tremendous conflict and frustration in most organizations. Too often, several people believe that they have the right to make certain decisions. In other cases, no one wants to or is permitted to make decisions.

Consequently, you have to be clear about who has the final word about any key decision. As the leader, do you need to make the decision? Do you simply *want* to make the decision? Or should a member of your team be empowered to make the decision? Who makes the call? You or someone who reports to you?

Participation is the other important element of decision making. If people with critical information are not involved, it is unlikely that a high-quality decision will be made. If people who have to live with the consequences of a decision are not involved, it is unlikely that they will be committed to implementing it. On the other hand, if people are asked to participate when they are not affected by the decision or they have nothing meaningful to contribute, they are likely to resent the unnecessary demand on their time. It is important that you understand when participation is needed and be clear about people's roles as participants in the decision-making process.

Figure 3 depicts the four leadership styles in terms of responsibility and participation.

On the right, with Styles 1 and 2, the leader is responsible for making the decisions. On the left, with Styles 3 and 4, a member of the team is responsible for making the decisions.

On the top, with Styles 2 and 3, both the leader and team members participate in the decision-making process. On the bottom, with Styles 1 and 4, only one party is involved, either the leader or the team member, but not both.

So, if you are the type of leader who prefers to retain responsibility and doesn't tend to invite other people to participate in the process, then your preference is for making decisions on your own, and you probably come across as a Style 1 leader.

If you encourage people to bring problems to your attention and ask for their recommendations but still like to be the one who is in charge, then you tend to make decisions based on team members' input, and you probably come across as a Style 2 leader.

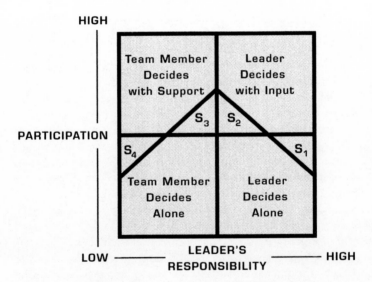

Figure 3 Leadership and Decision Making

If you like the members of the team to have the responsibility for making decisions but still like being an active participant in the process, then you tend to support others as they make decisions with your input, and you most likely come across as a Style 3 leader.

Finally, if you let the members of the team have the responsibility without your being involved in the decision-making process, then you prefer to let others make decisions on their own and probably come across as a Style 4 leader.

HOW ARE YOU AS A COMMUNICATOR?

What you say and how you say it can be as important as anything else you do as a leader. When you think of your leadership in terms of communication, the question is, what happens when you open your mouth? To answer that question, try thinking of your communications in two broad categories, *giving information* and *seeking information.*

Giving information requires the use of *influencing skills.* These communication tools include

- Providing directions
- Giving advice
- Giving explanations
- Pointing out consequences
- Giving feedback

At the beginning of a project, people need clear directions that include complete information about what is to be accomplished and when it needs to be done. They also need complete explanations about why actions are needed, including background information and interpretation of key events. People are also prompted to action if they understand the consequences at stake, including the potential payoffs or pitfalls for them, the organization, and the customer.

As work progresses, people also function better if they have access to timely advice or constructive suggestions. They also benefit from ongoing feedback about their performance and their progress toward the intended objectives.

If you tend to use these influencing skills frequently, then you are probably good at giving others the information they need to perform successfully and influencing them to take action.

Listening skills are the communication tools for seeking information. Listening is not a passive act. It means actively seeking information from people and then using their thoughts and feelings to identify problems and resolve them. Listening skills include the following:

- Paying attention
- Encouraging openness
- Asking probing questions
- Paraphrasing ideas
- Empathizing with feelings
- Summarizing key points

Paying attention to other people's concerns, listening to the problems they are facing, and hearing their recommendations for corrective action are critical skills for any leader. Whenever people have ideas to share, it is important to give them verbal and nonverbal messages that encourage them to be as open as possible.

Nonverbally, that means using an inviting, nonjudgmental tone of voice that encourages people to speak candidly. It also means avoiding body language that says, "Go away; don't bother me," or makes people feel intimidated.

Verbally, that means asking relevant and thoughtful questions that help everyone fully understand the situation. It also means valuing others' points of view by empathizing with their feelings and paraphrasing their thoughts. In addition, whenever problems are complex or many people are involved in discussing them, it is essential for the leader to keep everyone on track by summarizing the key points of a conversation.

If you tend to use these listening skills frequently, then you are probably good at encouraging people to be open with you and making them feel like valued contributors.

Figure 4 shows the four leadership styles in terms of influencing and listening.

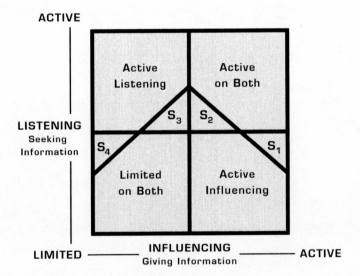

Figure 4 Leadership and Communication

On the right, Styles 1 and 2 are active influencing styles. On the left, Styles 3 and 4 are limited influencing styles. At the top, Styles 2 and 3 involve a lot of interaction between the team leader and team members. At the bottom, Styles 1 and 4 require less two-way communication.

Think about yourself again as a leader.

Focus on the lower right window. If you are the type of leader who tells people what to do, when to do it, how to do it, and why, or if you provide close supervision and frequent feedback, then you are an active influencer and will be perceived as using Style 1.

Look at the upper left window. If you like to be a sounding board to help team members think through their decisions, if you ask good questions, pay careful attention, reflect back their ideas, and empathize with their feelings, then you are more of an active listener and will be perceived as using Style 3.

Now look at the upper right window. If you tend to listen to people's problems and then tell them how to fix them, or if you explain problems to others and then invite their input to your decisions, then you use a balance of influencing skills and listening skills and will be perceived as a Style 2 leader.

Finally, in the lower left window, if you tend to leave team members on their own without giving them lots of information or spending a lot of time keeping yourself informed about what they are doing, you will probably be perceived as using Style 4.

WHAT DO YOU GIVE PEOPLE RECOGNITION FOR?

Recognition is another factor that influences the way you are perceived as a leader. Recognition refers to anything you say or do that lets team members know they are doing what you want them to do. When you give people assignments, give them feedback, and evaluate their performance, you send them formal messages about the ways you expect them to behave. When you give people pats on the back, smile, or simply pick up on some topics while ignoring others, you send informal messages that also let people know if they are doing the right things. As much as anything, the behaviors that you reward or pay attention to establish the way you come across as a leader.

Everyone wants recognition. When they get it, they and the people around them are more likely to continue behaving in the ways that led to recognition. Conversely, if they are reprimanded, they and the people around them are more likely to avoid doing the things that led to criticism. In addition, if people are used to receiving some form of recognition and it stops coming, they are likely to stop acting as they did in the past and start looking for new ways to get recognition.

Recognition is not the same thing as support. Styles 2 and 3 are high on support, but Styles 1 and 4 are low. Styles 2 and 3 also require high participation and active listening, but in Styles 1 and 4 someone decides alone, and there is limited communication. Recognition is different. It is not connected to just Styles 2 and 3, the high support styles. Instead, since recognition has such a strong impact on team members, it is a significant dimension of all four leadership styles. However, each style is associated with a different type of recognition.

Figure 5 shows the four leadership styles in terms of recognition.

If you tend to value people who like you to call the shots, praise team members for asking what to do, when to do it, and how to do it, and reward people who follow directions and do what they are told, then you are sending out Style 1 messages.

If you like people who bring problems to your attention so you can resolve them, appreciate people for making recommendations, and encourage them to provide input into your decision making, then you are giving off Style 2 messages.

If you are available and willing to help people when they get stuck, encourage them to ask for your support and use you as a resource, respond positively when they need help, and appreciate them when they ask for your advice, then you are broadcasting Style 3 messages.

If you surround yourself with people who are willing to assume responsibility and make their own decisions, encourage them to be creative and take risks, and reward them for solving problems on their own, then you are giving team members Style 4 messages.

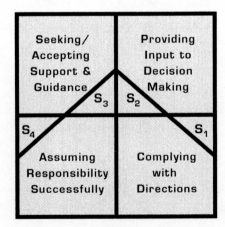

Figure 5 Leadership and Recognition

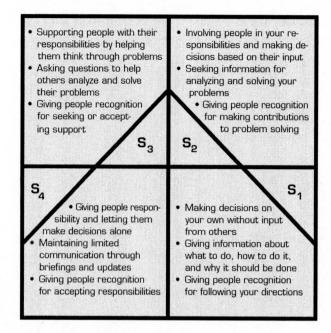

• Supporting people with their
  responsibilities by helping
  them think through problems
• Asking questions to help
  others analyze and solve
  their problems
• Giving people recognition
  for seeking or accept-
  ing support

S_3

• Involving people in your responsibilities and making decisions based on their input
• Seeking information for
  analyzing and solving your
  problems
  • Giving people recognition
    for making contributions
    to problem solving

S_2

S_4

• Giving people respon-
  sibility and letting them
  make decisions alone
• Maintaining limited
  communication through
  briefings and updates
• Giving people recognition
  for accepting responsibilities

S_1

• Making decisions on
  your own without input
  from others
• Giving information about
  what to do, how to do it,
  and why it should be done
• Giving people recognition
  for following your directions

Figure 6 The Four Styles of The Leader's Window

WHICH LEADERSHIP STYLES DO YOU USE?

Now that you understand what behaviors are associated with each style, let's look at Figure 6, which shows the four styles of The Leader's Window.

Each window contains a summary of the decision-making, communication, and recognition behaviors that will get you a reputation for using that style. As you look at these summaries, ask yourself which behaviors you use with the people who work with you. What do you typically do? How do you think you come across to the people around you? Are you a Style 1, Style 2, Style 3, or Style 4 leader?

NOT SURE WHICH ONE IS YOURS?
TRY THESE LABELS ON FOR SIZE!

In Figure 7, on the next page, you will see that each style can be effective or ineffective. People will speak of you admiringly with the effective labels if you use the right styles at the right times. But they will use the ineffective labels to complain about you if you use the same behaviors at the wrong times. Look at these labels and the descriptions that follow and maybe they will help you discover the type of leader you are.

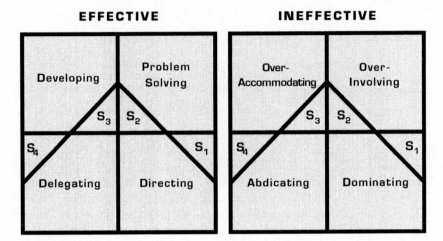

Figure 7 Effective Versus Ineffective Leadership Styles

Style 1: Directing

A leader using S1 effectively gives people clear directions about what they are expected to deliver. These leaders also provide complete explanations and honest appraisals of consequences. They give people the information they need to do their jobs and structure work carefully when team members are not sure how to get started. They offer advice when it is requested and help people avoid negative consequences with frequent feedback. In these situations, *directing* is appreciated.

Style 1: Dominating

A leader who is highly directive will be ineffective if team members have more information than the leader, already understand the situation clearly, know what needs to be done, and have already been taking appropriate actions. In these situations, the leader is *dominating*, taking control when it is unnecessary, interrupting the efforts of team members, and overriding their initiatives.

Style 2: Problem Solving

Most leaders who use S2 effectively have a systematic approach to problem solving that involves

- Identifying problems
- Clarifying goals
- Generating alternatives
- Choosing the best solution

- Building an action plan
- Monitoring implementation

The effective leader involves people in this process by listening to their concerns and making them feel like important identifiers of organizational problems and necessary participants in finding solutions. The leader seeks input from those people who have to live with the consequences of decisions, meets only with those people who need to be involved, runs effective meetings when they are needed, and makes assignments that speed up the decision-making process.

Style 2: Over-Involving

When S2 is used ineffectively, including people in decision making is perceived as *over-involving*. Team members feel frustrated with the amount of time they spend in meetings or with the leader's over-involvement in decisions that others could make on their own. Committees and task forces slow down the organization's responsiveness to problems and issues are discussed at too many levels. The important problems never get heard or are ignored while attention gets diverted to forms and charts and new names for old ways of doing business. Leaders who seem to meet for the sake of meeting, discuss issues but do not listen, involve people but produce no action are *over-involving*.

Style 3: Developing

When S3 is used effectively, the leader assists members of the team when they need support with decision making. The leader asks open questions that support team members with their problem solving:

- How have you defined the problem?
- What is the goal in this situation?
- What alternatives are you considering?
- Which alternative is the best for achieving the goal?
- What is your plan for implementing the solution?
- How will you monitor the implementation?

The leader listens to the responses, paraphrasing key points, paying attention to nonverbal cues, and summarizing the issues. The leader may provide information or opinions but stresses that responsibility for decision making is still with the team member. By encouraging people to discuss problems openly, the leader is *developing* them to assume responsibility. People feel supported and gain confidence in their own problem-solving skills. Conversations focus on organizational problems. They occur when people want support and need help managing their responsibilities.

Style 3: Over-Accommodating

Listening to people's problems and giving them support can also be perceived as an *over-accommodating* style. Often leaders are too focused on relationships for their own sake. They try to be liked by everybody and keep everyone happy. They come across as friendly but are not well respected. They listen but don't let people know if they're on the right track. They agree with anything, bending over backward to be supportive even when requests are inappropriate or recommendations don't make sense. Their need to help can also be distracting to people who work better on their own. Having to check in with the leader and seek guidance takes such people away from productive activities.

Style 4: Delegating

When S4 is used effectively, the *delegating* of responsibility and authority empowers members of the team to make decisions and take action in areas in which they have expertise and are motivated to follow through. Communication is limited to receiving periodic progress reports and expressing renewed confidence in people's work. Team members feel trusted, believe that the organization's success depends on them, and know that they are responsible for their area as well as for coordination with related areas. These people respond enthusiastically to the opportunity to use their knowledge and skills, be involved in challenging work, and achieve results. These intrinsic motivators satisfy them and, consequently, the only encouragement they need is recognition for their performance.

Style 4: Abdicating

When S4 is used ineffectively, the same act of giving responsibility and authority takes place. However, the leader is also perceived as losing accountability. If team members lack the ability to identify problems or the confidence to take necessary actions, they feel like they are out on a limb or in over their heads. As frustrations mount, the leader is blamed for dumping responsibilities on them. People complain about lack of support, ambiguous authority, and absentee management. In time, this *abdicating* becomes the focus of people's attention, distracting them from the organization's business problems. Members of the team may try to provide substitute leadership, often resulting in factions or strife.

COMPARE YOURSELF TO THESE LEADERS

If you're not sure how you come across as a leader, one way to clarify what each of the styles looks like is to identify familiar people who use each style. A fun way to do this is to think about some well-known TV characters whose two-dimensional personalities make them dramatic examples of a style. Understanding the labels that describe these leaders should help you be objective about your own tendencies as a leader. Some of our favorite examples follow. If these examples aren't enough, think of your own favorite TV or movie characters to see if you can identify their main styles and analyze their effectiveness.

*M*A*S*H* Memories

The long-running (and now syndicated) comedy series *M*A*S*H* offers a rich array of leadership styles. Here's a quick rundown of what we see when we look at that venerable M*A*S*H unit.

Henry Blake, the original M*A*S*H commander, is a classic example of an ineffective Style 4 leader, *abdicating* at every turn. Henry is usually distracted from his work, off on a fishing expedition, returning from a trip to Seoul, or hung over. He is best known for asking company clerk Radar O'Reilly to make most of his decisions for him. Had he not been so ineffective in performing his own duties, he might be seen—as evidenced by Radar's flawless completion of his duties—as a masterful delegator.

Henry's replacement, Colonel Potter, is much more of a leader than his bumbling predecessor. Potter doesn't hesitate to give orders and can be quite *directing.* He is also a good listener. Sometimes he is *developing* as he supports the doctors with challenging cases. On occasion he even plays the father figure for an enlisted man like Radar. His *over-accommodating* side shows up in his tolerance for Klinger's cross-dressing in hopes of getting discharged. With a solid command of both the influencing and listening skills, most of the time he comes across as a *problem solver*—aware of people's problems, letting them talk about how to fix them, but never hesitating to make a decision.

When Blake or Potter has to be away from camp, Frank Burns sometimes becomes acting commander. He is a classic Style 1 leader, expecting everything to be done by the book. Since all the other officers are more interested in breaking the rules, no one takes Frank seriously. He would actually like to be *dominating,* but he comes across as nitpicking and whiny—and is totally ineffective as a leader. The only person in the 4077 camp who is more *dominating* than Frank is Margaret Houlihan, who is an expert at dominating him!

Occasionally Hawkeye Pierce is left in charge of the camp. As a leader Hawkeye is a good example of Style 3, *over-accommodating.* The problem is that he spends most of his time indulging the troops' (and his own) social needs by throwing parties, running his still, and chasing nurses. Most of the time he is ineffective, but sometimes he rises to the occasion and uses his Style 3 skills for *developing* a fledgling recruit or listening to needy patients and giving them the support they need to survive.

Enterprise Leadership

Perhaps the best models for effective leadership are the TV Star Fleet captains, from James T. Kirk of *Star Trek* to Jean Luc Picard of *Star Trek: The Next Generation* to Katherine Janeway of *Star Trek: Voyager.* All of these leaders demonstrate the uncanny ability to use the right styles with the right people at the right time.

Each of these Federation commanders spends a good deal of time operating in Style 2. When there is a problem that requires their attention, they summon their experts to the bridge or the boardroom and engage in intensive *problem solving* to find a resolution. How many times has Kirk called down to engineering to ask Mr. Scott if the thrusters are ready? And when Scotty gives the predictable answer that he needs more time, Kirk listens up to a point but will order him to full power if another threat is more dangerous.

Sometimes the captains will defer to the knowledge or skills of their officers but stay in the Style 3, *developing,* mode by asking questions and encouraging them to find a solution. If the problem is of a highly technical nature regarding an aspect of the ship they know little about, they may form a team of experts and support their efforts in solving the problem.

They also demonstrate their ability to use Style 1 when making routine decisions like what galaxy to go to or whether to take the *Enterprise* up to warp speed. They also use Style 1 whenever time or circumstances make it necessary for a single person to make a decision. And their use of Style 1 always comes across as *directing,* since none of them has failed to make the right decision or issue the proper order when faced with imminent annihilation from the Klingons, the Romulans, or the Borg!

Finally, when faced with a crisis requiring action away from the ship, they employ their Style 4 skills by *delegating* a landing party or, if leading the landing party, *delegating* control of the ship to their trusted first officer. And they all delegate with exceptional timing. If there is an attractive partner on the planet, they lead the landing party. If there is an ugly creature, they delegate.

Peterson's Personalities

In one of the funniest episodes of the classic sitcom *Cheers,* Norm, or, as Woody calls him, Mr. Peterson, owns a small house-painting business. In the opening scene, Norm is at his permanent seat at the bar complaining, "I just can't get used to bossing people around. I can't seem to make my workers do the things they're supposed to—like increase their productivity, exceed their goals, show up."

Rebecca asks, "You're not letting your employees take advantage of you, are you?"

He answers, "Yeah, maybe a little bit. Like yesterday the guys decided to knock off early and go bowling."

"So what did you do?" she asks.

He shrugs. "I broke 200."

Psychiatrist Frasier Crane, another *Cheers* regular, *over-involves* himself, as he usually does, and counsels Norm to create a new and different personality. After screwing up his courage, Norm calls the crew chief, Rudy, and tells him that the crew can't go to the Patriots game because they're going to have to work on the weekend. He holds the phone away from his ear for a few seconds and then explains, "No, no, it's not me. It's my new business partner, Anton Kreitzer."

When Rudy wants to speak to Mr. Kreitzer, Norm disguises his voice and yells into the phone, "All right, this is Kreitzer! Now listen up, you bunch of gutless, sniveling little wimps. I don't care what Peterson said; that low life does not lay down the rules!" After a pause to listen, he goes on, "Hey, hey, any more lip out of you and I'll rip your face off and stick it in your lunch bucket!" Then he slams down the receiver and says, "That was kind of fun."

In the next scene, Norm tells Frasier, "I love being Kreitzer. I don't have to paint anymore, business is booming, I've hired a secretary, I've rented us offices."

Frasier asks, "Us?"

And Norm explains, "Well, Kreitzer's door only opens into the alley, but I gave strict orders that no one could go in there, so it's okay."

Of course, that's when the crew demands to talk to Kreitzer in person: "We're not taking this anymore—football tickets, weekends, nights!" Norm promises to talk to Kreitzer for them, but Rudy tells him, "You don't have a spine, Norm. We're going over there ourselves and bash his head in!"

Norm decides it's time to get rid of Kreitzer and arrives at the office just before the crew. Over the protests of the terrified secretary, who insists that Mr. Kreitzer left instructions not to be disturbed under any circumstances, Norm the *over-accommodator* steps into the alley to confront his alter ego, Mr. Kreitzer the *dominator*. Behind the closed door, Kreitzer yells at Norm, and Norm tells him he's got to stop abusing the crew and insulting people. Then Kreitzer insults Norm and asks what he's going to do about it, and Norm says, "Well, Anton, I'll just have to quit, and I'm taking my guys with me."

Kreitzer yells, "Peterson, you can't do that!"

Norm replies, "Oh, don't beg, Anton; it doesn't become you." Then he walks back into the reception area.

Rudy has a horrified look on his face and says, "Norm, you had no right to do that. Now you've really upset him!"

Norm tries to reassure him. "We don't need him. You can work for me."

Rudy says, "Norm, look, no offense—you're a nice guy, but you're not boss material. Everyone knows Mr. Kreitzer was the brains behind everything." And the crew walks out.

The entire episode is a beautiful illustration of what ineffective leadership—in all its forms—looks like in action.

Friends Should Never Manage Friends

The characters on the popular show *Friends* also provide some humorous examples of leadership. In one episode Chandler is seen telling Nina, an attractive young employee, that she has to stop post-dating her reports because it is making his WENUS look bad. She asks him what that is, and when he explains that it's the Weekly Estimated Net Usage number, she coyly responds, "I certainly wouldn't want to do anything to hurt your WENUS."

The next morning Chandler's boss tells him that the ANUS—the Annual Net Usage—is down and they have to let some people go, including Nina. When Chandler tries to fire her, he stammers, "Nina, Nina, Nina, uh, uh, I hope you don't take this the wrong way . . ."

She prompts him, "What is it?" and he chickens out and asks her out on a date. In successive scenes, he offers her a promotion and a big raise before she eventually figures out what's going on and saves him from his *over-accommodating* ways.

In Chandler's relationship with Monica, he is also *over-accommodating*, but that is a good fit with her control freak, *dominating* style. Monica has a place for everything and strong opinions about how everything should be done. In one episode Chandler decides to apologize to Monica by cleaning up their apartment despite Ross's warning that he'll never be able to get everything back right. He goes ahead, and when Monica comes home, she does her best to pretend she's grateful as she moves around the room putting things back in their proper places.

In another episode, Monica is the head chef in an Italian restaurant where she has replaced the beloved chef of many years who is also the father of five members of her kitchen staff. The staff all hate her and are doing whatever they can to make her life miserable—and it's working. She concocts a scheme with Joey to hire him as a waiter just so she can fire him in front of the others and show them who's the boss.

The next day she gathers the whole staff, including Joey, in the kitchen and tells them, "For two weeks I've tried really hard to make this a positive atmosphere, but I've had it up to here. From now on it's going to be my way or the highway! Does anyone have a problem with that?"

This is Joey's cue, but he is so happy with his tip money that he says nothing. Monica looks at him and says, "How about the new guy. Do you have a problem with that?"

"No, ma'am," says Joey, and Monica is ready to kill him.

The next day things get worse for her, and when Joey sees how mercilessly the others are teasing his friend, he finally speaks up and says, "You know that thing you said yesterday, Chef Geller? I have a problem with that."

Monica jumps at the cue. "Well if you want a problem, I'll give you a problem!"

Joey retorts, "What are you going to do, fire me?"

And she yells at him, "You bet your ass I'm going to fire you, and get out of my kitchen. Get out!"

Then she turns to the rest of the staff and says, "All right, anybody else got a problem?" and they all look away. She confronts one waiter who had been giving her a particularly hard time. "How about you, Chuckles. You think this is funny now?" He shakes his head. And Monica is back in the *dominating* business, barking out orders. "You, take those salads to table four. And you, go get that swordfish. And you, get a haircut!"

The Perfect White House

It will be no surprise to anyone living in the United States that the perfect White House is in fact the fictional White House of the widely acclaimed television series *The West Wing*. And it's no surprise that during the unprecedented contentious presidential race of 2000 a running joke was that the only president that the entire nation could get behind was President Bartlett, played by Martin Sheen, who presided in prime time every Wednesday evening.

Bartlett is in fact a role model of effective leadership. We can see through him what effective execution of each style looks like. In one episode Bartlett finds himself in a room with a group of radio personalities. One of the more obvious attendees is a woman known for her extreme right-wing views. Bartlett, usually decidedly left of center, proceeds to challenge the woman's position in a rather combative fashion. The woman, the only person in the room not to stand up when Bartlett entered, gets told by him in quintessential Style 1, *directing,* fashion, "When the president of the United States enters a room, everyone stands." He continues to stare at her until she shows due respect and stands.

Bartlett's use of Style 2, *problem solving,* is also evidenced frequently. Whenever there's a policy decision to be made he quickly gathers his advisors in the Oval Office, grills them on topics that they often know more about than he does, and then, once fully informed, makes his decision. In one episode, he is getting so bombarded with input that Leo, his chief of staff, orders everyone to reduce his or her thoughts to one page of bulleted recommendations. After they struggle to comply, Bartlett briefly skims their papers and asks them to resume the debate so he can fully grasp the issues.

In a particularly poignant moment, President Bartlett is faced with a dire situation. Earlier in this episode he dispatched a fleet of naval ships into an area now under siege by hurricane conditions. All hands on a particular carrier are on deck trying to protect the ship from going down—except for a young seaman who is manning the radio. Bartlett is seen talking to this seaman, whose voice reveals that he is clearly terrified. Bartlett asks if there is anything he can do, even though he knows that there isn't. In a moment of leadership brilliance, Bartlett assesses the situation and realizes that all he has to offer this young man is moral support—not insignificant for a twenty-year-old seaman coming from the president of the United States. He says to the young man, "I'm going to just sit here with you, son, as long as we remain in radio contact." The young man responds, "Yes sir," mustering whatever courage he can just to be able to speak. It is Style 3 at its finest.

In an episode involving flashbacks to the election campaign we get a glimpse of candidate Bartlett exercising his mastery of Style 4, *delegating*. The scene involves his campaign manager reviewing the results of a poll showing that Bartlett is losing ground in his election campaign. Rather than try to control a situation he knows less about than his lieutenant (part of Bartlett's appeal is that he is more statesman than politician), he defers to the political expert and empowers him to make key strategic decisions. The campaign manager fires all but one of his staff and replaces them with all the characters who end up becoming those we have come to know and love for their intelligence and political savvy—the *West Wing* White House staff.

KEEP READING TO GET MORE
VIEWS OF EACH WINDOW

In each of the next four chapters, you will read about well-known public figures who typify each leadership style. The profiles of these real leaders should leave no doubt in your mind as to what each window of leadership looks like.

Window 1: The Leader as Director

Chapters 3 through 6 will help you understand what The 4 Windows of Leadership look like in real life. Each chapter is filled with profiles of real leaders in many different settings. As you read these profiles, you can clearly envision the range of behaviors associated with each leadership style.

In each chapter, the profiles will highlight the way leaders make decisions, the way they communicate, and the recognition they give to team members because, as mentioned earlier, these are the essential behaviors that determine how a leader comes across to the rest of the world.

Each chapter will show you the effective use of that leadership style as well as the result of the right style being used with the right people at the right times. It will also show you the ineffective use of that leadership style and the result of that same style being overused with the wrong people at the wrong times.

As you read this chapter and the ones that follow, it is important to understand that most managers use all four styles on a regular basis. The powerful people you will read about could not have been successful without using all four styles (more about that in later chapters). The profiles in these chapters focus on the main styles these people are known for, the ones that define their reputations but not everything they do.

In addition to using all four styles, most managers have a main style, and you probably do, too. So as you read these next four chapters, think about the choices you made on the cases in chapter 1. Which window were you looking through when you responded to those cases? Which one is your favorite view?

Let's start with Window 1. Taking charge, being in control, steering the ship, being at the helm, commanding the troops, and giving people their marching orders are all images that most people associate with strong leaders. The view through Window 1 will show you a number of effective leaders who come across as *directing*, decisive people who are good at getting things done.

Window 1 will also show you some leaders who are so good at directing that they overdo it and therefore are perceived as *dominating*, squelching other people's attempts to take the initiative.

UNIFORM RESULTS

Ray Kroc, the founder of McDonald's, was the quintessential Window 1 leader. He had a vision that the key to his success would be to create a uniform product—the hamburger—that could be replicated and accessible at a reasonable price anywhere in the country—and eventually the world. "Ray Kroc pictured his empire long before it existed, and he saw how to get there. He invented the company motto—'Quality, service, cleanliness, and value'—and kept repeating it to employees for the rest of his life" (Labich 1988). The key to his success was establishing a standard and adhering strictly to that standard. Kroc's *directing* leadership style was (and is) echoed throughout his organization. When you put on a McDonald's uniform to work as a cook they don't ask you what you think is the best way to make a hamburger—they tell you in no uncertain terms precisely how you will make it. "Kroc left nothing to chance. He wrote manuals specifying exact grill heats, cooking times, amounts of ketchup and mustard. Score marks on every burger were to be precisely the same distance apart" (Ola and D'Aulaire 1987).

While some may argue that the Kroc approach breeds conformity and stifles creativity, it would be difficult to argue with the success of his venture. Further, while this type of management approach might not be attractive to some, it is well suited to the frontline workers at McDonald's, most of whom work part-time. From high school kids to moonlighters, workers can walk in, put on an apron, and turn out perfect quality with little difficulty.

One way Kroc was able to create and sustain such consistent conformity was by creating a corporate culture that reinforced his personal approach to hamburger production and sales. The creation of Hamburger University is a vivid example of Kroc's legacy of control. "Franchisees, accountants, lawyers, managers, and executives—everyone in the decision-making process—are required to attend Hamburger University in Oak Brook, Illinois. During 12-day courses, 28 'professors'—actually ex-restaurant operatives—lecture to thousands of students a year. Here they learn the essentials of restaurant management, human relations and grill skills" (ibid.). Essentially, they learn the gospel according to Kroc.

An even more vivid manifestation of Kroc's legacy of control is Kroc's "presence," years after his death, at corporate headquarters in Oak Brook. "Ray is not only quoted, he is, uh, sort of there in Oak Brook today. In a headquarters exhibit called 'Talk to Ray,' a visitor can phone up Ray, as it were, on a videoscreen, and with a keyboard ask him questions. Over several years he recorded his thoughts for the company archives, and his appearances on talk shows were taped as well, so those left to carry on can find out about nearly everything they might need to know" (Moser 1988).

Perhaps the greatest testament to Kroc's ability to use his *directing* approach to sustain his vision for his organization comes from his successors, Michael Quinlan and, most recently, Jack Greenberg. Says former CEO Quinlan, "If there's one reason for our success, it's that Ray Kroc instilled in the company basic principles. Standards of excellence" (ibid.). And while current CEO Greenberg has experimented with new ways of maintaining McDonald's competitive advantage in the increasingly high-stakes fast-food marketplace, he too does not hesitate to pay homage to founder Kroc and his vision. Says Greenberg of Kroc's golden arches, "That symbol is recognizable everywhere in the world and what it stands for is instantly understood" (Hume 1999).

Finally, what makes Kroc's Style 1 approach so successful is that, as with most successful visionaries, he has given the public what it wants. People go to McDonald's because they know exactly what they are going to get—and they are rarely surprised. Consider these reflections by journalist Penny Moser: "Rather than being bored with McDonald's sameness, we learned to appreciate it. In a world where one of my ancestral homes became an on-ramp for the Illinois tollway and another was claimed for an atomic accelerator site, McDonald's became a symbol of stability. A McDonald's meal tastes pretty much the same everywhere. It can cure homesickness and make strange places less strange. I brightened up considerably when, after a long day on Guam earlier this year, the golden arches greeted me around a bend" (Moser 1988).

FUN FOR THE ENTIRE FAMILY— ON DEMAND

Another extraordinarily successful Window 1 leader was Walt Disney. Examination of Disney's leadership style throughout his career paints a picture of a relentless Style 1 leader, committed to realizing his vision of his organization through a carefully controlled orchestration of every detail. Disney used to walk into the theme parks and pick up errant cigarette butts, sending a clear message to each "cast member" working on the street-cleaning crew. In every aspect of Disneyland and Disney World, Walt demanded that things be picture perfect. Every detail was important, to ensure that each guest would experience the total illusion. In fact, the entire Disney dynasty was built on the premise that success would be predicated on the theme parks' ability to practically guarantee perfect vacations—and this goal was accomplished through a very directive mode of leadership.

As with Kroc's approach, the organization is driven by the leader's vision and *directing* leadership style down to the last detail. Every employee has a specific role in Disney's plays, and every play is scripted. Whether an employee is leading an adventure cruise down a jungle river or directing guests to their desired destination, there are scripts, or, as everyone at Disney calls them, spiels, for what to say and what to do to ensure that the desired effect is created and conveyed. This prescriptive control gets played out in every aspect of the organization. Whether an employee is walking the streets of the Magic Kingdom as Goofy or behind the scenes in the accounting department, there are instructions as to what to wear, how to behave, and the role to play in the organization.

Disney's approach to managing his dream was with him throughout his career and continues to drive the Disney organization even after his death. Even early on as a fledgling animation editor, Disney would take control of ideas developed by other studio employees and create the finished product himself. In fact, he was the first in his business to utilize the storyboard approach for animation, which involves taking general ideas and plotting them out meticulously, step-by-step, to create a cohesive, integrated result.

Perhaps the most vivid view of what drove Disney to maintain his high-control approach to his business can be seen through his own eyes. "In a story typical of his tendency to portray his actions in mythic terms, Disney was fond of telling how he first got the idea for his Disneyland. He was sitting at a park bench with his daughter at a traditional amusement park, when, in looking around, he angrily mused to himself that there ought to be fun-oriented parks that are clean and wholesome enough for the whole family. In planning his park, Walt Disney created a relentlessly clean environment through an almost compulsive passion for order and control" (Croce 1991).

This patriarchal presence also gave a *dominating* aspect to the Disney dynasty, playing itself out particularly in Disney's relationship to his employees. "Disney's most important control was that which he exercised over his subordinates. He may have appeared avuncular to the public, but on the job, he played the stern and powerful father. Animator Ward Kimball was one of many who explicitly acknowledged this relationship: 'Walt was our father figure. We both respected and feared him. He ran the studio as a sort of benevolent and paternal dictatorship. He was the total boss . . . , but we all knew he was a genius whose tough demeanor seemed to stimulate and bring out the best in all of us. . . . We were inwardly proud to be part of his organization" (ibid.).

LARRY ELLISON, THE ORACLE
OF THE INTERNET

If there is an exemplar of Style 1 in the new economy it is Larry Ellison, CEO of software giant Oracle. The consummate visionary, motivator, and influencer, Ellison prides himself on being able to repeatedly re-invent his company to compete with arch rival Microsoft—and to get others to follow him. He is betting the bank that the right thing for his company is to make Oracle the one-stop shop for database and application software for the corporate world. If he is right, he could end up unseating Bill Gates as the overseer of the most dominant software company in the world.

Where Ellison differs from archrival Gates is in style. Gates, the relentless *problem solver*, banks on his intelligence and the intelligence of those around him to come up with the right answers as the means to the pot-of-gold end. Ellison, while no intellectual slouch, is far more flamboyant and relies on his personal power to influence and instill faith in both his customers and his employees.

By all accounts Ellison is the heart and soul of Oracle—and its driving force. Consider this description of a recent Oracle user group conference: "The Larry faithful line up outside an auditorium for hours before his speech. When the doors open 8,000 programmers race into the hall as if they're in some kind of frontier land grab. . . . And then Larry and his entourage march in. . . . It's almost like a rock star thing. . . . The whole thing is like a group of Romulan ministers surrounding their Romulan-in-chief" (Serwer 2000). And Ellison's charismatic dominance is not reserved for just followers. It extends to the most challenging and powerful potential customers. "I went with Larry to visit Sandy Weill at Citigroup," says Oracle EVP Jay Nussbaum, "and after Larry pitched Sandy, Sandy said, 'You don't have to sell me anymore. I'm a numbers guy. This is awesome. I want some of that'" (ibid.).

While Ellison's highly *directing* style in building his company from the ground up has served him—and investors—well, the problem with his decidedly egocentric style is that he has not groomed a replacement or built any bench strength. The concern on Wall Street is that if something were to happen to Ellison, or if he were to lose interest in favor of one or more of his many hobbies or side interests, there would be no one in place to steer the ship. In fact, the person many thought would be Ellison's heir apparent, Ray Lane, stepped down as president in June 2000, reportedly under contentious circumstances, unwilling to live in the shadow of his *dominating* boss. Only time will tell whether this Style 1 leader, a good example of *directing* and *dominating*, will prevail over the greatest success of the new economy—or the greatest failure.

CONTROLLING THE GAP

For the past ten years the retail clothing industry in this country has experienced great volatility, with many merchandisers experiencing tremendous losses. The Gap, which has spawned brands like Banana Republic, GapKids, and the increasingly successful Old Navy, is and has been run for nearly twenty years by Millard "Mickey" Drexler. As president of The Gap, Drexler exemplifies the power a Window 1 leader can wield—if he or she is right. While over the past ten years The Gap has experienced its share of fluctuation in value, industry analysts look at it as the model for how to run a successful enterprise. And Drexler's leadership is given credit for the company's enduring success. Like all successful Style 1 leaders, Drexler has a compelling vision that drives every aspect of his company's staggering success. Part of Drexler's vision was to create a network of stores that provided consistent products of good style, good quality, and good value—a network of stores that would be appealing to many markets, including children, teenagers, young adults, and baby boomers. What Drexler did to create a corporate culture where consistency ruled was to focus on two principles: simplicity and control.

Consider this description of Drexler's actions soon after his taking charge of The Gap: "Drexler handed out signs with a single word in white letters on gray background: Simplify. He meant not just the clothes, but the whole way The Gap does business. He got rid of executives who relied on complicated quantitative research. Instead, he hired people who understood his approach of quickly testing his fashion intuition in new products." (Mitchell 1992). With a personal worth in excess of $1 billion, Drexler has continued his Style 1 approach. In a recent listing of the Forbes 400 (October 1999), Drexler was described as a hands-on manager who reads customer letters and regularly visits stores.

Drexler's penchant for maintaining consistency through control can be seen throughout his organization, from the way the clothes are manufactured to the way the stores are managed. "[T]he company has 200 quality-control inspectors working inside factories in 40 countries to make sure specifications are met right from the start. Because The Gap designs its own clothes, chooses its own materials, and monitors manufacturing so closely, it can keep quality high and costs low" (Mitchell 1992). While this highly systematic, methodical approach ensures consistency of product, it's the way the stores are managed that ensures the consistency of service. "The tight control extends to the stores themselves. There's no more room for creative expression at a Gap store than there is at McDonald's—maybe less. Gap merchandise goes through a major shift about every two months, and store managers receive a book of detailed instructions that tell them exactly what clothes go where" (ibid.).

Perhaps the most telling view of Drexler's Style 1 approach can be seen by looking at his day-to-day activities: "Drexler once oversaw every major design decision, and he still keeps a close watch. He visits stores constantly and rarely comes to rest at headquarters. A typical day at The Gap's San Francisco office finds Drexler roaming the halls, popping in unexpectedly on staffers to praise or criticize dozens of projects in design, advertising, and merchandising. . . . Insiders say newcomers either adapt easily to Drexler's vision—or they quickly walk" (ibid.).

It is clear to all who work with and for him that this high-control leader is determined to maintain the control that has served him and his company so well: "Drexler's opinionated style comes through at a meeting in San Francisco. About 30 merchandisers are showing the proposed fall collection for GapKids to Drexler. The woman in charge of jackets holds up a hooded design cut to look very puffy. Everyone holds a collective breath while Drexler eyes the jacket: 'I hate it,' he says" (ibid.). The design is killed.

As with any Style 1 approach, the danger (more on this later) for Drexler and The Gap is that, as the company matures, the ability and benefits of maintaining such tight control come into question. Drexler's *directing* approach can be problematic. Merchandiser Kay Vewrmeulen, who left the company in 1992, had this to say: "The Gap has gotten so big you have to go through several people to get anything done. You have to sign off with this department and that department" (ibid.).

While Drexler's strong Style 1, hands-on approach has enabled him to build an incomparable retail dynasty, the impact of his domineering style may be wearing thin. Earlier this year, facing slumping performance, sales, and stock price, The Gap experienced an unprecedented exodus of executive talent, including Gap brand head Robert J. Fisher, marketing head Michael McCadden, Banana Republic head Jeanne Jackson, and chief operating officer John B. Wilson.

While one can only speculate as to the reason behind such a mass exodus, significant in all of this is Drexler's response. He has not brought in any significant new hires but instead has chosen to oversee marketing and product development. And since he did not replace COO Wilson, he has many more people reporting directly to him. "You could say Mickey Drexler is stretched thin," said Richard N. Baum, analyst at Credit Suisse First Boston (Lee 2000).

However, given his track record, Drexler should not be counted out prematurely. "You never bet against a great merchant, and Mickey Drexler is a great merchant," said Gordon Segal, CEO of Crate and Barrel (Greenberg 2000).

POLITICAL PERCEPTIONS: THE GOREY DETAILS

The 2000 presidential election between George W. Bush and Al Gore was the closest and most bitterly contested in U.S. political history. Even after Gore accepted (while not agreeing with) the Supreme Court's decision to halt manual recounts in Florida and conceded the election to Bush, it still was not clear which candidate had captured the "will of the American people." We know that Bush won the electoral college vote, and that is all that matters. We also know that Gore won the popular vote, and many believe that Florida's voters also cast more ballots for Gore.

Our intent here is not to reopen the debate about that election or to explain why one candidate lost and the other won. It is to explore the styles of the candidates, because in the absence of substance, style was more visible in that election than in most. In this chapter we will talk about Al Gore as he was perceived in the election. In chapter 6 we will talk about George W. Bush. We will let history decide which style the people preferred.

Before the 2000 campaign, Gore had a reputation for being bright, a good debater, and stiff. Regarding his intelligence, Gore was a policy wonk like Bill Clinton. Both men had a tremendous grasp of details, an ability to formulate complex theories, and a passion for debating broad policies. His debating skills were well regarded among other White House staffers and on display to the viewing public in his 1996 election debates against Jack Kemp and Ross Perot. And his wooden demeanor was legendary. Every talk show host roasted him for being stiff, and even Gore got into the act by telling a joke to Jay Leno: "What's the difference between Al Gore and a marionette? The marionette is the one who moves."

After Gore defeated Bill Bradley in the primaries, the emphasis of his campaign was on distancing himself from Bill Clinton's highly publicized private life. In doing so, he moved away from the political center that Clinton had reclaimed and fashioned an image of himself as the people's advocate. Choosing Joe Lieberman as a running mate helped on both fronts. Lieberman had risen from a blue-collar heritage to become the first Jewish vice presidential nominee, and he was one of the first Democrats to speak out against Clinton's behavior during the Lewinsky scandal.

The Democratic National Convention was orchestrated to keep Clinton in the background, introduce Lieberman as a testimony to the American dream—and a very moral one—and showcase Gore as a family man kissing his wife and hugging his children. To complete the populist message, the theme of Gore's acceptance speech was, "If you vote for me, I will fight for you." He must have said the word *fight* at least a hundred times.

From a style perspective, he was casting himself as a Style 1 leader. He wanted to be seen as his own man, with a clear vision of the future and a passion for making sure that the masses would share in the wealth of the economic expansion. For the first few weeks after the convention, that message played very well, and he experienced a tremendous surge in the polls. His supporters were ready to accept him as the *directing* candidate who would fight for their concerns.

His detractors accused him of being a *dominator*—saying and doing whatever it took to fulfill his personal ambition, shifting his position on issues, and even lying when he thought it was to his advantage. Whenever this side of Gore showed during the campaign, it was noticed. In the first debate, he was criticized for interrupting, dominating the airtime, making the same point repeatedly, and making condescending sighs when Bush said things that he disagreed with. In the aftermath, very little was said about the content of the debate—most observers thought neither candidate said much. It was all about style, and the knock on Gore was all about dominating. *Saturday Night Live* had great fun portraying him as answering questions that were intended for Bush, interrupting the moderator to tell a long-winded and exaggerated story, repeating the term *lockbox* ad nauseum, looking down his nose and sighing, and asking if he could give two closing arguments.

In the second debate, Gore was so overly polite that he was accused of being dishonest about who he was—motivated to win at all costs. He also inundated people with a lot of facts and figures, feeding the perception of him as a micro-manager. By the third debate, he went with his strength and offered detailed, in some instances very detailed, proposals for every issue. He also repeatedly pointed out the differences between himself and Bush and took every opportunity to criticize Bush's record in Texas. His message was "I'm in charge, I know where I'm going, I've got plans, and the plans are in the best interests of working people." Even though Bush's themes that night were higher level and far less specific, whatever points Gore scored on content were neutralized by his coming across as attacking Bush and the state of Texas.

After November 7, when he conceded and then rescinded his concession, Gore tried to portray himself as fighting for the people and battling for the disenfranchised to have their votes counted. But as the legal maneuvering dragged on, increasing numbers of people saw him as fighting for Al Gore. His detractors said this was the real Gore—mind made up, determined he's right, willing to fight to the bitter end, and therefore someone who couldn't govern even if he did prevail. For a while, his supporters thought the fight was about the principle of counting votes and appreciated his determination to fight for what was right. But their ranks dwindled as most people started to tune out and show the true will of the people—to get back to their usual TV programs and start their holiday shopping before it was too late.

Whatever your political persuasion, whether you saw him as *directing* or *dominating*, Al Gore in the 2000 election was a good example of the upside and downside of Style 1.

EQUAL TIME FOR THE INDEPENDENT CANDIDATES

While we are on the subject of presidential elections, it is only fair to give a little press to independent candidates. Even though no independent has come close to getting elected, several have had a major impact on various elections. In 1980, John Anderson was a liberal who split off from the Republican Party after Ronald Reagan was nominated. While he undoubtedly had a lot of outside input in making his decision, in the summer of 1980 most Republicans perceived John Anderson as marching exclusively to the beat of his own drummer. Initially, it appeared that he would take the party down with him through this willful act, but, as it turned out, he drew liberal votes away from Jimmy Carter and actually helped Reagan get elected.

In 1992, Ross Perot used his own money to finance the Reform Party as a platform for his candidacy. While he professed no love for Bill Clinton, he seemed to have a much stronger antipathy for George Bush the elder, and he certainly took away enough of Reagan's centrist coalition to help Clinton win. He was also a factor in 1996, making it almost impossible for Bob Dole to muster enough support to seriously threaten Clinton, even though many Republicans despised him.

People don't always see themselves the same way that others do, and Perot is a good example of that. We believe that if you were to ask him about his leadership style, he would probably describe himself as a *problem solver*. As a candidate, what was his answer to almost any tough problem facing the nation? His plan was to assemble some of the best experts on that particular subject, listen to their opinions, and make the tough decisions. His biggest criticism of traditional Washington decision making was the endless debates and horse trading. He often said during the 1992 and 1996 campaigns, "We don't need any more plans running around Washington. They've got plans for everything. What we need is someone who will pick the best plan and then just do it."

In all fairness, no one should forget Perot's reputation as one of the best businessmen in the country. His ability to succeed at IBM, then build EDS from scratch, then start over again with Perot Systems is clear evidence that he is able to take input from key people and make good decisions. There are also many people who have worked with him who tell stories of bringing proposals to the boss and getting his approval.

Even though he sees himself as a good listener who hears other people out before he moves ahead, he didn't come across that way in either of his political campaigns. If he listens, he processes the information so rapidly and responds so quickly that he doesn't appear to reflect on other people's perspectives. Then, when he responds, his answers are so full of detail that he can overwhelm others with his point of view, facts, and figures. He comes across as a salesman (which he once was) who listens just enough to get his foot in the door and then launches into his pitch.

In business, this has probably served him well and may even enhance his reputation as a *problem solver*. But in the political arena most observers saw Perot as a Window 1 leader. His supporters saw him as the *directing* type—a strong-willed and decisive leader who makes up his mind and then charges full steam ahead. He was their candidate to clean up the gridlock in American politics. If anyone could break the old system, Ross could.

His detractors also saw him as Style 1, but more on the *dominating* side. They told tales of his controlling ways of managing his companies and tried to make him out to be a paranoid megalomaniac. Being the strong and decisive person he is, Perot gave them plenty of evidence to work with. He often came across as *dominating* discussions by talking at great length and then crossly reprimanding reporters who would ask a focusing question. He would chide those who tried to stop his monologues by snapping, "Are you gonna let me finish?"

His firing of campaign advisors and totally independent selection of a running mate whom no one had ever heard of also fed this perception. So did his seemingly unilateral decisions to get into and out of and into the race again.

When it came to the 1992 election, many people still saw him as the guy to shake up the establishment and tackle the deficit. Most voters saw him as overly focused on one issue and too much of a loner to be effective under the intense public scrutiny of the presidency. By 1996, he had a lot of supporters, but his style had hardened, and most observers saw him as too *dominating* to be a serious contender.

Maybe an independent candidate has to be a bit of a loose cannon just to get heard. That was certainly true of Ralph Nader and of Pat Buchanan in 2000. Ralph Nader's campaign to put the Green Party on the map started out as a highly principled drive to protect the environment from the lobbyists and industrialists who, according to Nader, controlled both major parties. As the election got closer, Nader refused to listen to the argument that he was helping defeat the strongest environmentalist on the political landscape and helping elect a candidate whom he loathed.

In *dominating* fashion, Nader stayed focused on his view of the world as he siphoned off more than enough votes to enable George W. to win. Not only did he make Gore focus a lot more attention than he wanted to on states like Michigan, Minnesota, Washington, and Oregon; he got more that 92,000 votes in Florida, where the margin of victory was a few hundred.

Pat Buchanan was also a factor in 2000. Like Nader's, his campaign was driven by a strong ideology, and he had many ardent supporters who followed him from the Republican primaries to the Reform Party. As a leader, he was more persuasive on the conservative fringe of a major party than he was at the helm of an independent one. When confronted by the threat of a vote to determine the Reform Party candidate, he came across as very dominating as he maneuvered the rules to guarantee his own success. He still had his followers but didn't get much support from the party Perot had created.

Even so, he had a major impact on the election. His fractionalized Reform Party drew far fewer votes away from Bush than a unified party would have. And the location of his name on the ballot in Palm Beach may have unwittingly altered the course of U.S. history.

LOSING CONTROL

The view of the ineffective leader through Window 1 is equally striking. Consider the case of the 1992 visit of the big-three car dealers to Japan. Anyone who understands the nature of influence at all would wonder at the motives of Lee Iacocca when he conveyed to the Japanese that they'd better hear our message or else. In attempting to get the Japanese to buy more American cars, Iacocca chose to be directive at a time when a collaborative approach was needed. Consequently, he came across as *dominating* and was totally ineffective.

The ripples of that failed trip continue to be felt throughout the American automotive industry. Iacocca is an interesting case because he has long projected himself as the consummate team player, working with others, asking for a lot of input, building consensus, and generating team spirit. Yet those who work closely with him describe him as *dominating*. He loves to be in the limelight, they suggest, and say that with Lee it's "his way or no way."

Not that his way has always been bad for him and those around him. Iacocca was the visionary for such automotive industry successes as the Ford Mustang and the Chrysler minivan. He has been called the John Wayne of marketing and is by most accounts, including his own, first and foremost a pitchman, using his *directing* style to get others to do and buy what he wants them to.

He has also had his share of failures, backing a broad range of ventures, from a health-conscious fast-food chain called Koo Koo Roo Chicken to a Branson, Missouri, casino and a space-tour company. In the 1990s he entered the Internet commerce world by attaching his visage to an online asset exchange and, most recently, to an electric bicycle company. This latest venture is intended to promote interest in electric transportation by first hooking people on bicycles and then leading them to invigorate the fledgling electric car industry. His strategy here is his typical Style 1 approach. "If I can get enough bikes into garages, then eventually kids are going to pressure the old man to make an electric vehicle the family's third car" (Gibney 1999).

A far more extreme example of a *dominating* Style 1 leader is Iraqi dictator Saddam Hussein. There is little doubt that Hussein's intent is to be in total control of every aspect of his dictatorship. He controls the military, the economy, the educational system, and every cultural aspect imaginable. He aggressively tells Iraqis, Kurds, Kuwaitis, and everyone else in the world exactly what he wants and threatens consequences if people don't do what he wants. His decision-making style leaves no room for input from others, his communication is exclusively downward, and his reward system clearly emphasizes compliance: You do it his way or you get shot.

Perhaps the most astounding thing about him is his staying power—he continues to survive year after year of turmoil in perhaps the most volatile region in the world. And he has continued to lead in his *dominating* and self-aggrandizing way. According to an article in *Newsweek*, "The sanctions haven't made Saddam back down, but they have been devastating to ordinary Iraqis. With his people suffering from sanctions, Saddam is on a spending spree." He rebuilt a revolving luxury restaurant in Baghdad and "renamed it the Saddam Tower" and was building a "mammoth complex" that would become "yet another of Saddam Hussein's palaces" (Nordland 2000).

The article goes on to state that "The government remains very much a family business. Saddam's chosen successor appears to be his older son, Uday, 35, a notorious thug who is still recovering from wounds sustained in a 1996 assassination attempt. Another son, Qusay, 33, runs the secret police and other security forces and could be a less controversial contender for the succession. Internal opposition seems to have been completely suppressed, and while the Kurds in the north remain quasi-independent, Saddam's control elsewhere is total" (ibid.).

WINDOW 1 BEHAVIORS

If you analyze the above situations with regard to key leadership behaviors—decision making, communication, and recognition—you can begin to see how The L4 System works.

Kroc was an effective Style 1 leader because he retained decision-making power in a situation where the most important goal was delivery of a consistent product. He relied primarily on downward communication rather than two-way since the realization of his vision was what was important to him. And he built a reward system based on employees' abilities to meet his specs, or follow his rules. Disney employed many of the same strategies. The vision of delivering a consistently predictable experience kept the decision making in his hands, conveying that vision led to almost exclusively downward communication, and rewards were given for adhering to designated roles.

In the case of Iacocca's trip to Japan, a very different picture unfolds. Iacocca was in a position to influence a collaborative alliance between the Americans and the Japanese—a task requiring a great deal of give-and-take in which there was sharing of ideas and problem solving. Instead of taking an open position and engaging in joint decision making, Iacocca presented an ultimatum, a mistake unless you're ready and able to deliver on it—which he clearly wasn't. Instead of opening two-way channels of communication, he spoke down to his Japanese counterparts, thus diminishing the chances of any serious dialogue occurring. Since Iacocca had no real power to reward or recognize, this factor did not come into play in a significant way. However, while he certainly didn't have the power to reward in a directive leadership role, had he engaged in a more cooperative approach, he could have recognized any successful joint problem solving and rewarded his Japanese counterparts with kind words of appreciation—something highly valued in Japanese culture. Instead, he chose a heavy hand that resulted in widening the gulf between these two superpowers and lessening the chances of any true collaboration.

Hussein's dominating Style 1 behavior has certainly not served him well. While he is still in power, he now rules over a country in shambles. His unilateral decision making has caused his people untold suffering, his inability to take and use input from others has caused him humiliation and disgrace, and his heavy hand has alienated him from his people to the point where he is in constant fear for his life.

THE WINDOW 1 LEADER: DIRECTOR OR DOMINATOR

As you can see, the success of the Style 1 leader lies in the ability to make decisions unilaterally, communicate those decisions unequivocally, and reward behaviors that are in line with the leader's wishes directly. These leaders tend to be focused on their own goals and are not particularly concerned with the attitudes or developmental needs of followers. They are likely to maintain a high degree of control around decision making and task management. They rely on motivating subordinates by imposing punishments and penalties for lack of compliance and reward followers primarily for following their directions.

The Style 1 leader's top priority tends to be to get the job done as he or she believes it should be done. These leaders are most effective when they have a vision that they want others to implement, and when they are willing to take full responsibility for the results of that implementation. Some advantages of this approach are that the leader has control over completion of the task, knows precisely how things are going, and can readily identify and respond to problems as they emerge. Some disadvantages of this approach are that the leader has to be highly involved at all times, limits problem-solving capacity to his or her own abilities, and carries the burden of success or failure on his or her shoulders exclusively.

ERRORS IN AEROSPACE—A CASE STUDY

Herb was the manager of a small plastics factory. One of his key accounts was an aerospace company for whom his company manufactured plastic parts for jet engines. Over several weeks Herb received an inordinate amount of returns on a particular part cited by the customer company as not meeting specifications. Since the part was to be used for a precise instrument, it was essential that it meet exact specifications.

Herb's usual approach with his employees was to present them with clear instructions and leave them alone. He knew their jobs had the potential to be boring, so he encouraged them to be creative in developing ways to do the work. As long as quality work was getting done on time, he didn't mind that employees frequently socialized while operating their mold machines. To motivate people he would keep track of production output and occasionally announce how the shop was doing. If overall production was low, he would reprimand the group and suggest they find new ways of operating; if production was high, he would praise them and urge them to keep up the good work. As long as the work was getting done, Herb felt his hands-off approach worked well.

As it became clear to Herb that problems were emerging with the quality of the work being produced, he let the workers know this and engaged in conversations with them about what they might do to change. After a few days of observation, Herb grew increasingly concerned that the problem was not "fixing itself." In an attempt to remedy the problem without getting heavy-handed, Herb started making suggestions as to how to improve the quality of the work. He was surprised when he found the workers resistant to changing their patterns and became increasingly concerned as the delivery date for the new shipment rapidly approached.

Herb realized that in order to remedy the problem he needed to take increased control of the situation. He knew he could not afford to spend much time on the problem since competition was fierce and his contract could be jeopardized if there were any more delays. Thus, time was of the essence. Herb decided to get tough and be a directive leader. He quickly let his people know that under no circumstances would he continue to tolerate the production of substandard parts. He announced that there would be no more distracting conversation on the shop floor and began frequent inspections of parts to ensure quality. As soon as he began seeing improvements in quality, he voiced his approval to those responsible. For the next several days the tone of the plant was conspicuously sober. Any employees not producing high-quality, high-yield products were carefully scrutinized and monitored. At the end of a four-day period, the job was completed, and the parts were delivered and accepted. Eventually the plant returned to its pre-crisis state. However, the message was clear that poor-quality work would not be tolerated. Herb went back to his less controlling style but knew that if production problems arose again he would not hesitate to return to his *directing* approach. His crew knew it, too.

As seen in the above examples, the *directing* style can be quite effective when used with the right people in the right situations at the right time—and can be quite powerful and rewarding, as evidenced by the success of a Ray Kroc, Walt Disney, or Mickey Drexler. The key to Style 1's effective use is having a clear vision of what it is you're trying to accomplish, a keen understanding of how you are going to accomplish it, and an unwavering commitment to achieving your desired results.

Window 2: The Leader as Problem Solver

With every company challenging itself to improve quality, straining to become more customer oriented, and trying to find better ways to involve employees in top-level decisions, problem solving is a critical tool for every leader. The view through Window 2 will show you a number of effective leaders who are good at *problem solving*, skilled at managing the balance between openness and decisiveness.

Window 2 will also show you some leaders who rely too heavily on problem solving and therefore come across as over-involving themselves or others in the decision-making process. As you will recall from the discussion of the problem-solving style in chapter 2, a key aspect of this leadership style is that the leader retains control of the decision-making process. This is distinguished from the Style 3 approach, in which the leader supports team members' decision making in a way that develops their future problem-solving capability.

As you read this chapter, think about the choices you made on the cases in chapter 1. Is Window 2 the one you like the best?

MANAGING CRISIS THROUGH PROBLEM SOLVING

Jim Burke, the former CEO of Johnson and Johnson, is a good example of someone who effectively employed the problem-solving style of Window 2. During the Tylenol scare of the early 1980s, when traces of cyanide started showing up in bottles of Tylenol, leading to some deaths and more near deaths, most people thought that the life span of the popular painkiller was coming to an abrupt end.

What prevented Tylenol's seemingly inevitable demise was Burke's leadership in handling the crisis. Rather than merely relying on his own instincts in what was a very complex matter, Burke called on the combined brainpower of everyone around him and solicited their input on handling the problem. According to *Fortune* magazine, Burke utilized his staff's expertise to solve the problem. "Relying on his staff's sometimes noisy advice, Burke seized the initiative when seven people died from cyanide-laced Tylenol capsules in 1982. He recalled some 30 million Tylenol packages and sent out new ones with elaborate safety seals.

"When a poisoner struck again in 1986, Burke pulled all capsules off the market and sold the pain reliever only in tamper-resistant tablet and caplet form. . . . [H]e stayed cool in numerous media appearances in which he explained his efforts and soothed anxious consumers. All the while he was entertaining often sharply differing opinions about what he should do, and he believes he made better decisions as a result. Recalls Burke, 'People yelled and said what they thought and I synthesized it all. We had a tremendous fight over whether we should go on "60 Minutes."' Burke allowed CBS cameras into crucial strategy sessions, winning further public support of his efforts to contain the crisis" (Labich 1988).

What the above shows is a typical Style 2 approach in which a leader, after considering all alternatives, made an informed decision that led to surprising results and the resurgence of the product as a viable, safe choice for pain relief. This effective *problem-solving* approach should not be underestimated since, as the above example illustrates, it can mean the difference between success and failure. At the time of the Tylenol scare, most industry analysts were proclaiming the death of Tylenol as a pain-relief product. What Burke was able to do by inviting ideas from all his staff, no matter how divergent, was to make decisions that led to unlikely success and averted almost certain failure.

NOTHING "SOFT," BUT NO "MICRO" MANAGING EITHER

Arguably the most successful businessman in the history of commerce, Bill Gates is a *problem solver* extraordinaire. As the Microsoft dynasty continues to rule the software landscape—while having its very existence threatened by breakup at the hands of the federal government—Gates demonstrates his commitment to surrounding himself with people with brainpower and using them to solve problems. Whether it's preparing his case against government accusations of monopoly or figuring out how to make the Windows operating system three seconds faster, Gates is in the mix. While those around him complain that he can be a stickler for details, his dead-on instincts so often result in better resolution of problems that their complaints lose their punch.

One thing Microsoft does on a regular basis—typically every two years—is reorganize. And while Gates has plenty of lieutenants available to help him execute, his strong beliefs about the value of this activity reflect his Style 2, *problem-solving*, approach. "Done properly, reorganization can move people into new areas where they can be more creative and effective. People often hit plateaus, get too comfortable in their jobs, and no longer come up with new approaches. A realignment presents them with fresh challenges. Great results can happen when people who have worked in product areas get closer to customers, and when people who have been working with customers join the product-development cycle. This mixing helps customer-driven companies conceive and deliver better products" (Gates 2000).

When re-inventing his organization again and again, Gates carefully uses his problem-solving approach to increase the likelihood that they get it right. "In designing a new structure, you must strike a balance between keeping it logical and keeping executives happy and effective by giving them assignments they want and will handle well. During our most recent change we asked: What are our goals? How can we move them into practice? What does this imply for our structure? Will our people be excited about their new roles? Over two months our thinking evolved" (ibid.).

Gates and company are always careful not to overlook the formidable intellect present in their workforce. When executing a reorganization they take care, in true Style 2 spirit, to solicit the input of the troops. "We gathered thousands of employees together, put key executives on stage, and allocated one hour for questions and answers. We welcomed tough questions, and wanted employees to see first-hand how we responded. We wanted to know what employees were thinking" (ibid.).

While other successful entrepreneurs are often content to rest on their laurels and leave the messy task of running their organizations to others, Gates is ever present, whether the issue is business strategy or technical challenge. "I synthesize a lot of information to get a broad picture. So there are cases where I'll decide things a bit differently. But I'm the CEO and the technical strategy is in my hands. Sometimes I'm completely alone in my opinions if it's a technical question or a strategy problem. When it comes to a product decision there have been many cases when I analyze things in my own unique way. However if it's a business-type decision, rarely is my conviction sufficient to go it alone. Usually I'd take the time to get people to explain their views more clearly. That's my job and what's the point of having me here if I can't make my mind up" (Dearlove 1999).

Making up his mind can often be a very complicated process—one that historically has proven to have impact on how many of us live our lives and do our work. For example, Gates and Microsoft co-founder Paul Allen were two of the first to recognize the power of the microprocessor chip and its potential for leading to the explosive software revolution. Gates was also one of the first on the scene to see the value of building uniform operating systems resulting in a common platform for the entire PC industry.

As Gates looks down the barrel of the Justice Department's gun that threatens to split his company in two, he is faced with another formidable challenge that could once again shape our future and the tools we use to conduct our business. The challenge has to do with a new technology called XML and a new product that it drives code-named Microsoft.NET. The opportunity is enormous—to provide software that would be ingrained in billions of servers, PCs, cell phones, handheld computers, cable TV boxes, and other devices. To pull off this venture, however, requires cooperation from a variety of sources.

In order to *problem-solve* this issue, Paul Maritz, group vice president for the project, refers to Gates as "chief software architect," because he would have to gain the cooperation of archrivals like IBM, Oracle, and Sun Microsystems. And that's exactly what he's doing. Working closely with IBM and an industry standards body called the World Wide Web Consortium (which has the support of Sun, Oracle, Hewlett-Packard, Apple, and over 400 other companies), Gates and Microsoft are making a non-monopolist move toward achieving the kind of cooperation that could lead to the product's success.

What Gates is banking on is that if the consortium can achieve its goal of making a version of XML they can all get behind, then Microsoft will be the first player out of the gate, retrofitting the Windows operating system to interface successfully with all the devices utilizing XML. Taking an atypical approach—one of cooperation—toward a problem that historically would pit Microsoft against its competitors is yet another example of Gates's superior *problem-solving* abilities. Having the wisdom to bring the best technology minds in the world together rather than taking them on is perhaps "the single most courageous thing he's ever done," according to Dave Winer, founder and president of Userland, a Silicon Valley software tools company that is working on XML standards (Schendler 2000).

When he's not using his superior *problem-solving* skills to conquer the world, Gates's Style 2 philosophy about how to lead and his bias toward adopting a problem-solving mindset can be found in his description of what it takes to be a great employee: "Use your head. Analyze problems but don't fall prey to 'analysis paralysis.' Understand the implications of tradeoffs, such as acting sooner with less information and later with more. Prioritize your time effectively. Learn how to give advice crisply to other groups" (Gates 2000). This relentless pursuit of input for the sake of making things better is evidenced as well in his advice regarding customer relations: "Cultivate a genuine interest in engaging customers. Have discussions with customers about how they use your products to understand your customers' needs and likes . . . know where your company's products fall short and could be better" (ibid.).

While the big-picture issues like the Justice Department, XML, and Microsoft.NET are undoubtedly what keep Gates awake at night, his love of *problem solving* keeps him uncannily in touch with the day-to-day workings of the company. In fact, he is famous for replying to e-mails from any employee and, of course, offering his two cents on the problem. Consider the following not uncommon scenario: "Bill is exceedingly present at Microsoft. Even ordinary employees can brag about having gotten 'this close' to him. Maybe they didn't shoot him an e-mail but, as happened to Chris Hahn, a young programmer who has been at Microsoft less than a year, they sent an e-mail to their manager who forwarded it to his manager who sent it to Bill who returned it with comments. And voilá, they were part of an e-mail thread with the chairman" (Gimein 2001). And they had the benefit of Gates's input into their own *problem solving*.

ENTERTAINING EXPERTS: TWO WOMEN AT THE TOP

While a Window 2 approach can work well in the corporate arena, where both control and access to experts provide a balanced approach that many have utilized, it is also evident at the upper echelon of the entertainment industry. Consider the cases of two dynamic, high-profile women at the top—Oprah Winfrey and Madonna. For the past fifteen years both women have demonstrated an uncanny ability to manage their careers by continuously reinventing themselves and recasting their positions in the marketplace.

Oprah has continued her reign at the top of the TV talk show circuit even as she proved herself a formidable marketer of other people's books via Oprah's Book Club. She has also demonstrated the ability to transfer her appeal to additional media via the magazine *O*, launched in the late 1990s.

Madonna spent the 1990s proving she could keep the public's attention by improving her singing and acting in the well-received *Evita* and continuing her chameleon-like singing career, shifting almost effortlessly from one persona to another, setting trends along the way. Her most recent coup was a $46 million deal she cut with Microsoft for the webcast of a concert that was seen by 9 million viewers.

Both are enormously successful entertainers—and businesswomen—with net revenues in the millions. And both, it seems, are essentially Style 2 leaders. According to an article in *Working Woman* magazine, both women run carefully controlled operations where they retain all the important decision making, utilize a select group of advisors, and reward people for helping them make sound judgments and business decisions. "In an industry where stars traditionally turn business matters over to others and wealth is measured by how much money isn't bilked each year, Oprah and Madonna are notable for their independence. Each charts her own course and keeps her hand firmly on the corporate tiller, putting in long hours managing her holdings, investments and public image. As businesswomen, they share one important trait: both are control freaks" (Goodman 1991).

However, since they are both entertainers first and business moguls second, each seems to recognize the need for expert advice. For example, Madonna has a stable of the best businesspeople helping her manage her affairs—Bert Padell, the leading music industry accountant, Paul Schindler, a well-known entertainment attorney, and Liz Rosenberg, considered one of Warner Brothers' top publicists. In true Style 2 form, Madonna uses these independent experts in accounting, law, and publicity to help her make decisions, rather than hire a group of lesser talent that she could more readily direct. This strategy allows her to maintain a hands-on approach while still benefiting from the wisdom and experience of others.

"She has a very strong hand in deal-making and financing of her enterprises. Nothing gets done without her participation," said Jeffrey Katzenberg, then chairman of Disney Studios, who dealt with her during the production of *Dick Tracy*. He added that she used her lawyers, accountants, and advisors "as aides in making her own judgment, as opposed to having them run her life" (Schifrin 1990).

Oprah uses a similar Style 2 formula for ensuring her dynasty's success, although she relies heavily on one person, Jeffrey Jacobs (one of only two of Winfrey's full-timers). Consider the following from a *Ms.* magazine article on Winfrey: "Winfrey describes Jacobs' presence in her life as a gift. 'He helped me to see that I really could have control and didn't have to be simply a talent.' Jacobs insisted that she be 100 percent in charge of her business. 'It's my job to present research, options, and opinions to her,' he says. 'We discuss them and then she makes the decisions. I work for her and with her,' he adds, 'and because of that, we've built an organization where she knows exactly what's going on at all times. She signs the checks, she makes the decisions. I protect her and look at things from a legal as well as business standpoint, but she understands this organization from top to bottom.'

"With Jacobs' help, Winfrey operates similarly to Madonna, utilizing panels of experts to provide input into her decision making. Says Jacobs, 'I tried to find the best and the brightest people in the financial and banking communities here in Chicago. . . . We all meet periodically and come up with a consensus opinion. Sometimes Oprah sits in the meetings and sometimes—because of her travel schedule—she can't. But she's always presented with the information, and then she makes a decision. So she's really in control of her money' " (Gillespie 1988).

BUILDING ALLIANCES—
THE LEADERSHIP OF POLITICS

George Bush the elder, president from 1988 to 1992, provides another good example of a Window 2 leader, as long as you focus on his presidency in terms of foreign policy. If you focus on domestic policy, his view was not through Window 2 at all, but you will read more about that side of Bush in the next two chapters.

Bush's greatest successes as president came in the international arena. Early in his administration, he pushed for the invasion of Panama to capture accused drug lord Manuel Noriega. Using a *problem-solving* approach, Bush gathered the input of knowledgeable military advisors, ignored the political counsel of those who said that such an invasion would violate the international sovereignty of Panama, and went forward with the plan. This gathering of expert opinion and subsequent decision making based on that informed opinion are hallmarks of the *problem-solving* leadership approach.

Some accused him of grandstanding in order to overcome the "wimp" image that had haunted him during the campaign against Michael Dukakis. Others accused him of trying to silence Noriega, who supposedly knew too much about Bush from his CIA days. But most people saw Bush as a strong leader who was willing to use force in pursuit of his agenda, which, in this case, was the "interdiction" of large-scale drug trafficking from Latin America. In fact, the biggest criticism of the Panama invasion was that Bush should have been more decisive when he got input that Panamanians were holding Noriega. Better use of *problem solving* might have saved lives and helped the Panamanians at the same time.

Later, when Saddam Hussein became a threat in the Middle East, Bush seemed to have strengthened his ability to use Style 2. Before and during Operation Desert Storm, Bush was masterful in his ability to build a strong coalition with other world leaders, including several from the Middle East whose countries had been in conflict for centuries. He also used the United Nations skillfully by persuading that international body to pass the resolutions that he fully intended to enforce and was very adept in his timing as he picked the right moment to bring the issue before the U.S. Congress.

Throughout the conflict with Iraq, Bush spent incredible amounts of time in ongoing communication with other world leaders, in part to keep the coalition alive, but also to get continuous input to his decision making. He also listened closely to advice from the military. Most important, the perception of George Bush throughout Desert Storm was that he was a leader who could forge solid alliances and would listen to input from all key people but still be the one in charge. Bush was a perfect Style 2 leader in this situation, and his popularity in the polls was, just after the war, higher than that of any president since the polling game began.

Ironically, Bush's powerful use of Style 2 in the foreign policy arena actually hurt him a year later when he was running for reelection. We will say more about that in the next chapter.

FROM WAFFLER TO WINNER

In 1992, the successful presidential campaign of Bill Clinton illustrated how a Style 2 strategy can work to combat accusations of ineffectiveness. Perhaps the biggest threat to Clinton's successful race to the White House was the accusation by the Bush campaign that Clinton was a waffler—indecisive and *over-accommodating*. Ads showing two faces of Bill Clinton filled the airwaves, and the suggestion by Bush that Clinton could not be trusted seemed to be cutting into Clinton's lead just weeks before the election. Indications were that the Bush campaign had struck a nerve, that perhaps Clinton's Achilles' heel was his inability to be decisive and his tendency to be overly compromising (more on this later).

What Clinton managed to do in response to this threat was to shift from what by most observers' accounts had been an overly solicitous, crowd-pleasing approach, laden with generalities about change, to a very focused, specific delineation of what he would do if he were president. Concrete, well-thought-out plans to overhaul the health care system, rebuild the nation's infrastructure of bridges and highways, and revitalize the government's approach to employment and training led to a dramatic shift in perception that Clinton was not just a smooth talker but an active *problem solver* with a plan.

Many political observers believe that while Bush continued to focus on the nebulous issue of character, it was Clinton's attention to the issues both during and after the debates that led to the Democrat's victory.

Most important, Clinton was able to keep the focus on the domestic agenda; in the words on his campaign wall, "It's the Economy, stupid!" Knowing that Bush's strength was in foreign policy and that his weakness was the sluggish economy, Clinton had to convince the voters that he was the leader to turn the economy around. He had to make them believe that he would be more likely than George Bush to use Style 2 on economic issues. His message was that he would listen to a much broader constituency than Bush had and that he would be much more decisive in responding to their concerns.

Then he specifically defined his constituents as everyone making less than $200,000 a year, which, of course, included most people who could vote. To demonstrate his willingness to be decisive on their behalf, he promised to raise taxes on that same upper-income group that had profited during the Reagan–Bush years. He also promised not to allow taxes to be raised on those people making less than $200,000.

By election time, it was almost irrelevant whether his policies would work or not. As a leader, he had dodged a bullet by not letting Bush's accusations stick him with the *over-accommodating* waffler label. He was able to convince the public that he would listen to them and then make the tough decisions as the Style 2 leader of the downtrodden masses.

Defining himself as a *problem solver* was a struggle for Clinton from the outset of his presidency. His first stake in the ground after his inauguration was about gays in the military, an issue where his attempts to please everyone made him appear extremely *over-accommodating*. Another one of his earliest actions was convening an economic summit, which looked like rampant *over-involving* to most of the public and the press. Before his first year was half over, he looked so wishy-washy that he added David Gergen, a former Reagan advisor, to his staff specifically to improve his image. Gergen's job was to help Clinton appear more decisive. Within a few weeks, *Newsweek* ran a lengthy article about a typical presidential day, in which Clinton came across as open but very decisive. We were reassured that he always had been solving problems, but we didn't know it. A few weeks after that, Clinton used all of his political muscle to get his deficit-reduction budget passed and again was back in the driver's seat.

As Clinton matured into the presidency, he became increasingly adept at hardball politics. He frequently turned to the media to gain support for his position, convincing enough people that he was acting on their behalf that he was able to beat back congressional adversaries like Newt Gingrich. When he called the Republican leaders' bluff on shutting down the government, he looked like a problem solver—taking input from all sides but holding a firm ground against his opponents.

When he ran for reelection against Bob Dole in 1996, in many ways the election was a referendum on his *problem-solving* skills. Like George Bush in 1992, Dole wanted the main issue to be character. At the Republican National Convention, his wife, Libby, told the American public about his roots in Kansas, his military history, and his years of service to the country. Dole and his running mate, Jack Kemp, told us how untrustworthy Clinton was and how honorable they were. And on a personal level, maybe they were.

But on the political level, they didn't convince many people to make a change. Why? In Dole's acceptance speech, he said the number one problem facing the country was that the economy wasn't performing as well as it could. And his proposal for fixing that problem was a 15 percent across-the-board tax cut. Unfortunately, very few people believed the economy was sputtering, and only a handful of economists would endorse the tax cut. Dole had identified a problem that people didn't see and proposed a solution that they didn't believe would work. Then he said, "Trust me."

Many voters had some serious reservations about Clinton as a person, and that was even before the Lewinsky scandal got him impeached and nearly removed from office. But they did trust him to understand the issues that were important to them and use his *problem-solving* skills to make changes that would keep the economy growing. That's what he advertised in 1992 and we believe that is why, despite the concerns about his character, he got reelected in 1996.

UNPRECEDENTED PRESIDENT

The 2008 presidential election guaranteed an unprecedented outcome—the first black president or the first female vice president. There are many reasons why Barack Obama won, but his *problem solving* leadership style was a key factor.

"No drama Obama" was the mantra of his campaign. In part that was a reflection of his ability to be cool under fire, but it was also a clear statement that he expected his staffers to behave professionally and avoid the internal conflicts that often haunt political campaigns. He was decisive and directive about what he wanted. Obama was also a good listener. Warren Buffett and Republican Colin Powell were effusive about his thirst for knowledge, his asking of probing questions, and his ability to grasp a wide range of topics.

He was seen as an intellectually curious leader who would seek input before making key decisions.

This approach was in contrast to John McCain's Style 1. As a fighter pilot he had learned to make quick, independent decisions, including rapid changes of course. As a presidential candidate, changing positions didn't inspire voter confidence, and making unilateral decisions—especially poor ones like his choice of running mate—hurt him even more.

Shortly after the election, Obama showed his preference for *problem solving* when he said he would select cabinet members who would voice strong opinions and fully engage in debates. In his words there would be no "groupthink" in his administration.

In office, Obama's *problem solving* was most visible in hunting down Osama Bin Laden as he asked questions, listened to advisors, pushed for more alternatives, but by all accounts made the call. Some people viewed his response to the recession the same way—listening to a wide range of opinions and making tough decisions to prevent a deeper recession. Others accused him of being *over-involved* in the private sector.

Some critics also said he was *over-involving* with the Accountable Care Act, aka Obamacare. The debates, town hall meetings, negotiations, and compromises went on forever, and at the end it was hard to tell what the outcome was. But like any true *problem solver*, Obama said this was always intended as a first step toward a more complete solution.

WHEN HANDS-ON IS OFF BASE

Window 2 leaders are not always effective. Sometimes they operate out of Window 2 too much, leading to accusations of being *over-involving*.

A historical case in point was President Jimmy Carter, whose grasp of the details turned his *problem-solving* strength into an *over-involving* handicap. Carter was a voracious reader who would absorb so much information that people used to joke that he knew who was using the White House's tennis court at any hour of any day. To many, Carter's downfall as a president was caused by his inability to know when to allow others to take the reins.

The most glaring example of this was the abortive attempt to rescue American hostages who were being held captive in Iran. After that mission failed, Carter himself said that he should have listened better to his military advisors. Instead, by his own admission, he got too involved and made a lousy decision.

Imagine what would have happened if that mission had succeeded. Carter probably would have been a hero and most likely would have been reelected. This is a strong example of how a leadership style can impact one person's career as well as world history.

Ironically, Carter's *problem-solving* style, which he demonstrated superbly during the Camp David meetings between Anwar Sadat and Menachem Begin, has served him well in his post-presidency as a hands-on leader of the low-income housing organization Habitat for Humanity. In this situation, his willingness to get his hands dirty and to personally involve himself in the details has inspired many others to participate in solving one of the nation's most pressing problems.

Carter also demonstrated his willingness to be a creative *problem solver* by offering up his services and those of his Republican counterpart, Gerald Ford, as overseers of a recount of the contested Florida vote in the 2000 presidential election. While his offer was swiftly shot down by Republican candidate George W. Bush, his solution to bring integrity to the process by involving two widely respected former presidents demonstrated his *problem-solving* style.

THE BEST OF TIMES AND THE WORST OF TIMES

Another example of a politician who fits the profile of a Window 2 leader is John F. Kennedy. Even when he was in office, long before he had been elevated to mythical status, Kennedy was admired as a leader who surrounded himself with the best and the brightest advisors. He was known for being able to absorb tremendous amounts of information and was certainly willing to be decisive in pursuit of his agenda. He is highly regarded for the commitment he made to the National Aeronautics and Space Administration (NASA), a commitment which included his compelling vision to put a man on the moon. His handling of the Cuban missile crisis is still reviewed as the textbook for showdown diplomacy.

Kennedy also provides a good demonstration of how a leader's greatest strength can also become a liability. The most glaring example of his ineffective use of Style 2 was the *over-involving* activity that precipitated the Bay of Pigs fiasco. A classic case of ineffective decision making, the Kennedy team's process was the subject of a chapter in *Victims of Groupthink*, by Irving Janis. Janis's book paints a vivid scenario of Kennedy as both an ineffective Style 2 leader and (a year and a half later) an effective Style 2 leader, and it provides us with a compelling portrait of that style in action.

First, some background. In January of 1961, the CIA and the Joint Chiefs of Staff briefed President Kennedy and his leading advisors about a plan hatched by the Eisenhower administration. The idea was to overthrow the Cuban government of Fidel Castro by secretly placing a small brigade of Cuban exiles on a beachhead in Cuba. According to Janis, Kennedy and his top advisors assumed that "use of the exile brigade would make possible the toppling of Castro without actual aggression by the United States" (Janis 1967, p. 15).

The plan proved to be what historians describe as a perfect failure. In examining the leadership approach in this situation we can see, with the help of Janis's analysis of the decision-making process, a classic case of *over-involving*. According to Janis, group norms had developed within Kennedy's inner circle of advisors around the belief that they were, in fact, the best and brightest.

Janis refers to "mindguards" and an aura of invincibility as two of the traps that cloaked their discussions.

Discussing issues without full debate is another symptom of *over-involving*. Janis writes, "Whatever may have been the political or psychological reasons that motivated President Kennedy to give preferential treatment to the two CIA chiefs Dulles and Bissell, he evidently succeeded in conveying to the other members of the core group, perhaps without realizing it, that the CIA's baby should not be treated harshly. His way of handling the meetings, particularly his adherence to the extraordinary procedure of allowing every critical comment to be immediately refuted by Dulles or Bissell without allowing the group a chance to mull over the potential objections, probably set the norm of going easy on the plan. . . . Evidently, the members of the group adopted this norm and sought concurrence . . . without looking too closely into the basic arguments for such a plan and without debating the questionable estimates sufficiently to discover that the whole idea ought to be thrown out" (Janis 1967, p. 48).

More specifically, at one point in the debate, in an attempt to resolve the crisis, Kennedy pressured his cabinet to comply with his views on what should be done. As a result of this pressure, decisions were made that led to near disaster.

When interviewed after the fact, several of Kennedy's chief aides said that they felt uncomfortable stating their true opinions because the charismatic, influential Kennedy was so adamant about what should be done. In this case the retention of control that is characteristic of the Style 2 leader clearly led to his *over-involvement* and lack of ability to tap the formidable talents of his staff.

Interestingly, it seems in retrospect that Kennedy learned from his mistakes. A year and a half after the Bay of Pigs incident, the Kennedy administration was faced with another challenge, the Cuban missile crisis. In this instance Kennedy once again acted as a Style 2 leader; however, this time he was an effective *problem solver*.

Again, some background. One of the outcomes of the Bay of Pigs fiasco was the establishment of a deal between the Soviet Union and Cuba to set up nuclear bomb installations on Cuba targeted at the U.S., establishing Cuba as a powerful military satellite of the Soviet Union. The result of this action was the Cuban missile crisis, considered by most historians to be the greatest risk to mankind since the advent of nuclear weapons. The crisis spanned a period of thirteen days during October 1962. Speculation had been growing that in spite of Cuba's insistence that it was doing nothing more than reinforcing its own air defense system, it was in fact building an arsenal of deadly missiles aimed at the United States. On October 16, 1962, photos taken by a U-2 plane over Cuba confirmed that speculation, and the crisis began.

JFK's initial response to the threat was to launch air attacks against Cuba, but rather than go with his own inclination he decided, given the stakes involved, to once again call on his panel of experts. However, this time he employed the effective *problem-solving* approach of Style 2. Rather than ride herd over his cabinet and risk stifling their *problem-solving* capacity as he had in the previous incident, Kennedy intentionally took actions designed to lead toward the best possible solution.

Consider the following analysis of Kennedy's actions: "[I]nstead of inducing the group at the opening session to focus on the air-strike action he favored, President Kennedy emphasized the need to canvas alternatives. His message was that 'action was imperative' but he wanted the members to devote themselves to making a 'prompt and intensive survey of the dangers and all possible courses of action'" (Janis 1967, pp. 149–50). In addition, reports Janis, he called on outsiders to get their opinions as well, such as UN representative Adlai Stevenson, representatives from other government agencies, and distinguished outsiders. So committed was Kennedy to avoiding contaminating the *problem-solving* process with his own *over-involvement* that he even absented himself from cabinet meetings for two days, leaving instructions that communicated his desire to hear all divergent views and recommendations from those most capable of helping him solve the problem. Many observers believe that the actions taken as a result of this strategy led to the aversion of a major military confrontation.

In this case, Kennedy found a way to remain in control and be seen as the final decision maker while encouraging his team members to give him their most complete and uncensored advice.

INTERNATIONAL WINDOW 2

Sometimes the very nature of the political arena demands a certain style of leadership. Consider the case of Israel. Whether or not you agree with its policies, a study of its political structure can be enlightening in terms of the way that Style 2 leadership can work.

From David Ben-Gurion to Golda Meir to Yitzhak Rabin, Style 2 emerges as the predominant style in this wide-open democracy. The Israeli Knesset probably has more open and freewheeling debates than any other parliamentary body in the world. Israeli leaders tend to be strong-willed and outspoken, representing a multitude of small special-interest parties that must be brought into a coalition for any of the major parties to form a government. All the successful leaders have been able to take input from a wide range of sources who often hold differing points of view and formulate policy that the various splinter groups are willing to follow.

In Israeli politics, any leader who is not a good *problem solver* would have a very difficult time surviving. In fact, Menachem Begin and his successor, Yitzhak Shamir, were both strong Style 2 leaders, but they chose to take input from different groups of constituents than those their rivals in the Labor Party had consulted. In time, Shamir's steadfast refusal to accept input from the forces seeking a resolution of hostilities with the Palestinians led to the perception that he and his party were not focused on *problem solving*.

As a result, the Labor Party and its leader, Yitzhak Rabin, were returned to power with a platform based on a *problem-solving* style that would include input from the Palestinians.

Rabin was a pragmatist. Most Israeli leaders tend to be driven by their Zionist zeal to conquer their enemies. Rabin was probably the first to realize that, while the answer was not to do the unthinkable by embracing Israel's enemy, it might be found by engaging them in a process for mutual coexistence. "In the 1992 elections, Rabin campaigned as the man who could bring the country peace with security. But to succeed, Rabin told Israelis, they would have to relinquish a central part of their identity—their sense of fearful isolation. 'For many years, by necessity, by threat from wars and terror,' he explains, 'we developed a feeling of a besieged country that the whole world is against us.' This created a certain national psychology: Don't trust anyone; everybody is against you. It created a mistrust of peace" (Rabin and Arafat 1994).

This thinking was Style 2, *problem solving,* of the highest order—take input to a seemingly unsolvable problem from all vantage points, even from those whom you loathe and see as a very threat to your existence. Perhaps the most poignant moment in Rabin's lifelong crusade to solve this problem took place on the South Lawn of the White House on September 13, 1993. On that day, Rabin found himself in the awkward position of shaking hands with archrival Yasser Arafat—a symbolic gesture to emphasize his commitment to finding an answer. Unfortunately, Rabin's crusade to form a lasting peace by orchestrating an inclusive *problem-solving* approach to this inordinately complex problem was cut short in 1996 by an extremist's bullet.

The February 2001 election of right-wing leader Ariel Sharon as prime minister of Israel, replacing the more moderate Ehud Barak, suggests that the days of quiet diplomacy between Israel and the Palestinians under the stewardship of former U.S. President Bill Clinton are, for now, over. In 2001, the all too familiar violence between these two populations is once again reaching tragic proportions. Whether any Israeli leader and Palestinian leader Yasser Arafat can find their way to the negotiating table to create a lasting peace relies in large part on whether anyone can solve a problem that up to this point appears unsolvable.

WINDOW 2 SOVIET STYLE

While we're on the subject of international politics and culturally acceptable leadership styles, Russia (and the former Soviet Union) offers an interesting leadership story. From Lenin to Stalin to Khrushchev to Brezhnev to Kosygin and Andropov, the Soviet Union experienced a series of very strong Style 1 leaders who were every bit as *dominating* and ruthless as the czars whom they replaced.

Finally, when Mikhail Gorbachev came into power, a truly different breed of leader arrived at the top of the Communist Party. Gorbachev was far more willing to listen to input from within his country and from foreign sources.

He was far more tolerant of open dissent and candid debate than any of his nation's previous leaders.

As with many leaders, his strength became his undoing in the long run. He also provides a good illustration of what can happen when a leader says one thing and does another.

When Gorbachev began negotiating with Eastern European satellites about a new relationship with the Soviet Union, he began the discussions using Style 2. He wanted to listen to their concerns but made it clear that he (and the Soviet Union) were in control of the final decisions. However, as the negotiations proceeded, he did more listening than controlling. As a result, he allowed the satellite leaders to make their own decisions with his advice and counsel. To the Western media, he came across as Style 3, *developing*, and was hailed as a new-age leader who was willing to listen. To his constituents, he came across as Style 3, *over-accommodating,* and was seen as open and democratic, but potentially weak.

Shortly thereafter, the Baltic states began their own negotiations to re-structure their relations with the Soviet Union. In this situation, Gorbachev was inconsistent again. He began the negotiations with Style 3, saying that he would listen, be supportive, and work with them to find a mutually agreeable solution. In practice, however, he drew back to Style 2 by making decisions that did not reflect input from the Baltic leaders. The hard-liners praised him for listening to their input and saw him as *problem solving,* while the Baltic states accused him of *over-involving,* going through the motions with them while accepting too much input from the hard-liners.

Beyond these foreign-policy decisions, Gorbachev's gravest problem was the Soviet Union's staggering economy. Here, too, he walked an ambiguous line. His main style was Style 3. He wanted open debate and believed that good solutions would emerge from listening. On the other hand, he followed a long tradition of strong-willed Style 1 leaders who listen to no one. The masses wanted input, but they also wanted strength at the top. The politicians also required a strongman at the helm. As a result, Gorbachev had to use Style 2 more than he wanted and came across as an ambivalent leader in the process.

With his style changes, the people turned to the streets, ousted their local Communist Party officials, and turned to the outside world for recognition as independent states. As Gorbachev attempted to retain power, the union crumbled beneath him.

The leader who followed Gorbachev, Boris Yeltsin, actually was more of a Style 2 leader than Gorbachev, even though his political views were more liberal.

Yeltsin, a very strong anti-communist and a very strong advocate of free-market forces, was quite willing to dismantle the Soviet Union to get a fresh start with those countries who truly wanted to be in a union by choice, not force. As a leader, because he was much stronger and willing to be more decisive, he actually was able to gain more respect within the Soviet Union. His use of Style 2 was a smoother transition from the centuries of *dominating* leadership to an acceptable level of *problem solving.*

The ascension of Vladimir Putin to the leadership of Russia continues the trend toward a *problem-solving* style of leadership that began with Gorbachev and Yeltsin. Putin operates in a more modernistic way than the oligarchs of previous eras, focusing on bringing his country into the twenty-first century. His problem—and, appropriately, his focus—is on bringing economic prosperity to a part of the world that has not seen it in a long time.

Economists who study the region believe this is an opportune time to improve the economic landscape but that there are many challenges to doing so, including the need to modernize Russia's production facilities, infrastructure, and labor force. In response to this need, early after his victory, Putin declared his intention to create a nation of "maximum economic freedom" and established the Center for Strategic Research (CSR), made up of pro-market scholars whose charge was to provide him with input and advice on economic policy.

In his first eighteen months as Russia's president, Putin has had his *problem-solving* skills challenged considerably. His entrepreneurial strategy for reviving his country's economy has not been well received in other parts of the world. In fact, his willingness to supply arms to China and Iran has recently resurrected the specter of a cold war between Russia and the United States. His hesitance to enter into talks regarding arms control—under pressure from internal defense hardliners—could further threaten U.S.-Russia relations. On the domestic front his efforts to construct a more independent legal system have met serious opposition from both federal prosecutors and regional governors. While Putin appears to be committed to a *problem-solving* approach, only time will tell whether he will be able to bring his country—both socially and economically—into the twenty-first century.

THE STYLE 2 LEADER:
PROBLEM SOLVER OR OVER-INVOLVER

What the previous examples allude to is the centrality of information gathering and assimilating that is key to the Style 2 leader. Like the Style 1 leader, this type of leader retains control over decision making, but, unlike his or her Style 1 counterparts, this leader pays close attention to what others have to say. This style of leadership can be particularly effective in situations where others have access to key information but are not in a position to make the decision.

In a classic study of the difference in effectiveness between a Style 1 leader and a Style 2 leader, industrial psychologists Robert Blake and Jane Mouton (1964) tell of a situation that highlights the potential effectiveness of *problem solving* and the potential liabilities of *directing*. The case has to do with a major airline that was experiencing an inordinate amount of "near misses" by its pilots. The airline decided to bring in consultants to train the pilots to be more decisive. After the decisiveness training, airline officials were puzzled by the lack of reduction of near-miss incidents. With the help of the consultants, they came to the realization that they were operating under a false assumption—that the problem *was* one of decisiveness. What they learned after studying these crisis situations was not that the pilots were indecisive, but rather that they were underutilizing the resources in the cockpit. In other words, when faced with a quick but crucial decision, pilots were using a Style 1 approach and making unilateral decisions without consulting the other members of the cockpit crew.

What finally led to a reduction in near misses was training the pilots in how to more effectively gather information from other crew members, synthesize that information, and then make an informed decision. They needed to be better *problem solvers*, not quicker unilateral decision makers.

Like the political leaders discussed earlier, the pilots in this situation had to learn to be better listeners and information processors. The role of the Style 2 leader is to take in as much information as possible, sort it, and act as a result of a full understanding of the parameters of the situation. When this style is used with the right people in the right way, it can be a powerful tool for any leader for whom responsibility and control are primary.

What it offers a leader is the opportunity to utilize the knowledge and experience of followers. The advantage of a Style 2 approach is that the leader taps the talents of followers yet still maintains control over the process and the end result. The disadvantage of this approach is that it can result in a time-consuming process in which followers or the leader are more involved in making decisions that could be more efficiently made another way.

FROM CRUNCHING NUMBERS TO CREATING QUALITY—A CASE STUDY

Dick had just become the manager of human resources for a large computer company after having worked in the organization's accounting department. The shift, although unusual, made sense since he had been studying human-resource development in graduate school and had been a loyal employee. More important, he was seen as someone who was very decisive and was good at working with other people.

Dick had an advantage moving into his position since he was an insider and had thus seen the operation from that viewpoint. He knew coming in that he was going to make some changes. The human-resource department, in his opinion and in that of his superiors, was "soft." The training they offered was focused primarily on self-development, and it seemed apparent that the management of the department emphasized the development of the human-resource staff itself as a priority.

Dick was brought in after the previous manager of human resources was let go amid complaints that there was no consistency in the training coming out of the department and that there was no way of measuring the effectiveness of the department's work. In management's view, the department had become a "consensual free-for-all" where no one was accountable and no one was at the helm.

Upon arrival in the department, Dick announced to his new staff that all programs currently in progress would be halted immediately and that he would spend the next month entertaining proposals for training programs. He stressed that he would be making the final decision on whether a program would run but encouraged staff members to present their most creative and innovative ideas for consideration. Programs would be judged, he informed staff, on the extent to which they were measurable and clearly tied to the goals of the organization. Each new proposed program, he stated, would have to pass his rigorous requirements and would have to be viewed by management as worthwhile and substantive.

For the next four weeks, Dick maintained an open-door policy and spent most of his time listening to and evaluating proposals. He made a point of informing people of the status of their proposals as soon as possible. Those whose proposals passed his strict criteria were given the go-ahead to develop their programs; those whose ideas didn't pass were told what was lacking and were encouraged to revamp and resubmit their ideas.

Within a couple of months, Dick's *problem-solving* leadership style had turned the department around. Enrollments in the department's classes were up and there was a general feeling throughout the company that training was now a viable professional development department that added value to employees' repertoire of skills.

As with any shift in leadership, there were some problems. Several trainers, frustrated with the new controls exerted over them, quit, while others complained to top management about the changes. (Since Dick had the sanction of his superiors, this was not a problem.) He eventually lost some staff to transfers to other departments, but he was able to replace the people he lost with new staff who were willing to comply with his approach.

In addition, the people who survived were happy to work in a department that could demonstrate measurable results. To not be under the gun as a department, as they were with their previous manager, was quite a relief.

While Dick feels the pressure of shouldering the responsibility for the department's accountability, he is pleased with the company's shifting view of human resources from one of a questionable contributor to one of a department that gets things done. And he is confident that once some of his senior trainers establish their footing, he can begin delegating some of the decision making to them.

Window 3: The Leader as Developer

The leadership style that receives the most lip service in today's more forward-thinking organizations resides in Window 3. Many leaders attempting to meet the demands of an increasingly sophisticated workforce adopt a *developing* approach by listening to people, implementing job rotation strategies, and offering skill building and other career-enhancement opportunities. This developer approach can be a powerful leadership tool at the right time; however, it can be disastrous if used with the wrong people at the wrong time. At its worst, it creates a perception that the leader is unwilling to take a stand and is *over-accommodating,* trying to listen to every point of view and to make everybody happy.

As discussed in chapter 2, the key to understanding the *developing* approach is in looking at the ways communication, recognition, and, perhaps most important, decision making play themselves out in this style. In Style 3, the leader is primarily on the receiving end of communication, listening actively and helping the team member sort things out. Recognition is provided for asking the leader's help in solving his or her own problems.

This leads us to the primary distinction between a Style 2, *problem-solving,* approach and the Style 3, *developing,* approach. The difference is—and it's an important one—that the shift from Style 2 to Style 3 involves a fundamental change in the way decision making gets handled. In Style 3, the leader defers responsibility for solving the problem to team members and thus assists and supports them in solving the problem but does not, as in the case of Style 2, solve the problem for them. Keep this distinction in mind as you read this chapter and it will help you better understand the essence and distinct nature of the *developing* window.

Again, as you read about these people, think about yourself. In what ways do you resemble these Window 3 leaders?

EMPOWERING SELECTIVELY

A good example of a *developing* leader is Warren Buffett, CEO of the holding company Berkshire Hathaway. Buffet is not your typical acquisitions mogul. He buys only companies that he believes in and can get behind; then he gets behind them. What he does as a developer is quite simple. Periodically, he sits down with the top people of a newly acquired company and listens to them—using his experience to help them sort out their own problems. He can be quite pointed in his advice if he needs to be, but his preference is to help others solve their own problems.

In fact, Buffett functions as a kind of consultant to those in his charge. "His operating managers can call him whenever they wish with whatever concerns they have, and none pass up the opportunity to draw on his encyclopedic knowledge of the way businesses work" (Loomis 1988).

This accessible but non-domineering approach is the hallmark of a Style 3 leader in that it emphasizes Buffett's preference for supporting people rather than controlling them—and it pays off in many ways to those charged with running Berkshire Hathaway's companies. For example, Ralph Schey, chairman of Buffett's Scott & Fetzer Company, says that working with Buffett has provided him with more autonomy and support than he's experienced anywhere else. "If I couldn't own Scott & Fetzer myself," says Schey, "this is the next best thing" (ibid.).

There can be a downside to this type of hands-off approach, suggest some who work for Buffett (although he is almost unanimously praised by all who report to him). Robert Heldman, who runs Fechheimer Brothers, a Cincinnati manufacturer and distributor of uniforms, also under Buffett, reluctantly suggests that there are times when he would like to see Buffett be a little more hands-on. " 'He never second-guesses us. Maybe he should do more of that.' Buffett roars upon learning of this complaint: 'Believe me, if they needed second-guessing—which they definitely don't—they'd get it' " (ibid.).

One of the keys to Buffett's success as a high-support leader is that when buying companies he looks for not only quality in the company, but quality in the management as well. He is often quoted as saying that what he looks for is "wonderful businesses run by wonderful people." According to *Fortune,* that was one of the main reasons he bought Fechheimer Brothers, a company smaller than his usual acquisitions. Robert and George Heldman, owners of Fechheimer, "seemed so completely the kind of managers he looks for—likable, talented, honest, and goal-driven" (ibid.). Perhaps the key to Buffett's success, aside from having a gift for smart investing, is that he finds people who know what they are doing and helps them do it.

He also rewards them for making good decisions that lead to improved performance. Many people had never heard of Buffett before he was asked to become CEO of Salomon Brothers. "Just two years after the Salomon scandal brought the firm to the brink of collapse, Wall Street's preeminent trading house has been thoroughly reformed. Buffett's secret: stressing two themes critical for running any business—proper allocation of capital, and management incentives tied to producing shareholder value.

"You can't pay for performance unless you really measure it—and pre-Buffett, Salomon didn't. . . . Accordingly, they allocated expenses to the business units, and since compensation is now linked directly to each operation's earnings, managers are inspired to squeeze out costs" (Fisher 1993). Buffett's predecessor at Salomon, John Gutfreund, "had exercised absolute power and ran the business more like a clubby partnership than the gigantic publicly held company it has become" (ibid.). Buffett shifted decision-making responsibility downward and rewarded managers for seeking whatever input would enable them to impact the bottom line. This is one more hallmark of a *developing*, but certainly not *over-accommodating*, leader.

Currently one of the world's five richest people with an estimated net worth of 31 billion dollars, Buffett has continued to use his hallmark Style 3 approach to further enrich the coffers of his company, Berkshire Hathaway, and enhance the fate of the companies he acquires. Like a true *developer*, Buffett finds many ways to support those blessed with his attention.

Throughout the 1990s he has continued to acquire well-run companies and support them by recognizing what they do well and letting them do it, as he has done with recent acquisitions Geico and National Indemnity. Says John Cashin, executive vice president of Willis Faber North America, "Buffett has a track record for buying proven companies and letting them do what they do best without intruding" (Banham 1998).

While certainly not always as hands off as he is described in this instance, Buffett has a long-standing reputation centered on providing a high level of support. Sometimes that support is in the form of managerial advice and counsel, as described earlier. At other times, the support takes on a very concrete form, as was the case with the recent acquisition of General Re, a reinsurance business. In this case the support came in forms beyond the managerial or relational—what in L4 nomenclature we might call organizational and technical support of the highest order.

One of Buffet's first moves was to appoint Ron Ferguson, chairman and CEO of General Re, to the board of Berkshire Hathaway, thus supporting his continued leadership of his own company. Next he offered a variety of means of technical support that he would call "synergies." He removed constraints on earnings volatility, offered greater tax flexibility, encouraged global franchise development, and provided probably the ultimate in technical support: money.

What's significant about Buffett's approach is that rather than do what many in the position of acquisition mogul choose, i.e., dismantle the new purchase and integrate it into other holdings, he chose to build on and leverage its current strength in the marketplace by supporting and reinforcing the company's development. Said Grace Osborne, a director in the reinsurance division of Standard & Poor's Insurer Rating Agency, "Buffett is tolerant of unusual spikes in earnings. That's not to say General Re will be given carte blanche. It has always been a very well run, prudent and conservative company. The modus operandi won't change. What the merger does do, however, is liberate it from reliance on retrocessions and gives it more freedom to take on larger risks. All in all, this is a win, win deal for both companies" (ibid.).

Impressive about Buffett is his vast range of investments. The recent acquisition of ice cream vendor Dairy Queen is probably as far afield as possible from the reinsurance business. Again Buffett's Style 3 approach comes through. He left the executive team intact. Says John Mooty, IDQ chairman, "He looked at our management group and felt we did have an outstanding team. We had 23 years of uninterrupted improved earnings each quarter" (*Restaurant Business* 1998). Said Buffett of his approach to managing the acquisition, "I mainly attend to capital allocation and the care and feeding of our key managers" (ibid.).

ELECTRIFYING THE RANKS

Perhaps the most surprising high-profile Window 3 business leader is Jack Welch, CEO of General Electric. Most observers of this CEO of one of the largest corporations in the world would not guess that this tough-as-nails corporate leader who demands excellence in every corner of his organization would be a champion of a style that suggests words like *listening* and *employee involvement*. Certainly his reputation as "Neutron Jack" implies more of a Style 1, *dominating*, approach than a Style 3, *developing*, orientation. But even if Welch used to be a hard-nosed driver, he has certainly changed his tune in recent years.

Jack Welch also explodes the "soft" or "touchy-feely" mythology that often distorts people's ideas about Window 3. On the contrary, Style 3 can and should be highly demanding of those who are charged with doing the work. Jack Welch understands this and has taken on the enormous task of transforming a company steeped in traditional approaches to management into one that runs on the premise that those in the trenches have the know-how to create change and ought to be listened to carefully.

Consider the following from an article on Welch in *Fortune:* " 'We've got to take out the boss element,' Welch says. By his lights, twenty-first-century managers will forgo their old powers—to plan, organize, implement, and measure—for new duties: counseling groups, providing resources for them, helping them to think for themselves" (Stewart 1991). This shift reflects, in every way, the hallmarks of a Style 3 leader—one who listens to followers and helps them to solve their own problems.

Welch's approach to Window 3 is the brainchild of James Baughman, head of faculty at GE's Management Development Institute in Crotonville, New York. The approach is called Work-Out. In its typical format a group of forty to a hundred people, increasingly coming from the lower ranks of the organization, spend three days with one another talking, with the help of an outside facilitator, about problems and how to solve them. At the end of the three days those in the Work-Out present their recommendations to superiors who are charged with doing one of three things: saying yes, saying no, or asking for more information. The distinction between the Work-Out and the typical two- or three-day retreat is that those participating in the Work-Out are empowered to make decisions, so much so that there are serious consequences for those at the top for not "driving decision making down" and for not following through on the decisions that get made during the Work-Out.

As is characteristic of a Style 3 approach, decision making is handed down the line to the lowest possible level, and accountability is maintained at that level. Welch has gone to great lengths to institute culture-wide change at GE to support this high-participation notion, from informally sending the message that not supporting Work-Out teams is bad for your GE career to formally building evaluation of support for Work-Outs into formal annual reviews.

One result of this *developing* approach has been increased success for GE's operations. In addition, this has made GE one of the best training grounds for CEOs of other companies. After being an executive at GE, you would be ready to lead most corporations.

This point was dramatically driven home as Welch planned his departure from GE at the end of 2001. The day after Welch tapped Jeffrey Immelt as his successor, the two runners-up, W. James McNerney and Robert Nardelli, instantly became the two hottest properties in the CEO market. That same day, the three men—who remain friends—spent time e-mailing one another congratulatory notes: Immelt for his ascension to CEO of GE, McNerney for being named CEO of industrial giant 3M, and Nardelli for accepting the position of CEO of merchandising behemoth Home Depot.

It is clear that the mark Welch has left on the business world will endure as other companies continue to pick their new leaders from the ranks of General Electric. In fact, executives on the receiving end of Welch's Style 3 approach are almost guaranteed success.

MICHAEL DELL, DEAN OF COMPUTER EDUCATION

Michael Dell, founder and CEO of Dell Computer Corporation, could be the high-tech poster child for the Style 3 leader as *developer* approach. Whether focused on his own learning and development, the development of Dell employees, or creating learning opportunities for children, Michael Dell sees the role of developer as key to the success of any manager. To the furthest extent possible he behaves as a Style 3 leader and has built an organization from Style 3 principles.

One of the many ways Dell instills a commitment to employee learning via mutual development is through the use of 360-degree feedback. "Instead of gauging an employee's annual progress against subjective views of one person— usually her direct supervisor—this full circle review solicits input from everyone an employee works with. It's a great measurement for identifying those areas that might require further development or improvement, and it keeps people focused on achieving their goals as a team. It's the closest we've come to objectifying the data on our people, minimizing interpersonal politics. As a result, we've seen stronger team members spend extra time and effort with others who seem to be having trouble keeping up because it's in their interest to do so. One of the ways they do that is by openly sharing the results of their 360 evaluations with one another. This allows our management teams to work together on individual areas for improvement. This kind of teamwork suggests a different way of building a company together. It's not about people staying our of each other's way, or working hard to be competitive but not political. It's about people who are thoroughly invested in each other's growth" (Dell 1999, p. 115).

When Dell talks about development as a corporate priority his vision is clear. In a recent annual report he stated, "Ultimately, in any business, it is people who produce results. Building a talented workforce remains our greatest single priority and challenge" (Cone 2000). And Dell puts his money where his mouth is. While most large corporations have learning and development centers, Dell Learning (formerly Dell University) is distinctive for several reasons. One distinction is that Dell Learning operates on the premise that learning needs to be available 24/7. Another distinction—which drives home Michael Dell's Style 3 mindset—is that employees are in charge of their own development. "The learner controls what she or he will learn, when the learning starts and stops, whether to interrupt it, and what elements to include" (ibid.).

Dell has been conscientious about surrounding himself with people who share this mindset. Says Darin Hartley, manager of Dell Learning Technology Services, about his target audience, "These are people who raise children, maintain households, manage budgets, and solve incredibly complex problems every day. We ought to be able to trust them to manage their own learning" (ibid.).

Michael Dell's commitment to development extends beyond his company. At Dell's website there's a section called Direct to Dell, part of which is Dell Kids, where you get a greeting from Michael himself and can pose questions to the CEO. He has also invested recently in the Austin Public Library Foundation with Dell Wired for Youth Centers, creating ten youth computer centers throughout Austin.

Dell's Style 3 approach extends to his day-to-day work and stewardship of his company. He holds semi-annual executive conferences bringing together his leadership from around the world, the expressed purpose of which is to build stronger relationships with one another. And he has an annual vice presidents' conference to build leadership knowledge and skill. On the personal level Dell prides himself on being a good listener, the hallmark of a Style 3 leader. "I go to brown-bag lunches two or three times a month, and meet with a cross-section of people from all across the company. It's easy to sit in a product meeting and say, 'We have these new products and our salespeople will sell them.' But this may not be the reality. So I go to a brown-bag lunch and listen carefully to what the sales force has to say. It's a great way of learning what people are really dealing with on a day-to-day basis, and provides a forum for the exchange of ideas and solutions" (Dell 1999, p. 117).

While some of his peers—other giants in the high-tech world—spend their time impressing others with their mastery of the industry and knowledge of their business, Dell takes a decidedly different approach. Whether focusing on employee or customer needs, Dell maintains that the key to his company's astounding success is never assuming you know the answers and relentlessly asking the right questions, listening to the responses, and helping those accountable take action. "Our people are obviously motivated by the ways we link our goals to their compensation and incentives. But more importantly, there are ways in which we work to instill ownership thinking in our people and better leverage their talents so they can reach their full potential . . . I approach learning from the standpoint of asking questions: What would make your job at Dell easier? More successful? More meaningful? What do our customers like and not like? What do they need? What would they like to see us doing better? How can we improve? I start by asking a lot of questions and doing a lot of listening" (ibid., p. 122).

In summary, what distinguishes Michael Dell from some of his monolithic counterparts is the importance he places on learning and support as fundamental tenets of his philosophy. Says Dell, "Everyone has to be open to learning all of the time, starting with me, and everyone must support and encourage their teams to make sure they have the knowledge and skills to succeed (Cone 2000).

SURROUNDED BY EXPERTS

Another high-profile business leader who used Window 3 successfully (for a while) is former Apple Computer chairman John Sculley. When Sculley first came to Apple after having been a marketing vice president for PepsiCo, his knowledge of personal computers was severely limited. In order to become an expert in his new business he had to spend a lot of time listening to those in the know. He understood that for him to lead this organization effectively, he first needed to pay close attention to those around him who had the expertise to produce products that would eventually dominate their industry.

He also knew that he had to be careful. He was walking into an environment that, under the leadership of Steve Jobs, had inspired creativity among its employees. Jobs had created a culture that enjoyed teamwork, engaged in free-spirited brainstorming, and was extremely open-minded. Had Sculley entered this highly collegial environment with a heavy-handed, highly controlled approach, he no doubt would have met with formidable resistance. Instead, he effectively met the technically savvy workforce on its own terms and was able to learn from them in a way that led to the development of his own expertise. He was careful, as are most *developing* leaders, not to take decision making away from those who knew more about the decisions to be made then he. As a result, eventually he was able to take greater control once he knew more about the nature of the game.

In fact, when it came to a showdown between Sculley and Jobs, Apple's board of directors chose Sculley—even though he lacked Jobs' technical wizardry—for his business sense. By listening to his people and supporting their decision making around technical issues, he was able to make some tough business decisions, like letting go of some employees and forming a partnership with arch rival IBM.

A few years later, Sculley erroneously concluded that he knew enough to assume technical leadership, pushed out the company's technological leader, and shifted to Style 2, *problem solving*. A few years later, with the product line in disarray, he was ousted in favor of Michael Spindler. Spindler, unable to turn Apple's rapid decline around, was then replaced by Gilbert Amelio who also failed to stop the hemorrhaging and lasted a short 500 days as CEO.

Ironically Jobs returned as the knight in shining armor. By most accounts, he "pulled the horses out of the burning barn" by reinvigorating the company through the design innovations of the iMac, the sleek distinctive desktop models that followed. He not only simplified the product line, he once again showed his uncanny ability to anticipate where the industry was heading and drive the Apple team with his painstaking attention to detail and demands for user-friendliness.

He also strengthened Apple's board by adding Larry Ellison of Oracle and other industry heavyweights as directors. And in his most stunning move that offended many Mac devotees but probably saved the company, he formed an alliance with Bill Gates who invested $150 million in exchange for a commitment to keep Apple products Microsoft-compatible. After returning Apple to high profits, he then transformed the company, and several industries, by developing revolutionary products like the iPod, iPhone, and iPad.

Depending on whom you ask, Sculley's post-Apple career tells a different story. Many saw his departure from Apple as a fall of mythic proportions—one he has never recovered from, but if you ask the man himself you get quite a different story—one that further elucidates his propensity for Style 3 leadership.

While his next venture was indeed a disaster by all accounts including his own, the story gets better. Immediately after leaving Apple he joined a group of unscrupulous characters at Spectrum Information Technologies that turned out to be a charade. After that he bounced back—choosing he says, to work in the small business area, moving from one start up to another helping other people manifest their creative ideas in a role he describes as "venture catalyst."

WORKING TOGETHER FOR CREATIVE ENTERPRISE

Perhaps the most renowned Style 3 leader of the corporate world is the late Sam Walton, founder of the Wal-Mart dynasty. Walton built his unparalleled retail chain (over 1,650 stores) on the basis of involvement and participation, beginning with his family, who make up the board of Walton Enterprises and make all major decisions by consensus.

While Walton was modest about his role in the making of Wal-Mart's strong participatory culture, it is clear that his folksy style and insistence on maintaining the corporation as a partnership were in great part responsible for bringing that culture to life. "We don't pretend to have invented the idea of a strong corporate culture. We're constantly doing crazy things to capture the attention of our folks and lead them to think up surprises of their own. We like to see them do wild things in the stores, things that are fun for the customers and fun for the associates. If you're committed to the Wal-Mart partnership and its core values, the culture encourages you to think up all sorts of things to break the mold and fight monotony" (Walton 1992).

What's critical to Walton's approach—and the success of his corporation—is that he built in mechanisms for problem solving that recognized the importance of openness, involvement, and shared responsibility. "At Wal-Mart if you have some important business problem on your mind, you should be bringing it out in the open, so we can try to solve it together. . . . From the very start we would get all our managers together once a week and critique ourselves . . . and it worked so well that over the years, as we grew and built the company, it just became part of our culture" (ibid.).

The best way to understand Walton's commitment to a Style 3 approach is to take a look at the principles by which he guided the business and the rules he followed in playing out those principles. First, he placed a high value on communication occurring up, down, and across the entire organization. "Communicate, communicate, communicate: If you had to boil down the Wal-Mart system to one single idea, it would probably be communication because it is one of the real keys to our success. What good is figuring out a better way to sell beach towels if you aren't going to tell everybody in your company about it" (ibid.).

He also focused on pushing responsibility down through the ranks. Walton believed that the people on the front line, the department managers, those who stocked the shelves and talked with customers, were the ones who should make as many decisions as possible—and he supported their doing so.

"What sets us apart is that we train people to be merchants. We let them see all the numbers so they know exactly how they're doing within the store and within the company; they know their cost, their mark-up, their overhead, and their profit. It's a big responsibility and a big opportunity" (Huey 1991).

This sharing of responsibility with the people in the trenches created a dynamic within the network of stores that made those managing the stores realize that they really did have responsibility for their own success. Walton was also very careful to acknowledge success and use one person's accomplishments to achieve greater success systemwide. For example, he took ideas that would emerge from the ranks and spread them throughout the company, creating a dimension to problem solving that he would call "bubbling up." In true Style 3 form, this involved careful listening and support of others' decisions. Walton became notorious for his store visits, traveling around the country, dropping in unannounced, looking for good ideas to support.

Consider the following scenario, as reported in a cover story in *Fortune:* "On store visits, Walton's 'primary tool of empowerment' is his tape recorder. 'I'm here in Memphis at store 950, and Georgie has done a real fine thing with this endcap display of Equate Baby Oil. I'd like to try this everywhere.' Georgie blushes with pride" (ibid.).

Some observers of Walton's style have been critical of his open approach, suggesting that this sort of broad-based access to information for everyone in the organization creates a vulnerability to outsiders that can be damaging. Walton counters those accusations by suggesting that any corporation serious about gaining commitment from employees can ill afford the secrecy that many corporate leaders engage in. "Communicate everything you possibly can to your partners. . . . If you don't trust your associates to know what's going on, they'll know you don't really consider them partners. Information is power, and the gain you get from empowering your associates more than offsets the risk of informing your competitors" (Walton 1992).

WHEN PLEASING THE MASSES
SPELLS DISASTER

Window 3 clouds up when the perception of those around the leader is that the leader is more concerned with being popular than with being effective. This brings us back to George Bush the elder and his reputation as a domestic policy leader. During his reelection campaign in 1992, Bush received a great deal of criticism from both ends of the political spectrum for failing to articulate a clear, strong position on many key issues confronting the nation. Conservatives in his own party accused him of being too wishy-washy on issues like abortion and support for religious schools. Liberals, on the other hand, saw him as bending over backward to *over-accommodate* the Pat Buchanan side of the Republican coalition at the expense of issues such as health care, education, and, most important, the economy.

This really should not have come as a reelection year surprise. When Bush ran for the presidency the first time, he told the American public that he wanted to give us a "kinder and gentler" form of leadership. His hope was to use the power of the presidency to encourage the private sector (the businesses that had been making huge profits during the Reagan years) and the volunteer sector (the "thousand points of light") to come forward and solve the social problems facing the country.

Even George Will, a staunch conservative, said very early during Bush's term in office that George Bush couldn't make a decision without consulting four or five polls. The man was trapped by the fear that he might offend one of his constituencies. He preferred to step back and let the natural forces of the marketplace bring prosperity to everyone.

This apparent tendency to *over-accommodate* everyone is typical of the ineffective side of Window 3. Most analysts agree that part of Bush's downfall was his inability during the 1992 campaign to shift to a more directive style and demonstrate his ability to solve the country's economic problems.

Instead he tried to paint Bill Clinton as more *over-accommodating* than he was. The clear message was that if people thought Bush was bad, they should know what was coming if they elected a "pork-barrel, rainbow-coalition, misery-index Democrat." Unfortunately for Bush, he was already seen as so *over-accommodating* to the wealthy that it was easier for Clinton to make the "trickle-down economics" label stick to Bush than for Bush to stick the "Waffle House" image on Clinton.

One reason Bush couldn't make the Waffle House label stick was the way Clinton positioned himself as the Style 2 leader of the masses. A second reason was that many people already perceived Bush as *over-accommodating* a much smaller and wealthier constituency. A third reason was Bush's own success in foreign policy. He had clearly demonstrated during the Persian Gulf War that he knew how to build a strong coalition, listen to divergent points of view, and mobilize a well-coordinated effort to combat worldwide problems. Ironically, his foreign policy success left Bush open to the criticism that he did not care about the economic woes of poor and middle-class Americans. The problem wasn't that he didn't know how to address the economic problems; he was simply choosing not to.

So his penchant for *over-accommodating* on the domestic front, colored by his skill at *problem solving* on the international front, made it easy for the Democrats to create the perception that he was *abdicating*. Many saw him as operating in an uncaring, aristocratic manner, aloof from the problems of the real world, leaving the homeless and the jobless to fend for themselves. To this day, when we ask about Bush's style, most people say he *abdicated* on economic issues even though his intentions were to make everyone happy.

THE RAZORBACK PRESIDENCY

In the last chapter, we talked about how Bill Clinton had to convince the voting public that he would be a *problem solver* and not an *over-accommodator*. One reason he had to make that case was his penchant for telling people what they wanted to hear, empathizing so strongly with their point of view that they thought he agreed with them. Another was the reputation he brought with him from his years as governor of Arkansas.

Despite his ability to sell himself as a Style 2, *problem-solving,* leader, his gubernatorial style reveals a strong Style 3 approach. According to John Brunnett, an Arkansas journalist who covered Clinton, "First he gives great lip service to his proposals. Then when the bill comes in and the legislators and lobbyists chip away at it, he says, 'That's okay, that's okay.' In the end, it's watered down to forty percent of what it was, and he declares victory" (Alter 1992).

This *over-accommodating* reputation is the result of overusing a Style 3 approach. A strength that Clinton brought to the White House was that he carried with him a formidable list of experts he used to shape his own thinking on a wide range of topics. An early example of this was his acceptance speech at the Democratic National Convention in 1992. It was peppered with language that reflected the thinking of a variety of pundits on everything from economics to social psychology to pop music. The speech was in fact a carefully woven presentation of many people's ideas, another hallmark of Style 3.

Many analysts believe that Clinton was well served by his Style 3 approach in his first run for the presidency. Consider this excerpt from a *New York Times* front-page story: "If a man is known by the company he keeps, Bill Clinton is clearly a left-leaning liberal. Also, a right-leaning moderate. In foreign policy he is a United Nations multi-nationalist and an America-first interventionist. In a city where every Democrat suddenly wants to be a 'friend of Bill,' Mr. Clinton is a man for all advisers" (Gelb 1992).

The upside of Style 3 was also visible in one of the most defining moments of that campaign: the third debate against then president Bush. It was in a town hall format, and a young black woman in the rear of the auditorium asked Bush a question. Bush's response was, "I don't think I understand the question." The woman restated her query and Bush again said, "I don't understand." Clinton stood up, walked over very close to the woman, and, oozing with empathy, said, "I understand your concern." He then demonstrated his ability to listen by paraphrasing her question, and after she nodded that she felt heard, he gave her an answer. In that simple moment, he conveyed the message that he was able to listen to people whom his adversary couldn't even understand. And for the eight years of his presidency, despite his cavalier attitude toward women, women and minorities supported him in disproportionate numbers.

The downside of Style 3 also reared its ugly head with Clinton. In his early attempt to reform health care, he let his wife, Hillary Rodham Clinton, chair the commission while he stayed in the background supporting the initiative. Not only did Hillary come on too strong for many of the involved parties, but Bill was perceived as not being strong enough. Early critics faulted him for being unable to say no to his wife's drive to share the power. Later critics, including his most ardent supporters, eventually saw that he couldn't even say no to a White House intern, by far the most sordid chapter in his "Dr. Feel Good" administration.

Clinton was also criticized for trying to be all things to all people in the foreign policy arena. The failed mission in Somalia was ill advised and clearly the result of his willingness to "feel their pain" and try to do something about it. The UN peacekeeping force that entered Bosnia was also a hotly debated venture. While many argued that the Serbs' "ethnic cleansing" had to be stopped, the United States' involvement moved forward haphazardly as our negotiators listened to Milosevic's hollow promises in the hope of finding a nonmilitary solution. Demands were made and withdrawn, deadlines were set and extended, threats were issued and not backed up while the Serbs continued to kill their neighbors. Even when the military action was organized, Clinton was criticized for allowing an overwhelmingly American force to be commanded by the United Nations.

Even in his final days in office, both sides of Style 3 were visible in Clinton's attempts to help Israel and the Palestinians reach a peace accord that both sides could live with. As with any attempt at mediation, he couldn't make this decision, so his role was to listen to both sides, help them find areas of agreement, and encourage them to convert disagreements into compromises. It was a credit to his listening skills that the warring parties stayed in dialogue with him for much of his eight years in office. On the other hand, many saw his efforts as the misguided folly of a leader who wants to help everyone, including those who don't want to be helped. To quote George Will, "Bill Clinton may have saved his very worst for last. With remarkable—even for him—self-absorption, as he tap-dances toward the exit he is pursuing as his crowning legacy something that only the cynical or delusional could call a 'final' Middle East 'peace agreement' " (Will 2001).

TOO MUCH POWER TO THE PEOPLE

The ascendancy of Corazon Aquino to the presidency of the Philippines provides an enlightening view of the dangers of overusing a Style 3 approach. Cory Aquino defeated Ferdinand Marcos, a very strong tyrant and a *dominating* Style 1 leader who controlled every aspect of government, including the electoral process and the military. He ruled the Philippines in much the same way that the first Mayor Daly ruled Chicago, with an iron fist and a lot of patronage.

As happens to many *dominating* leaders, his ruthless behavior eventually caught up with him. The execution of Benigno Aquino (Cory's husband) proved to be Marcos's undoing. He seriously underestimated Aquino's widow, who eventually unseated him in a popular uprising against the dictatorship.

When Cory Aquino was elected president of the Philippines, it was on a power-to-the-people platform. In her first days in office she opened the presidential palace to the public, put Imelda Marcos's ostentatious collection of shoes on display, and tried to share her power with as many people as possible. She wanted to be the antithesis of Ferdinand Marcos. Aquino listened to her constituents, supported their causes, encouraged them to openly express themselves, and invited her supporters to take on substantial responsibility. In other words, her main style was a Style 3 approach of *developing.*

Unfortunately, the honeymoon didn't last long, and her effectiveness with Style 3, *developing,* diminished rapidly. The Philippines has a long tradition of power-dominated leadership, and Aquino had a rebellion on her hands within a few months of taking office. Apparently some of her cabinet and many of the military leaders felt that she was *over-accommodating* the people and some of her political adversaries.

She and her allies were able to squelch the coup and, as a result, she learned that she needed to be much stronger. She decided to be more selective in whom she trusted and more careful about whose input she used. She realized that in order to survive in a nation coming out from under Marcos's strong domination she had to become tougher.

And that's exactly what she did. She started taking input from a close-knit group of trusted advisors who were very powerful in their own right. She listened to their recommendations but made it clear that she was making the bottom-line decisions. As a result of her becoming more decisive and regaining some control, she was able to provide a more democratic form of leadership than her predecessor while still demonstrating her ability to be a strong leader of her nation and its competing factions.

She even used her hard-learned *problem-solving* skills to take herself out of office. In 1992, she went against the wishes of many of her supporters who wanted her to run for office again. The history in the Philippines would have permitted her to become as benevolent a despot as Marcos had become a self-serving one. Instead, Aquino refused the temptation of perpetual power. She preferred to use her power to guarantee a smooth transition from her to her strongest supporters, with the result that her candidate won the election. Not only did her party remain in power, but a small victory for democracy was achieved as well. Aquino is a good example of someone who shifted from an ineffective Style 3, *over-accommodating,* approach to a more effective Style 2, *problem-solving,* approach that was best for her country as she envisioned it.

Throughout the 1990s Aquino used her post-presidency clout to harness the "people power" so critical to her ascendancy to the presidency and her influence in shifting the Philippines to a more democratic model. By monitoring the actions of her successor, Fidel Ramos, and his successor, Joseph Estrada, Aquino has played the role of "watchdog for the people," ensuring that neither president falls prey to the corruption that was the hallmark of her predecessor, Ferdinand Marcos. Whether it be by organizing a demonstration or enlisting the help of other world leaders, Aquino has used her hard-earned *problem-solving* skills to continue to be an advocate of the people she so dearly loves and strives to protect.

THE STYLE 3 LEADER: DEVELOPER
OR OVER-ACCOMMODATOR

Perhaps the greatest difference between the Window 3 leader and the Window 1 and Window 2 leaders is a shift in responsibility. For the Style 3 leader, decision making is transferred to followers, communication is more upward than downward, and followers are valued for using the leader as a coach, not for following orders or going off on their own. In order for this to work, timing is critical.

We can see this from both the positive and negative cases discussed above. John Sculley used a Style 3 approach to effectively gain the trust and knowledge of followers when he needed them to help make decisions for which he was accountable. Cory Aquino used the same approach at a time when followers needed an unwavering decision maker at the top, and it almost cost her the presidency.

The Style 3 leader is decidedly more follower centered than the previous two. This leader considers the development of followers as the key means to an end. The Style 3 leader supports followers' decision making by asking lots of open-ended questions, listening actively, and praising them for asking for assistance. Primarily, the Style 3 leader promotes followers' development of their own problem-solving abilities. He or she does this by helping followers define their own problems, clarify their own goals, generate alternatives, evaluate and choose among alternatives, build action plans, and monitor and evaluate those plans.

The Style 3 approach works well when the leader is prepared to share significant responsibility with followers and followers are prepared to take it. There are many advantages to Style 3. Leaders get to share the burden of responsibility with team members. Chances of success are optimized because all human resources are utilized. And there is usually a high commitment to the task on the part of team members resulting from a sense of ownership over the work.

The disadvantages of this approach are that the leader gives up control over the process, has to tolerate followers' moving in directions not necessarily consistent with the leader's desires, and may have to accept decisions made by followers that differ from his or her own.

LEADING IN A LEARNING ENVIRONMENT—
A CASE STUDY

Julie was the new president at a university where her predecessor was described as someone who ran a "tight ship." In her first meeting with faculty and staff, she quickly discerned that there was a lot of frustration with the former president's tough, hands-on approach. The school was, she learned, a place that attracted a large number of nontraditional students—adults returning to school after several years in the workforce, homemakers whose children had grown, and people seeking skill upgrading in their jobs. At a meeting with this diverse, sophisticated student body, she learned quickly that they too had been feeling the constraints of an overly controlling administration.

Julie decided to take the feedback she was getting from faculty, staff, and students and do something about it. She knew that the school had been over-managed from the top down and that the best way to change things was from the top down. She met with the three executive deans individually and informed them that she intended to change the way the school was run. Beginning today, she announced to each, the deans would be responsible for making decisions in their areas. She would be available to them to lend her support and advice if they wished, but each of them would be charged with making the key decisions in his or her area. Further, she suggested that they might want to pass their authority down the line to those who could handle making lower-level decisions that they felt should not be within the domain of the dean.

At first, the three deans were shocked with their new level of authority. Within a few days two of them personally expressed to the new president their excitement over their newfound freedom. The president reminded them that she still intended to be involved with the decisions they were making and was simply shifting decision-making power for their overall responsibilities to each of them. The third dean was less enthusiastic about his newfound freedom—and responsibility. He expressed his concern to the president, and she assured him that he was not on his own in these matters but would have all the support he needed from her. Since he was less enthusiastic about the new setup, the president decided to set up a regular meeting schedule with him to help him develop and feel secure about his own problem-solving process.

While there was some initial confusion about who was accountable for what, the high-support style established by the president with her deans eventually took root, and she was able to spend most of her time dealing with her board of trustees and handling big-picture concerns of the university.

The three deans, including the reluctant one, eventually learned to model their own behavior on that of their president. They began appropriately deferring decision making down the line, often offering high support to their charges, particularly in the early stages of the shift in authority, when those with the new responsibilities felt somewhat hesitant to take control. As time went on it became clear throughout the system that the president's preferred way of operating was to share responsibility down the organizational hierarchy to the lowest reasonable level for any given set of decisions. What also became clear was that her way of creating this shift away from what she called "top-down gridlock" was to offer those engendered with new responsibilities all the support necessary for them to take on those responsibilities. As a result of this careful, thoughtful approach, Julie was able to retain her control over the overall direction of the university and empower those charged with meeting the goals of the organization with the authority and support to do it.

Window 4: The Leader as Delegator

One of the most common approaches to leadership in lean times, when resources of all sorts, human and otherwise, are scarce, is that reflected in Window 4. This same approach is also prevalent in times of rapid growth, when "wars for talent" cause managers and employees to be stretched thin to cover all the bases. Many companies today, in the face of increased global competition and the pressure to reinvent themselves, are flattening hierarchies, widening spans of control, and *delegating* increased responsibilities.

In many cases, the leaders try to wrap these changes in the mantle of empowerment. Our research consistently suggests that employees in many of these "empowered" organizations feel that the people above them are just downloading responsibility without providing the accompanying assistance required for them to truly be empowered.

What leaders often don't realize is that the downward shift of authority results in effective *delegating* only when the next level down the hierarchy feels that the expanded responsibilities make sense in light of organizational goals and offer greater opportunities. Giving people increased authority may just as likely be perceived as the *abdicating* of accountability when it doesn't serve either the needs of the individual or the best interests of the organization.

GIVING UP TOO MUCH

A highly visible example of both the upside and downside of Window 4 can be seen by examining the presidency of Ronald Reagan. Reagan was a popular president and an effective *delegator*. While he was very directive in establishing the foundation and ideology of his presidency, he was a consummate *delegator* once he chose the people who would carry his banner. The model for his presidency was to find competent people to do the work that needed to be done and, provided their values and agenda matched his, let them do it.

Perhaps to avoid repeating the mistakes of his predecessor, Jimmy Carter, whose excessive hands-on approach was partially responsible for the demise of his presidency, Reagan maintained a decidedly hands-off approach to the day-to-day management of the government. He was praised in the media for his skills as a communicator and a manager. Especially during his first term in office and early in the second term, there were articles all over the business magazines telling us what we could learn from Reagan the manager. He was touted for his ability to define a value-based vision and then get out of the way and let his people have the authority to run their departments as they saw fit. Despite the occasional reprimand, such as when he scolded David Stockman for being too open with the press, Reagan always handled people in a gentle, avuncular manner and was an expert at letting go.

As with any leader who views his role primarily from a single window, this myopic view got him into trouble. From the outset, his detractors accused him of being too laissez-faire, or *abdicating* on critical issues. Some said that he spent too much time at the ranch. Others claimed that he let his wife, Nancy, make too many decisions. And rumors circulated that he would often doze off during cabinet meetings.

The Iran-Contra scandal marked the peak of dissatisfaction with his Window 4 leadership when his claim not to know what Oliver North was doing raised concerns about his competence. He doggedly maintained that he was unaware of what was going on. Interestingly enough, it seemed that most people who followed the Ollie North hearings did not mind the fact that North had been given so much authority. Where they drew the line was with the president's attempt to dodge accountability for his role as commander in chief. Consequently, the press hounded him mercilessly until he finally accepted full accountability for what had happened under his leadership. Of course, in the next breath, he still insisted that he didn't know.

An interesting footnote on Reagan's presidency is how the public's perception of him has shifted over the years. When he was in office and we asked audiences about his style, we always heard vehement arguments about whether he was a *delegator* or *abdicator*. In the years right after Reagan retired, when Bush was at his strongest during the Persian Gulf War, most people we talked to described Reagan as *abdicating* in comparison. Then, when Bush's popularity waned, many Republicans started longing for the good old days, and Reagan's reputation as a *delegator* returned to the discussions. Since he was diagnosed with Alzheimer's, the debates about *abdicator* or *delegator* have started again. Some applaud him for managing like a visionary CEO, while others insist that he lost his touch long before the public knew.

Ultimately, history will judge the effectiveness of Reagan's presidency. Nonetheless, he serves as a good study of both the pluses and minuses of

Window 4 leadership: Reagan's strength in *delegating* was also his weakness when it turned into *abdicating*.

LETTING EXPERIENCED LEADERS LEAD

In Chapter 3, we talked about the 2000 presidential election and looked at the positive and negative aspects of Al Gore's Style 1 approach. While his style was probably not the ultimate factor in determining the outcome of that election, it was part of the story. Style was also a piece of George W. Bush's winning the White House.

Before the election, the country as a whole didn't know as much about Bush as they did about the vice president. Most people knew that W's father had been president, that W was the governor of Texas and his brother was the governor of Florida, and he entered the campaign with the biggest war chest in history. As the public learned that he had been successful in business and in politics, questions were raised about whether he had succeeded because of his own efforts or his privileged background. Even though he had attended the best schools, he had a reputation for being more interested in partying than studying. Some of his detractors said he lacked the work ethic to be president and others accused him of not being smart enough for the job—an *abdicator* out of neglect or necessity.

Throughout the campaign the talk show hosts played on this *abdicating* theme showing him taking orders from Cheney or lost in the woods with George senior. They roasted him for not knowing the names of world leaders, fumbling with concepts, or stumbling over his own words. In one *Saturday Night Live* skit, the commentator read a completely mangled statement that Bush had made and asked him to explain what he meant. With a puzzled look on his face, the actor playing Bush slowly said, "I don't know." The commentator then put the statement on a screen so Bush could read it. He stared at the words, shrugged his shoulders, and again said, "I don't know." To underscore his dependency on others, the actor playing Gore jumped in and said, "What my opponent meant to say was . . . ," and Bush responded, "Yeah, that's it."

In an interview with *Time*, Bush defended himself saying, "I've never held myself out to be any great genius, but I'm plenty smart. And I've got good common sense and good instincts. And that's what people want in their leader." And despite the occasional gaffe and the endless jokes, most of the time Bush came across as sincere, personable, and highly articulate. The *Time* article also revealed some insights about his style saying, "Bush speaks convincingly about how important it is for a leader to assemble a trustworthy cadre of advisors. And he argues that there is no percentage, as Governor or as President, in trying to master every subject or micromanage every decision." (ibid.).

In his acceptance speech at the Republican National Convention Bush's refrain was, "They had their chance. They have not led. We will." As the campaign unfolded, it became clear that this refrain was intended to contrast his

Style 4 approach to Gore's penchant for getting into the details. W was saying he would be a leader, not a manager—a Ronald Reagan type who would *delegate* most of the decisions to his cabinet and expect high level recommendations from them on the decisions he has to make. His big picture approach also came through in one of the debates when he said, "I've been a leader, a person who has to set a clear vision and convince people to follow. We need a clear vision, that's what a leader does."

In another debate, Bush elaborated on this theme saying, "An administration is not one person but a team of dedicated people called by the president to serve. In Texas, we have been able to put together a good team of people. We have been able to set clear goals and bring people together to achieve those goals. That's what a chief executive officer does." By selecting Dick Cheney as his running mate and making it known that Colin Powell would be his choice for Secretary of State, W made it clear that he was not afraid to have extremely strong and well-respected people on his team. In terms of leadership styles, both choices showed that he intended to be a Style 4 leader, *delegating* as much responsibility as possible to people whose experience and expertise were stronger than his.

In response to detailed proposals from Gore, Bush would talk about his principles, his values, and broad concepts. His detractors accused him of being vague but his supporters insisted that he had been highly successful with this approach in Texas. As governor, he "set a few policy goals, outlined the principles by which he would judge success and gave other people the power to work out the details. 'We can make decisions based on his principles, which are very clear,' said Vance MacMahon, Bush's policy director in Texas. We don't have to run every decision up the flagpole." (ibid.). He also "preferred one-page memos to bound treatises, oral briefings to long meetings," pushed his advisors to make recommendations, and let his Lieutenant Governor handle many of his responsibilities.

During the dispute over manual recounts in Florida, W stayed in the *delegating* mode letting Jim Baker, another well-respected conservative from the Reagan and senior Bush administrations, orchestrate the legal battles and be the front man with the press. Bush shuttled between his ranch and the Governor's mansion, only speaking out when his advisors said he should, trying to keep smiling and stay above the fray. And as the country's patience for the deadlock waned, many people came to the conclusion that Bush would have an easier time governing than Gore would. Why? Gore wanted to fight over the details like the definition of a "hanging chad" while Bush's willingness to *delegate* to experienced people offered hope that he could work across the partisan divide that had nearly severed the electorate.

In his first year as president, George W. made good on his promise to be the first "CEO" of America behaving like the consummate *delegator* he claimed to be. Anointing seasoned professionals like Dick Cheney as ostensible Chief Operating Officer, Colin Powell as head of international relations, and John

Ashcroft as head of legal, Bush fashioned a cabinet that more resembled a corporate executive team than a group of close advisors to the head of government. Unlike his predecessor, but much like a typical CEO, Bush had *delegated* the day-to-day running of the country to these experts while preserving his energy and maintaining his focus on "the big picture."

The down side of this approach—as all *delegators* run the risk of discovering—is taking your eye off the ball. This happened shortly before the 9/11 attacks when W ignored reports of a potential threat that Condoleezza Rice tried to show him. Just after the attacks, he came across as *abdicating* as he read to kindergarteners while the world watched in horror. The *abdicating* persisted as W stayed at his ranch, red-eyed and ashen-faced, while Rudy Giuliani used his Style 1, *directing* approach to lead the first responders in New York.

After a few days, W shifted to his back-up style, *problem solving*. He decided (based on input from colleagues and allies) to retaliate by bombing Afghanistan, where Al-Qaida had trained the perpetrators of the attack, and driving out the Taliban who were actively engaged in state-sponsored terrorism. Speaking through a bullhorn amid the rubble at Ground Zero Bush announced his solution to the terrible problem the country was facing. Many other countries joined the coalition, and most of the world saw this as a justifiable response.

A few years later, he took his eye off the ball again by deciding to oust Saddam Hussein from Iraq. Most people saw this decision as Style 1. Bush's supporters saw it as *directing*—sending a strong message that he would take pre-emptive strikes to prevent further attacks on the US or its allies. But most people around the world saw it as *dominating* since W ignored vast amounts of input, including Colin Powell's strong objections, to pursue his own agenda. It could also be viewed as the ultimate *abdication* to Cheney who many saw as the true decision-maker. In the end, most people saw this as a bad decision that would make W go down in history as an ineffective leader.

BROADCASTING LEADERSHIP

Perhaps the most visible Window 4 business leader is CNN's Ted Turner. Turner, named *Time* magazine's man of the year in 1992 for his leadership in catapulting CNN into the ranks of the world's leading news outfits, has a knack for *delegating* responsibility that few leaders can parallel. Not content to simply transform the world of television news, Turner continued to build his dynasty throughout the 1990s and has been credited with "firing the first shot in the revolution that created all those television channels up in the air—he made the concept of cable networks work" (Briones 1999). In 1998 Turner was honored with the American Marketing Association's Edison Achievement Award for his extraordinary contributions to broadening the reach and impact of television on a global scale.

One key to his success, aside from his willingness to take risks and to dream, is his willingness to relinquish control of the day-to-day operation of his empire to others who are better equipped to handle things. He has thus effectively managed to *delegate* to a small group of journalists responsibility for decision making on world events and has created a cadre of what some say is now the world's most influential group of journalists. In doing so, Turner has created an organizational structure that consistently outperforms its network counterparts.

By eliminating the bureaucracy that plagues and inevitably slows down reporting of the news at the networks, Turner created a culture that consistently outperformed the competition for years. Consider this observation from CNN executive producer Simon Vicary regarding a fast-breaking news story: "My counterpart at ABC would have to go through 15 committees. I can just turn my head around and get a decision made" (Henry 1992).

From a leadership perspective, what Turner did in building his organization was to surround himself with experts in their field and give them the power and authority to do the job. While he still makes important decisions about overriding issues and overarching goals that determine the direction of the network, he lets those in the know make the decisions that lead to producing consistently high-quality programming.

Executive president in charge of news gathering Ed Turner (no relation), executive producer Bob Furnad, and CNN president Tom Johnson essentially run the network, making all the important tactical decisions on an ongoing basis. While this triumvirate of news hounds, unlike their leader, takes a decidedly hands-on approach concerning what gets aired, Turner's penchant for *delegation* seems to have rubbed off on how they work with people. Says Johnson, a refugee from the print medium: "I'm not going to try to become an expert in TV technology. I want to surround myself with people who are better than I am in the various disciplines. My job is to lead" (ibid.).

Perhaps the most striking thing about Turner's *delegator* approach and its impact on CNN's "product" is that it gets carried down to the consumer. Unlike its network counterparts, CNN does not tell viewers what to think about events. Says G. Cleveland Wilhout, professor of journalism at Indiana University, "Ideological critics of the media, left and right, agree on one thing—that the press is too arrogant, too ready to tell people what to think. By its very structure, CNN is populist. It provides the raw materials of the story and lets the viewers form their own opinions" (ibid.). People watch CNN because they get far more information than can be provided in a half hour of sound bites and are left to sort out and interpret that information for themselves.

Turner has continued to build and expand his holdings in the world of entertainment and communications, most notably joining forces first with Time Warner and then with AOL. His style of letting other people do what they do well has not abated, although it has come up against challenges in some of the merged organizations that do not operate at the same level of Style 4. Says Terry McGuirk, chairman of TBS and a longtime friend of Turner's, "At Turner we just felt something needed to be done, and we'd do it. Within Time Warner, Turner executives found themselves having to justify themselves more in front of their new colleagues" ("Merger Brief" 2000). Only time will tell whether Turner will be able to continue to replicate his signature style as his dynasty grows.

VIEWING LEADERSHIP AT MTV

Interestingly enough, another highly successful media mogul, Sumner Redstone, also brings a decidedly Style 4 approach to the management of his growing media empire. When we first wrote about these two media giants in 1993, Redstone was less known but no less impressive than his counterpart Turner. He has since eclipsed Turner in both holdings and personal wealth. Turner's wealth is estimated at $6.9 billion, Redstone's at $9.4 billion. As the chief of Viacom, which purchased CBS in 1999 for $37 billion, Redstone has created a media monolith. He and Viacom are forces to be reckoned with. Viacom's holdings include MTV, Nickelodeon, Paramount, VH1, and Blockbuster Video.

Perhaps it's the nature of the business, or the diversity of the holdings or the entrepreneurial leanings that these two giants have in common, that leads them to defer direct control of the management of their enterprises to others. Whatever the reason, it is clear that in their industry, under their circumstances, it has worked extremely well for both of them.

One of the keys to Redstone's success—and to that of most effective *delegators*—is the ability to surround himself with good people and let them do what they know how to do. For example, when Redstone took over Viacom, he kept key operating executives Thomas E. Freston, chairman of MTV Networks, and Nickelodeon president Geraldine Laybourne onboard and encouraged them to keep doing what they had been doing (which was working). He also brought on Frank J. Biondi to be Viacom's CEO rather than take the position himself.

In a *Business Week* article on Redstone's takeover of Viacom, Biondi, who formerly headed Viacom's archrival Home Box Office, imparts that Redstone's pledge to him as his boss was that he would not interfere with him. Biondi contends that Redstone indeed gave him a great deal of room. Said Biondi, "Unlike any other chairman I've worked for, he's enormously deferential" (Landler 1992). It's interesting that four years later, in 1996, after nine years of building Viacom into a media powerhouse, Redstone decided that Biondi's style, which was reportedly similar to his, was too laid back to fit the new Viacom. "Frank's style doesn't work in this company as it is today," said Redstone after firing him (Bryant 1999).

JEFF BEZOS: SLEIGHT OF HAND STYLE 4

When most people think about Jeff Bezos, CEO and the brains behind premier online retailer Amazon.com, they think first about his marketing brilliance. This is a man who for the past six years has accelerated his company's dramatic growth while not coming close to turning a profit. To date Amazon has lost $1.74 billion and borrowed $2 billion. The business press is full of stories questioning Amazon's ability to retain investor faith and keep the Wall Street hounds at bay.

Indications are that Bezos's capacity to avert serious criticism may be weakening. Recent articles have attacked his approach as being little more than smoke and mirrors. One such piece from *Barron's* went so far as to re-label Amazon Obfuscation.com (Veverka 2000). The insinuation was that, as Ronald Reagan was labeled the Teflon president, Bezos must be the Mylar CEO, resembling those metallic balloons that are slippery on the outside and full of hot air on the inside. Other critics of the "Bezos show" have toyed with their own speculation about the inevitable failure of his venture with names like "Amazon.toast" and "Amazon.bomb."

Whatever the future holds, there is no question that Bezos is a brilliant marketer and spin-doctor. His company, currently touting more than 25 million customers in 150 countries, is a household name in many parts of the world. There is perhaps more than a little irony that the first name for his brainchild was Abracadabra.com, shortened to Cadabra.com, and then finally abandoned in favor of Amazon when one person misheard "Cadabra" as "cadaver."

Whether or not Amazon and Bezos will ultimately succeed, his approach to building the first online retailing dynasty is very focused on the consumer. You might wonder how he manages to pay so much attention to the external world and still manage to run this rapidly growing empire. Bezos clearly knows his business from many angles and can drill deep into a variety of technical and marketing areas, but his approach to running his organization has been distinctively Style 4, *delegating,* from the start. He hires the best people he can find who are proven experts in their fields and, as much as any CEO can do, leaves them alone and lets them do what they do well.

His methods for finding people are somewhat unique in that he searches for people who share his penchant for having fun, are entrepreneurial, have compelling outside interests that give them a balanced perspective, and are decidedly independent. One of his first hires was Nicholas J. Hanauer, who at the time was head of sales for his family's business, Pacific Coast Feather Co., the nation's leading supplier of feathers for high-end pillows, comforters, and mattresses. Hanauer once posed in his pajamas for a national ad campaign that appeared in *Forbes, Fortune,* and *Business Week.* When he and Bezos met they became, he said, instant friends.

Another early hire was Shel Kaphan, considered by many to be "the go-to guy in Silicon Valley for building very fast databases." Recommended by a friend, like most of Bezos's early hires, Kaphan became Amazon's first VP for research and development. A former colleague of Kaphan sums up what it was about him, other than his technical prowess, that Bezos found alluring: "Shel has an intuitive idea of how things work . . . He's not really willing to accept other people's say-so (Spector 2000, p. 36).

More recently, as pressure to produce results has increased, Bezos has gone through a new wave of hiring but has stuck with the *delegating* formula of finding proven players and letting them do their thing. His highest-profile hire was old-economy player Joe Galli, a nineteen-year veteran of Black and Decker. Bezos made Galli chief operating officer and instructed him to play hardball to shift the company from rampant spending to dramatic earnings.

Galli, not Bezos, was the overseer of restructuring. He brought in an expert to apply Six-Sigma quality controls to the distribution centers, implemented an approval process for expenses, and oversaw the first layoff in company history, resulting in the departure of 2 percent of the work force. And while Bezos was totally behind Galli's actions, it was Galli who took the heat and eventually left the company.

In shifting his company from a "get big fast" mentality to a "make profits fast" approach, Bezos continues to hire seasoned executives to run various parts of the company. In the past two years he has brought in Jeffrey Wilke, Allied Signal's head of distribution; Ben Slivka, Microsoft's Internet guru; and Delta Airlines' former CFO Warren Jenson.

While Bezos is clearly the visionary of his company, his tendency to hire people who share his vision of empowering others to do what's best for the company runs through his senior staff. In the words of executive editor Rick Ayre, "I'm looking for people who want things to do that matter, a group of people who want a life with meaning, who want a career with meaning. And we offer that to people because it's a company that provides everyone with a voice and a responsibility for their actions (ibid., p. 108).

In fact, the basic tenet of Bezos's approach to recruiting is to hire people who are smart, open, creative, and able to think for themselves. Interestingly, this *delegating* approach is the underpinning of Bezos's goal to create the largest store in the world—one that is customer focused. "Our vision," reads one banner, "is the world's most customer-centric company. The place where people come to find and discover anything they might want to buy online." Bezos's *delegating* approach is at work even with the customer in his message: we don't tell them what to buy; we just make everything available to them and let them choose.

STYLE 4: DELEGATOR OR ABDICATOR

Delegating as a primary leadership style can be tricky to grasp because, on the surface, it looks like the classic laissez-faire approach whereby the leader defers to followers and appears indifferent to what goes on. That is definitely not the case, however, with the truly effective *delegator*.

One of the hallmarks of the Style 4 leader is that he or she respects and acknowledges the personal vision of followers. This does not mean that one's own vision becomes irrelevant in the leader/follower relationship. Consider for a moment the two cases that opened this chapter—Ronald Reagan and Ted Turner. While you might argue with Reagan's policies as a leader, you would be hard-pressed to argue with his ability to effectively choose people who were aligned with his vision and to delegate responsibility to them. Nor could you find fault with Ted Turner's ability to select people who would carry out his vision of a "thinking person's" news network, a place where people can come for information and make their own judgments about that information.

The point is that effective Style 4 leaders don't *abdicate* responsibility; they merely empower others who share their vision to orchestrate the realization of that vision. They find others who are ready and able to run with the ball and let them run, always continuing, however, to keep an eye on the ball as well.

CREATIVE AUTONOMY

Consider the case of another highly successful entertainment industry leader, Alan Ladd, who was president of Twentieth Century Fox Film Corporation. In a recent book on creativity and management, Harvard Business School professor John J. Kao documents how Ladd left Fox to create his own motion picture company that would foster optimum creativity in the film-making process. In so doing, Kao also paints a picture of a masterful Window 4 leader.

The case is a particularly compelling study for an industry that is normally dominated by people with strong egos and strong control needs—people far more likely to exhibit Style 1 characteristics than Style 4. Consider the following observations made by Kao about the film industry as background for understanding the significance of Ladd's approach.

"It is a highly speculative business where stakes are in the millions. Two out of ten make money, two break even, and the rest lose money. The production process is complex and depends on a diverse group of creative and technical people. In the 18 months to two years needed to complete the cycle, public taste may change, or the competition may have already released a similar product. People in the industry use gambling analogies to describe their successes and failures. They assert that charts and graphs led nowhere; Lady Luck, magic, and pure mysticism explained events just as well. You give the people what they want and they still don't come" (Kao 1991).

Considering the volatile, uncertain nature of the film industry, one might suspect that those at the head of production companies would respond to this uncertainty by imposing a measure of control and direction more reflective of a Style 1 or Style 2 leader. The case of Alan Ladd is a good example of how someone could effectively use the power of delegation to prosper in the context of uncertainty.

According to Kao, the first thing Ladd did, which set the groundwork for the Window 4 organization he would create, was to handpick a group of proven performers to start his venture with him. These included such people as Jay Kanter, his senior vice president of worldwide production, and Gareth Wigan, his vice president of worldwide production, as well as half a dozen other industry veterans who collectively were responsible for garnering thirty-three Academy Awards in 1978. They had produced *Star Wars* in 1976 and backed five critically and popularly successful "women's films" in one year: *Julia, The Turning Point, An Unmarried Woman, Norma Rae,* and *The Rose.*

In assembling such an illustrious cast of characters, what Ladd was doing was setting the stage for his Style 4 approach by staffing his organization with experts who knew what they were doing and creating the conditions for letting them do it. Observes Kao, "Production requires a sensitively and efficiently coordinated effort of subgroups—office people, technical crew, and talent groups—making full use of available technical resources for creative problem solving." Adds Wigan, "If things are going well, and the principal individuals are people who like to be left alone, then your personal contact can be slight. It's a question of judging between not nagging and at the same time appearing not to be disinterested" (ibid.).

This snapshot of Ladd's corporate culture suggests the hands-off approach characteristic of an effective Style 4, while sustaining the limited involvement necessary to avoid the threat of *abdication* present in the ineffective form of this style.

Another indication of Ladd's Style 4 approach can be seen by looking at the way day-to-day activities occurred. According to Kao, decision making took place all the time, anywhere people gathered. Though there was one person with primary responsibility for each project, everyone else was involved, and anyone could step in and become the project's spokesperson at any time. And consider these observations by Kao regarding Ladd's open, *delegating* style regarding meetings: Meetings simply evolved and included long silences, which Ladd seemed comfortable with. There was often no agenda—people spoke when they had something to say and decisions got made "by dissolve." Ladd was totally accessible to everyone in the company, all of whom he trusted completely—they would not be there otherwise. Certain people needed to be at certain meetings, but others weren't kept from coming. Whoever wanted to attend a particular meeting could. While this scenario might appear chaotic, and very well could be under the wrong circumstances, it highlights the need for the leader to let go of control when using the *delegating* style.

According to Kao, one of the main incentives people identified for wanting to work with Ladd had to do with his tendency and preference for leaving people alone and letting them do their work. He seemed to use this approach even when things were not going well. Says Ladd, "Well, there's leaving people alone and leaving them alone; the difference is how you approach your involvement . . . you don't say, 'I'm right and have all the answers, because they may be right too' " (ibid.).

As with most effective CEOs, Ladd's style was echoed by and evident in the approach of his key charges. Consider these words by Ladd's vice president, Gareth Wigan: "If things start not to go well—it gets behind schedule, or you don't like the material—then it becomes much more difficult. It doesn't help to be sitting on top of the creative person's back. You can't tell him or her what to do, exactly, and if you're standing there with a stopwatch, it can be counterproductive.

"It's very important with creative people to join them, and not to challenge them. It's always easy for them to turn around and say, 'You don't understand, you're not a filmmaker' " (ibid.).

This perspective on working with people in a delegating way even when the going gets tough is probably the greatest testament to Ladd's commitment to a Style 4 approach. Finally, consider these words by Ladd himself regarding his philosophy: "As long as you trust the people you're working with and feel that they are responsible, then you don't ask a lot of questions" (ibid.). While the volatility that is inherent to the motion picture industry has caused Ladd to move on to other ventures, he continues to be a major player in the American film industry.

WHEN THE SHOE DOESN'T FIT

While finding and surrounding yourself with good people to delegate to, as Ladd, Turner, and Redstone have done, can be a recipe fopr success choosing the wrong people to delegate to in the wrong situation can spell disaster. Consider the case of Paul Fireman, chairman of athletic shoe giant Reebok International Ltd., which since its inception has been battling for the top of the sneaker heap with Nike.

In 1987, according to *Forbes* magazine, Fireman reconceived his vision of Reebok from that of a shoe company to that of a consumer products company. To further his vision he brought in experts from other specialties—Joseph LaBonte, formerly president of Twentieth Century Fox; Mark Goldstone, formerly president of Faberge; and Frank O'Connell, formerly CEO of HBO Video—to run his operation. According to *Forbes* and to Fireman himself, his strategy of *delegating* control of the company to outsiders who were a bad match for Reebok's client base failed miserably and, as a result, looked more like *abdicating*.

Says *Forbes*, "the shoe business wasn't show business. The strategy flopped. Shoe retailers liked dealing with people who knew about shoes, and resented flashy Hollywood types. 'I really abdicated responsibility,' concedes Fireman" (Meeks 1990).

But Fireman's woes did not end with his misguided foray into products beyond athletic shoes. In fact, the number two post under him has been vacated nine times since 1986. Fireman has been accused of abdication many times. A column in the *Boston Globe* stated about his leadership style, "Fireman has espoused the idea of chaos as a way of management, it's his belief that constant change and turmoil creates energy. Chaos is what he's gotten" (*Boston Globe* 1999).

He has been accused of "being out of touch with today's consumer and more concerned with his golf game and real estate ventures than Reebok's declining market share" (Tedeschi 2000). Fireman's latest challenge—and perhaps his last chance for redemption—comes on the heels of the departure of brand president Carl Yanowski. In an uncharacteristic move Fireman has chosen not to replace Yanowski but to fill the void himself. Whether he can turn around the abysmal performance of Reebok—the company's earnings dropped 54 percent in 1999—will be in large part determined by his capacity to demonstrate a leadership style other than an ineffective Style 4.

LETTING EXPERTS BE EXPERTS— A CASE STUDY

One of the times when *delegating* can be most effective is when you're dealing with someone who knows far more than you do about a particular problem and how to solve it and is willing to tackle it. For example, in this age of rapidly advancing technology, it is entirely possible that someone who reports to you is more adept in a particular area under your purview than you are. Many managers resist this notion; nervous about their own accountability, they maintain control over things they know little about and end up decreasing their effectiveness along with the effectiveness of their reports. However, you'll see from the following example that it is possible to delegate and retain your accountability at the same time—and the rewards for both you and those who report to you can be considerable.

Roger was a senior manager in a medium-sized research lab specializing in software development for the microelectronics industry. He took great pride in the fact that his research group functioned as a team and always shared responsibility for both their successes and their failures. Roger was extremely knowledgeable in most of the technical areas his group encountered, so it was reasonable that he used a hands-on approach most of the time, working closely with his team to make sure their motivation and results were as strong as possible. Roger's personality was such that he liked this hands-on approach and enjoyed the control over his team's results that it afforded him.

His greatest challenge as a manager came one Friday when he was assigned a new employee, Steve, and the same day was assigned a project in an emerging technology he knew little about. The new hire, it turned out, was an expert in this emerging technology. The assignment was to create a software program employing the new technology, and to do it fast.

That Friday afternoon, Roger met with Steve to begin to establish their working relationship. He began by explaining to Steve that their unit worked as a team, that he prided himself on being a team leader who recognized that everyone on the team had a contribution to make, and that he saw his role as one that integrated everyone's contributions.

During the conversation Roger noticed that Steve seemed disinterested in what he was saying. As soon as Roger was done talking about teamwork,

Steve began asking him questions about the technical resources that would be available regarding the new project. As Steve talked, Roger grew increasingly uncomfortable, realizing that Steve was not a team player and that he seemed to know a great deal more about the upcoming project than Roger or anyone else in the group. Rather than bring up his concerns, Roger decided to spend the weekend thinking about the situation before attempting to address them.

That weekend Roger realized he had a dilemma. If he used his typical participatory style with Steve, he would likely end up slowing the progress of the project, which was up against a tight deadline. If he let Steve have free rein, he ran the risk of alienating the rest of the group, who were used to working together on everything under his leadership.

By the end of the weekend, Roger developed a strategy that he was hopeful would work. He decided that since Steve was the most qualified to take the lead on this project, he would try *delegating* responsibility for the project to him. That would solve the first problem—not slowing down the project. His second problem was the team and their expectations regarding involvement and their comfort in following Roger. He knew from his initial discussion with Steve about teamwork that it was unlikely that Steve would be an effective team leader. Perhaps the best thing to do, he thought, was to encourage Steve to work on his own, with assistance if he needed it, while the rest of the group worked on other projects.

On Monday morning he called Steve into his office, told him of his plans to delegate responsibility for the new project to him, and suggested that he let Roger know if he needed any assistance. Meanwhile, he told Steve, he would be talking to the rest of the team about what they would be doing while Steve worked on the new technology project. Steve seemed excited about being able to dig right in and admitted he had been nervous all weekend about having to work with a group that might slow his progress. Roger pointed out that at some point Steve would have to accept that he was in a team environment and that when the circumstances warranted he would be expected to work more cooperatively with the rest of the group.

As a result of Roger's careful *delegating* of responsibilities, he managed to get the project completed on time without disrupting the team spirit he so cherished.

Your Personal Window of Leadership

CHAPTER 7

By now, you should have a good understanding of the leadership styles of The L4 System. You know what they look like in terms of direction and support. You understand the decision-making methods, the communication skills, and the recognition strategies that are associated with each window. You also have many well-known leaders to use as a frame of reference. There should be no doubt in your mind as to what the four windows look like.

As you have been reading about the styles and famous people who use them, we have asked you several times, "Which leadership styles do you tend to use?" Now it is time to find out the answer to that question.

This chapter will help you interpret your responses to the cases from chapter 1. First, you will see which styles you selected in each case. Then you will see the overall mix of styles that you chose and the way your choice of styles compares to those of other managers. Finally, as you read about your main, backup, and limited styles, you will get a clear picture of yourself as a leader.

In the matrix on the next page, enter your responses to each of the cases in chapter 1. You will notice that the four actions have been reorganized into columns that reflect the leadership styles that you selected. Be careful to get your answers in the right spaces.

Add each column to determine the total number of points you assigned to each style. The four totals should add up to 50 points.

Finally, multiply each column by two to find out what percentage of each style you selected. The four percentages should add up to 100 percent.

We used to tell people that the style with the highest percentage was their main style, any style with 15 percent or more was a backup style, and any style

	Style 1	Style 2	Style 3	Style 4
Case 1	B 2	A 0	D 2	C 1
Case 2	C 0	A 0	B 3	D 2
Case 3	C 4	D 1	A 0	B 0
Case 4	D 0	B 0	C 3	A 2
Case 5	A 0	D 2	B 3	C 0
Case 6	B 0	C 0	D 3	A 2
Case 7	D 0	C 4	A 1	B 0
Case 8	A 0	B 1	C 2	D 2
Case 9	C 2	D 3	A 0	B 0
Case 10	B 1	C 2	D 2	A 0
Totals	9	13	19	9
Percentages MULTIPLY X 2	17	24	38	18

with less than 15 percent was a limited style. That is one way to look at your leadership profile; however, over the years we have learned that most people give themselves the benefit of the doubt on a self-assessment.

In our training programs, we always do an L4 Other Assessment—feedback from direct reports—so that managers can compare what they think they do to what other people say they actually do and ideally should be doing. For most people, their self-assessed leadership profile is very similar to their ideal profile but quite different from their actual profile.

In this book we can't administer the L4 Other to your team, but we can show you how your choices on the ten cases compare to other people's self-assessments. This comparison will give you a context for thinking about how others might perceive you.

HOW DO YOU COMPARE TO MOST LEADERS?

The way you come across as a leader is not just a question of what styles you use. It is a question of what you use in comparison to other leaders. The table below shows averages and ranges we have compiled from several industries. The averages enable you to see whether your use of each style is typical of most managers and the ranges show you how far you stand out from the pack.

As you can see, the averages vary somewhat from industry to industry. They also fluctuate within an organization's hierarchy as higher-level man-

	AVERAGES (PERCENT)			
INDUSTRY	Style 1	Style 2	Style 3	Style 4
Accounting	19	22	51	8
Financial Services	15	19	48	18
Consulting	16	20	49	15
Technology	12	16	50	22
Energy	12	13	53	22
Manufacturing	13	18	49	20
Pharmaceuticals	15	19	46	20
OVERALL	**15**	**20**	**47**	**18**
RANGE	**0–56**	**0–60**	**0–100**	**0–84**

agers in every industry tend to use more Style 3 and Style 4, while frontline supervisors tend to be more hands-on with Styles 1 and 2.

You can also see that in every industry, Style 3 has the highest average. That's because on the questionnaire you took in chapter 1 (and on the L4 Self—the longer version we use in training programs), the vast majority of people assign the most points to Style 3. Why is that? Just ask yourself two questions. First, "Do you think you give your team members a lot of responsibility?" And second, "Do you think you are available to give your people support?" If you are like most managers, you answered yes to both questions. Most of us think we give our people a lot of responsibility and we believe that we are available to support them.

So if Style 3 is the style you selected the most, you are not alone. However, as we have learned from our experience with L4 Other feedback, this probably is what you ideally should be doing but may or may not be what you actually do. We also know from the L4 Other feedback that a large number of feedback givers say they would perform better with more or less of each style. If you want to know your actual and ideal leadership profiles and learn which styles you need to increase and decrease, you should consider an L4 Other assessment. In the meantime, you can get an idea of how others might perceive you by comparing the percentages you just calculated to the averages and ranges above.

The overall average for Style 1 is 15 percent, with a range of 0 to 56. Thus if your score is around 15 percent, your use of the directing style is about average. If your score is near the low end of the range, you may not be doing enough directing. If it is at the high end of the range, you may be perceived as dominating.

For Style 2, the overall average is 20 percent, with a range of 0 to 60. If your score is close to 20 percent, your use of the problem-solving style is typical of the average manager. If your score is at the low end of the range, you may not be doing enough problem solving. If your score is at the high end, you may be over-involving yourself or others in decision making.

The average for Style 3 is 47 percent, with a range of 0 to 100. If your score is around 47 percent, you are using the developing style an average amount of time. If you have a very low score, you may not be giving people enough development opportunities. If you have a very high score, you may be perceived as over-accommodating.

For Style 4, the overall average is 18 percent, with a range of 0 to 84. If your score is near 18 percent, you are doing an average amount of delegating. If your score is at the low end of the range, you may not be delegating enough. If it is at the high end, you may be perceived as abdicating.

If your use of any style is significantly above or below average, you may be perceived as overusing or underusing that style, and that can affect your reputation as a leader. To help you visualize how your responses compare to other managers' responses, use the table on the facing page to convert your percentages to percentiles.

There is a separate column for each style. In each column, make a dot where your percentage falls. Connect the four dots to create a line graph illustrating your leadership profile.

The 75th percentile is shaded because any style that is at or above it is a main style. The 25th percentile is also shaded because any style that is at or above it is a backup style. Any style below the 25th percentile is a limited style.

Now you can see how using more or less of any style could color people's perceptions of you. For example, suppose you selected an even 25 percent of each style. Even though you chose all four styles equally, you would be at the 85th percentile for Style 1 and, therefore, are probably good at directing but may also be seen as dominating. You would be at the 75th percentile for Style 2 and most likely are a strong problem solver, but you may be seen as over-involving. You would be slightly above the 5th percentile for Style 3 and, therefore, are probably not doing as much developing as people need. And you would be between the 75th and 80th percentiles for Style 4 and are likely to be good at delegating but may also be seen as abdicating.

Now, read the charts on pages 104 and 105 for a more complete look at your leadership profile. You may want to highlight the borders of those paragraphs that pertain to you. That will make it easier to get a full view of your leadership profile.

Most people have one main style, one or two backup styles, and one or two limited styles. Some people have two main styles and a few have three. And some people have a balanced profile where all four styles are between the 25th and 75th percentiles. Every profile has its assets and liabilities. The goal in this chapter isn't to see if you have the right profile. It is simply to help you recognize the styles you use the most and appreciate that underusing any style can be a limitation for you and overusing any style can turn a strength into a weakness.

	PERCENTAGES			
PERCENTILE	**Style 1**	**Style 2**	**Style 3**	**Style 4**
100	56	60	100	84
95	32	36	72	35
90	28	32	66	31
85	25	29	62	28
80	23	27	59	26
75	21	25	56	24
70	20	24	54	22
65	19	23	52	21
60	17	22	50	20
55	16	21	48	19
50	15	20	46	18
45	14	18	44	16
40	13	17	42	15
35	11	16	40	14
30	10	15	38	13
25	9	13	36	11
20	8	12	33	10
15	6	10	31	9
10	5	9	28	7
5	3	5	24	5

The following sections provide a more complete interpretation of your Window of Leadership. The first section is for people who have one main style that stands out as their clear preference. The second section is for leaders who have two predominant styles and two styles that are used on a more limited basis. The third section describes leaders who use three styles with some degree of frequency as well as one limited style. The fourth section is for people who use a balanced amount of all four styles.

	Style 1	**Style 2**
Main Style	DIRECTING is your strength. You are decisive and don't need a lot of input to make a decision. You are good at giving clear directions and full explanations. You follow up to make sure work is done properly and value people who do exactly what you want. Your weakness is that you can be DOMINATING when people already know what to do or want more responsibility.	Your strength is involving people in the PROBLEM-SOLVING process. You are good at listening to team members' problems and making decisions based on their recommendations. You are also good at opening your problems to input from others. Your weakness is that you can be OVER-INVOLVING by getting yourself or others into the process unnecessarily.
Backup Styles	You can be DIRECTING when you need to be. Even though this is not your main style, you are good at making decisions on your own, giving team members clear assignments, and providing them with close supervision if it's necessary. You may come across as DOMINATING at times if you tend to use this backup style in situations when less directing is needed.	You are willing to involve yourself or others in the PROBLEM-SOLVING process whenever it is necessary. While this is not your main style, you are good at opening up problems, inviting input, and getting closure on decisions if you need to. You might come across as OVER-INVOLVING at times if you use this backup style in situations that call for less participation.
Limited Styles	DIRECTING is not your favorite way of leading. As a result, you may not be as decisive as you should in situations that don't permit time for deliberation. You also may not be as clear as you could about what you want and how you expect it to be done. On the other hand, you are not likely to be DOMINATING unless you use this style at times when people don't need it.	PROBLEM SOLVING is not your most comfortable way to work with people. Consequently, there may be times when you don't get others involved enough with your decisions. You also may not involve yourself with followers' decisions as quickly as you should. You are not likely to come across as OVER-INVOLVING unless you use this style at the wrong times.

	Style 3	**Style 4**
Main Style	DEVELOPING people is your strength. You are good at giving followers challenges that let them stretch and grow. You listen well and are good at helping them think through problems without undercutting their sense of responsibility. Your weakness is OVER-ACCOMMODATING by listening too much and letting followers make decisions that you should make.	DELEGATING is your strength. You are good at giving followers meaningful responsibilities and then letting go and allowing them to handle their assignments on their own. As long as your team members are prepared for this much authority, they see you as a challenging and trusting leader. When they feel overwhelmed, they are more likely to accuse you of ABDICATING.
Backup Styles	DEVELOPING is something you can do when you need to. While this is not your main style, you know how to support followers with their responsibilities when it is necessary. You can listen well, ask challenging questions, and offer helpful suggestions. On the downside, you may slip into OVER-ACCOMMODATING if you let followers call the shots when you need to decide.	When DELEGATING is needed, you are comfortable giving followers full authority. While you prefer some level of involvement, you are willing to let team members handle significant responsibilities in certain situations. Although this isn't your main style, you may come across as ABDICATING at times, especially if you are not available when people need you.
Limited Styles	DEVELOPING is not what you do best. You may leave followers alone to make some decisions, but when you get involved, you like to be the one who decides. As a result, you may miss some chances to give followers the support they need to handle their responsibilities. You are not likely to be seen as OVER-ACCOMMODATING unless you use this limited style at the wrong times.	DELEGATING is not easy for you. You are not comfortable with some level of involvement. Consequently, you may not give team members full authority as often as you could and may keep yourself more in control than you need to be. You are not likely to come across as ABDICATING unless your limited use of this style occurs when people need something from you.

You don't need to read every section—you will probably be most interested in the one that pertains to you. As you read about yourself, remember that this profile is based on a self-assessment. Even though you know whether your choices are above or below the mean, the only real test of your effectiveness is the impact you have on other people and the results they produce.

ONE-STYLE PROFILES

Style 1

If your clear preference is Style 1, *directing,* and you use the other three styles on a limited basis, you are the type of leader who likes to make decisions on your own, gives explicit instructions to team members, follows up with close supervision, and values people who comply with your wishes.

Your strength is your clarity about what you want, when you want it, and how you expect it done. You like being in control and are good at providing structure in situations that call for someone to take charge. You are particularly good at pointing people in the right direction.

Your weakness is that you tend to overuse Style 1. As a result, you come across as dominating to people who like to take some initiative or think for themselves.

Your reluctance to use Style 2 puts you at a disadvantage in situations that call for you to take input to your decisions. So there are times when you make decisions that are not well received or have trouble getting team members to buy in to your way of thinking.

Your limited use of Style 3 handicaps you at times when you should listen to team members and support them with their decision making. Consequently, you do not create as many opportunities for developing people as you might.

Your tendency to underutilize Style 4 makes you reluctant to let team members handle some responsibilities on their own. This leaves you unable to delegate as much as you should.

Style 2

If you have a clear preference for S2, *problem solving,* and a limited use of the other three styles, you are the kind of leader who enjoys getting others involved in helping you make tough decisions. You bring issues to the members of your team (and sometimes to peers, superiors, customers, or consultants) so that you can get as much input as you can on the problems you are trying to solve. You also feel important when other people bring their problems to you so that you can tell them what needs to be done.

Your strength as a leader is your willingness to roll up your sleeves and get your hands dirty to solve problems. You like to meet with people, one-on-one or in a group, to identify and fix whatever needs fixing. You are good at listening to diverse points of view, finding areas of agreement, and getting closure when there is disagreement.

Your weakness is that you may over-involve others in discussions that they would rather not participate in, or you may over-involve yourself in decisions that others could resolve, either on their own or with a little support.

Since you don't use much Style 1, you may appear indecisive to those who believe that you already have the relevant facts. You may also give unclear or incomplete directions when you have made up your mind.

Your limited use of Style 3 can make you come across as a poor listener in situations where others don't feel that you fully understand their point of view. It also limits your opportunities for developing team members by helping them think through tough decisions.

Finally, your reluctance to use Style 4 can make people feel that you don't trust them to handle meaningful responsibilities. By not delegating you actually reduce the possibility that team members will accept authority at times when you might want them to.

Style 3

If you have a definite preference for Style 3, *developing,* and use the other three styles on a limited basis, then you are the type of leader who excels at giving team members responsibility and supporting them as the need arises.

Your strength is your ability to listen in a way that makes team members comfortable approaching you with problems they can't resolve on their own. You ask good questions, encourage others to fully explain the problems and their ideas for solving them, and are more likely to reflect back others' viewpoints than to express your own. Most important, you give people opportunities to stretch their skills while knowing that you will back them up when they need it.

Your weakness is that you can spend too much time listening. Sometimes you become over-accommodating by virtue of wanting everyone to like you. You can also make yourself so available for assisting others that you don't have time for your own work.

Since you don't use much Style 1, you may appear incapable of making your own decisions. You may also give incomplete or unclear directions when you have made up your mind.

Your reluctance to use Style 2 puts you at a disadvantage in situations that call for you to make decisions based on others' input. There are times when you try so hard to please that you listen too much or are swayed to the point of view of whoever talks to you last.

Your tendency to avoid Style 4 makes you reluctant to let team members handle some responsibilities on their own. Your desire to be supportive may actually hamper your ability to delegate and may also limit team members' full capacity for growth.

Style 4

If you have a clear preference for Style 4, *delegating,* and a limited use of the other three styles, then you are the kind of leader who likes to let people handle major responsibilities on their own.

Your strength is your willingness to let others take full ownership of their assignments. You are comfortable letting go, staying out of the way, and letting team members make decisions as they see fit. You don't feel the need to give them your perspective or to check in to see how they are doing.

Your weakness shows up when team members find that they need your involvement. Often they find you unavailable. If they can find you, you will probably be unwilling to let the responsibility shift back to you. Either situation can make you come across as abdicating.

Since you don't use much Style 1, you may appear indecisive to those who believe that you have all the information you need to make a good decision. You may also give unclear or incomplete directions when you have made up your mind.

Your reluctance to use Style 2 makes you less than effective in situations where you need to make decisions based on follower input. Your preference to keep your hands off may convince them to turn to other leaders when they need timely decisions from above.

Your limited use of Style 3 can make you come across as a poor listener in situations where others don't feel that you fully understand their point of view. It also limits your opportunities for developing team members by helping them think through tough decisions.

TWO-STYLE PROFILES

S1–S2

If you use mostly Styles 1 and 2, *directing* and *problem solving,* you are definitely a hands-on type of leader. You like being in charge, you are comfortable with decision making, and you are good at telling people what you want, when you want it, how you want it, and why. Sometimes you seek input from others to make sure you fully understand a problem situation and have the benefit of their thinking before you make up your mind. You also like people to bring problems to your attention so that you are aware of what's going on and can make the right decisions.

The strength of this profile is your ability to be decisive, your willingness to be the focal point of decision making, and the fact that decisions will be made with a high degree of consistency based on the principles that you believe will drive your team to success.

The weakness of this profile is that you don't give team members much in the way of meaningful responsibilities. Consequently, they don't get many opportunities to think for themselves or to develop their capabilities. The other side of that coin is that your desk stays cluttered with decisions that everyone waits for you to make.

Your reluctance to use Style 4 may give others the message that you don't trust them or that you don't like the way they handle responsibilities. Your lack of delegating not only keeps the monkey on your back but it makes team members hesitant to accept authority at times when you might want them to.

This lack of trust is reinforced by your preference for Style 2 over Style 3. When you try to offer support, you only listen until you have made up your mind about the right course of action. As a result, when you are genuinely trying to be helpful, others are more likely to see you as checking up on them to be sure they are doing things your way as opposed to developing their skills.

S3–S4

If you use mostly S3, *developing,* and S4, *delegating,* you have a definite preference for giving team members responsibility. You are comfortable letting them make decisions and do not feel the need to control their actions. As a result, you are particularly good at leading people who like to think for themselves.

Under your leadership, these types of people feel challenged as they take on increased responsibilities and stretch themselves to handle them as well as they can. They will accept the authority that you delegate, in part because of who they are, but also because they know you will back them up with support when they need it.

The downside of this leadership profile is that there may be times when you need to step up to the plate and make some tough decisions or give clear directions. Since you don't use much Style 1, under these circumstances you may not come across as the kind of strong leader that people look to for decisiveness and action.

Your reluctance to use Style 2 makes you less than effective in situations where you need to make decisions based on follower input. Your preference to keep your hands off or to help others decide may convince them to turn to other leaders when they need timely decisions from above.

S2–S3

If you have a preference for Styles 2 and 3, *problem solving* and *developing,* you are the kind of leader who likes to be involved. You value talking to team members, peers, and superiors about problems that need to be addressed. You like participating in discussions and appreciate being asked to give your ideas to others.

Your strength is that you enjoy the problem-solving process. When you need to make decisions, you will seek out input from other people. When others are looking for input to their decision making, you are quite willing to share your best thinking.

Your weakness is getting caught up in too many meetings, endless discussions, and fruitless debates. You can be too quick to make others' problems your problems and involve yourself more than they would like. At times you may be giving people support that they aren't ready for or don't feel they need. At other times you may try to make decisions that others were expecting to make.

Since you don't use much Style 1, you may not do as much directing as you should and may appear incapable of making your own decisions. You may also give incomplete or unclear directions when you have made up your mind.

Since you don't use much S4, you are also not likely to let team members make decisions on their own. Consequently, you may not delegate as frequently as might be appropriate for the ability and motivation of the people working for you and may involve yourself more often than is truly necessary.

S1–S4

If you use mostly Styles 1 and 4, *directing* and *delegating,* you have a preference for using low-support, low-involvement leadership styles. For you, the question of who is responsible for decision making is black and white. If the ball is in your court, you just decide. If the ball is in someone else's court, you stay out of the way and let him or her decide. You don't seek a lot of input to the decisions you have to make, and you don't feel the need to provide a lot of input to decisions that others have to make.

The strength of this profile is very efficient decision making. You and the other people around you don't get caught up in lots of meetings, endless discussions, or fruitless debates. Either you make the decision or they make the decision, and you get on with it.

The weakness of this profile is that since decisions are not based on other people's thinking, they are not always the best ones that could have been made. Consequently, decisions you make may not have the full backing of those who have to live with them. There are also times when you don't fully endorse other people's decisions simply because you don't understand their perspectives.

Your tendency to underutilize Styles 2 and 3 can make you seem aloof and uninvolved. People may not seek you out to ask for support because they have learned not to expect it from you. They are more likely to take their problems to others who will offer them support and who will value their recommendations when tough decisions have to be made.

S3–S1

If you use mostly Styles 1 and 3, *directing* and *developing,* you tend to be decisive in those areas where the decision-making responsibility is yours. You know what you want, you know how you want it done, and you are quite clear with the people who work for you about the directions you would like to have followed.

When your team members are responsible for making decisions, you will listen and offer support when they need it. You are comfortable giving them responsibility but like to stay close to the situation to help them stay on course. If they are unable to make good decisions, even with support, your tendency is to take over completely. You will reframe the project to your own way of thinking and redirect people in the way that you think is most appropriate.

With this profile, you have the potential for being a very effective leader if you use Style 1 to give clear directions up front and then use Style 3 to provide support after people have had a chance to handle responsibilities on their own. Since you are less inclined to use Style 4, the challenge for you is to let go enough so that team members feel some sense of authority over their work. Without that, your attempts to support may come across as hovering.

With this profile, you also have the potential to hinder performance. If you are over-accommodating in the beginning, you may spend too much time helping people discover their own path. Then, when time is running short, your tendency would be to switch to Style 1 and undercut their sense of responsibility.

A leader who is more comfortable with Style 4 might let team members wrestle with the problem on their own for a longer period of time before taking over. A leader who uses more Style 2 would take control less abruptly by using team members' input to make decisions.

S2-S4

If you use mostly Styles 2 and 4, *problem solving* and *delegating,* you are good at giving team members meaningful responsibilities. You trust them and are comfortable letting them make decisions on their own. When you do get involved, you tend to jump in with both feet. Your inclination is to listen to problems that staff bring to your attention and then outline the best course of action for them to solve the problem.

Since you don't use much Style 3, team members don't experience you as someone who listens with a great deal of patience or who wants to understand their analysis of the situation. Instead, you listen only to that information which fits your perspective on the matter. As soon as you have heard enough, you will make your decision and move on. Consequently, your desk stays cluttered with other people's problems. Your tendency to take the monkey off a team member's back and put it on yours may be overstressing you, while simultaneously you may not be helping others make the tough decisions.

Since you don't use much Style 1, you may also be sowing the seeds for problems to return to your desk by making assignments without giving adequate directions. The result is that people come looking for you sooner than they might have if they had clearer expectations. Then, when they do seek you out, you move into the problem-solving mode and reclaim the problem.

THREE-STYLE PROFILES

S2–S3–S4

If you use Styles 2, 3, and 4 with some frequency, you are the kind of leader who is comfortable with *problem solving, developing,* and *delegating.* You are good at leaving team members on their own to handle significant areas of responsibility. You are equally effective at listening to them and providing support when they need some assistance. You are also willing to make tough decisions based on their input when necessary.

Because you use a limited amount of Style 1, directing, others may perceive you as lacking vision or decisiveness. They may see you as unable or unwilling to make a decision on your own. When you are in charge, they may see you as giving inadequate instructions or clear enough directions so that they can implement decisions in a way that meets your expectations or achieves the necessary results.

S1–S3–S4

If you use Styles 1, 3, and 4 with some frequency, you are the kind of leader who is comfortable with *directing, developing,* and *delegating.* You are good at giving team members clear outlines of what you expect. You are also good at leaving people on their own to handle significant areas of responsibility and are equally effective at listening to them and providing support when they need some assistance.

Since you use a limited amount of Style 2, *problem solving,* you may be perceived as the kind of leader who does not like to receive input to your decisions. It is rare that you will seek out others' analysis of a situation before you make up your mind about what needs to be done. When you are in charge, you make up your mind and tell team members what to do. When others are in charge, you let them handle it on their own. If they need support, you are happy to provide it, but you are reluctant to take others' recommendations and make decisions that they cannot or will not make. In addition, you are unlikely to bring problems to their attention and ask them to support you with your decision making.

S1–S2–S4

If you use Styles 1, 2, and 4 on a regular basis, you are the type of leader who is willing to use *directing, problem solving,* and *delegating.* You are good at telling team members what you want, when you want it, how you want it, and why. You are also willing to get out of their way and let them handle their responsibilities in the ways they consider most appropriate.

Since Style 3, *developing,* is limited in your profile, you come across as an impatient listener when team members discuss the problems they're wrestling with and the possible actions they are considering. While you are good at leaving people on their own to handle responsibilities as they see fit, once you get involved and begin to listen, ownership transfers quickly from them to you. In your mind, you may be doing the most efficient thing by shifting from Style 4 to Style 2, but from your team member's perspective you are undercutting their sense of responsibility.

A leader who is more comfortable with Style 3 would listen better and get a more complete understanding of the other person's situation. Listening often keeps the monkey off their backs. More important, from a long-term perspective, these leaders are developing people's potential for dealing with tough problems and finding good solutions.

S1–S2–S3

If you use Styles 1, 2, and 3 on a regular basis, you are the type of leader who is willing to use *directing, problem solving,* and *developing.* You are good at telling team members what you want, when you want it, how you want it, and why. You like asking them to bring problems to your attention so that you can solve them and truly value their input to decisions you need to make. You are equally comfortable helping them think through decisions they are wrestling with and giving them your best thinking without undercutting their sense of responsibility.

Since Style 4, *delegating,* is limited for you, your major weakness as a leader is your inability to let go. While you are comfortable giving team members assignments, your preference is to stay in close contact so that you can support them and ensure the quality of their decision making. You are less comfortable giving them the authority to make decisions and handle their areas of responsibility on their own.

People experience you as being a very involved leader, and since you use a lot of Styles 2 and 3, they will see you as open and communicative. Since you also use Styles 1 and 2, they will see you as being decisive and clear about what needs to get done. What they won't get is a feeling of being trusted to handle meaningful responsibilities or empowered to make decisions on their own.

A FOUR-STYLE PROFILE

If you use all four styles fairly evenly without having a clear main style, your leadership profile reads like a set of backup styles. At times, you are willing to tell team members what you want, when you want it, how you want it, and why. You are also willing to listen to people's problems, take their recommendations, and give them timely decisions. Sometimes you ask questions and offer support to help them think through decisions they are wrestling with. You are also capable of leaving team members on their own to handle significant areas of responsibility as they see fit.

The most unique aspect of this profile is that you don't overuse or underuse any of the styles. While this may make you more flexible than other leaders, your effectiveness will still be determined by your ability to use each style with the right people at the right times.

THERE'S MORE TO COME

In chapter 9, you will get some more feedback about how you responded to the first eight cases in chapter 1. Did you put the styles in the best places? Did you use the same styles with the women as you did with the men?

In chapter 12, you will get feedback about your responses to the last two cases. How did you decide to handle the two situations that involved groups? Did you use the best styles to get them focused and keep them productive for the long haul?

Keep reading. There's more to come.

MORE FEEDBACK

If you want to find out more about the mix of leadership styles that you actually use and the right combination of styles that you should use, the best way is to get feedback from people who work with you. At Charter Oak, we compile L4 Self and L4 Other profiles for the leaders we consult with. The L4 Self tells them what leadership styles they think they use. The L4 Other tells them what styles they actually use, and the styles that their team members ideally need so that they can perform to the best of their potential. These assessments are available in hard copy and online, and they can be self-scored or administered by us.

Let us know if you want to find out what your people have to say about you. You can call us at 1-800-741-7788 or go to our website at www.cocg.com. The cost is minimal, but the feedback is priceless.

Window Wisdom: The Name of the Game Is Leadership by Anticipation

Now that you have an understanding of your own Window of Leadership and the strengths and weaknesses of your leadership profile, you're ready to move on to the next crucial step for effective leadership. That requires taking the focus off your own style preferences and focusing on the needs of the people you're leading.

Working with people is a constantly shifting process requiring continuous adjustment and adaptation. Being able to anticipate and respond to the changing needs of team members and the situations they are dealing with is one of the great challenges of effective leadership. While no one can anticipate everything, a little bit of Window Wisdom will help you make quick style changes in smooth and predictable ways. The core of this Window Wisdom is what we call *leadership by anticipation*. There are four predictable leadership-by-anticipation patterns that will help you anticipate how to make style changes: frustration, empowerment, development, and intervention.

The *frustration* and *empowerment* cycles will help you anticipate shifts in the way you lead people on a day-to-day basis. The frustration cycle helps you avoid one of the most common traps of ineffective leadership by showing you one style change that you do not want to make. Empowerment, which we think is the most important of these four cycles, teaches you how to make style changes the way the best leaders do.

Empowerment is a guaranteed formula for real-world, day-to-day leadership. It teaches you a style sequence that will make your use of any main style successful. Any one of the four styles can be the right general approach to a given situation if it is implemented with the wisdom of empowerment. And without this Window Wisdom, your use of any main style runs the risk of failure.

The *development* and *intervention* cycles will help you anticipate shifts in the main style you use with an individual. Development shows you how and when to make smooth transitions upward through the styles. Intervention teaches you how and when to make smooth transitions downward through the styles. Both of these cycles will help you navigate the choppy waters of empowering real people in continuously changing circumstances.

HERE'S A LITTLE REALITY FOR YOU

Reality is the all-important context for leadership by anticipation. Reality, like beauty, is in the eyes of the beholder, which means that your reality may look quite different to other people. What you think you do as a leader is less important than other people's perceptions. In other words, perception is reality.

Knowing this, we have asked thousands of managers about their perception of the leadership styles they get from their managers. Most people in most organizations, when they talk about the leadership styles they receive on a day-to-day basis, say that they get told what to do (Style 1) and then left alone to do it (Style 4), as shown in Figure 8. If this is appropriate for the people and they like the way their managers work with them, the stories are very positive, and they describe their managers as delegating. If it's not right for them and they don't appreciate what their managers are doing, the tales are very negative, and they accuse their managers of abdicating. In either scenario, the net effect in terms of leadership styles is the same. Most people see their managers starting with Style 1 and moving to Style 4.

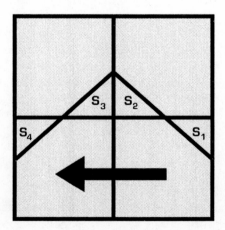

Figure 8 How Most Followers See Their Managers

Is that your reality? Is that what you get from the managers above you? Do they give you assignments and then let you figure out how to get them done?

And what about the people who work for you? Is that how they perceive you? There is a high probability that they do. But that's just the first part of the picture. It's your next move that determines whether you will be perceived as a good leader or a bad one.

FRUSTRATION!

If you are like most managers and are perceived as moving from Style 1, directing, to Style 4, delegating (or abdicating), and your tendency is to tell people what to do when they are having difficulties, you may be caught in one of the most unproductive patterns of leadership. We call it the *frustration* cycle, also known as the 1-4-1 sequence. This cycle is shown in Figure 9.

Unfortunately, a lot of managers get caught up in the 1-4-1 cycle. They start with Style 1, they move to Style 4, and when things don't work out, they move back to Style 1. It's guaranteed that when you move back from Style 4 to Style 1, you will be perceived as dominating.

In our work with leaders throughout the world, from all kinds of organizations—public and private, manufacturing and service, big, medium, and small—we ask people to talk with us about their experiences with particularly bad leaders. One of our biggest surprises has been the consistency of the stories that we hear.

We also ask people to quantify their experiences by distributing 100 percentage points among the four leadership styles to show us how much of each style these worst leaders use. Again, we have found amazing similarities.

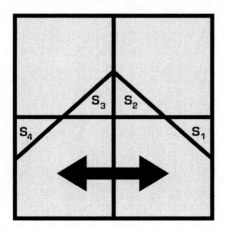

Figure 9 The 1-4-1 Frustration Cycle

We will show you the results next, but before you read any further, take a few minutes to play with this question yourself. Think of the worst leader you have seen in your organization. It could be a manager you reported to or it could be a situation in which you were close enough to observe this manager in action.

Think of the leadership styles this individual used. How much of Style 1, directing or dominating, was used? How much of Style 2, problem solving or over-involving? How much of Style 3, developing or over-accommodating? How much of Style 4, delegating or abdicating?

In the spaces below, distribute 100 points among the four styles to show how often this leader used each style.

YOUR WORST LEADER

PERCENT OF USE

_____   _____   _____   _____
Style 1   Style 2   Style 3   Style 4

Then look at Figure 10, so you can compare your experience with some samples from a selection of very different organizations.

In every industry, the worst leaders rely heavily on Style 1 and Style 4. They use significantly less Style 2 and Style 3. And when the people who have worked for these worst leaders talk about them, it is clear that the leaders are guilty of dominating and abdicating. The war stories we hear actually deal with three types of managers: the "all 1" dominators, the "all 4" abdicators, and the "1-4-1" managers who bounce back and forth.

The "all 1" stories refer to managers who need to join Dominators Anonymous. They like to control everyone and want everything done their way. They get stuck in the details, they micromanage, and they don't trust anybody.

Frank's story is typical of the hard-core dominators we hear about. A seasoned IT manager with twenty years of experience, Frank came from the "old school," having cut his managerial teeth in a rough-and-tumble manufacturing environment. Over the years, Frank did an impressive job of honing his technical skills and worked his way up to leading the IT organization in his plant.

Frank's pattern was to use his IT expertise as an excuse for watching his employees' every move. Any time anyone did something he disagreed with, he would yell at them using a string of expletives that would make the most off-color comedian blush.

The problem came to a head when a group of Frank's direct reports decided to go over his head and complain to his boss, the plant manager.

WORST LEADERS

INDUSTRY	AVERAGES (PERCENT)			
	Style 1	Style 2	Style 3	Style 4
Accounting	43	7	4	46
Financial Services	43	12	9	36
Consulting	39	13	8	40
Technology	49	11	5	35
Energy	37	19	8	36
Manufacturing	44	14	7	35
Pharmaceuticals	37	16	11	36

Figure 10 Worst Leader Profiles

Frank's boss told him that his top-down, hard-nosed, abusive-parent approach was not working and that if he didn't change he would risk a mass exodus that would leave his department crippled. His boss explained to him that today's employees demanded respect and did not take kindly to being taken to the proverbial woodshed. They saw themselves and needed to be treated as empowered individuals whose access to the same information as their boss left them fully capable of making informed decisions.

As is often the case with dominating leaders, this story has an unhappy ending. Unable to shift from his tried and true (or perhaps tired and true) style, Frank lost his management position and was relegated to a backroom, individual contributor slot where his alienating approach had little impact on others.

The "all 4" tales are about managers who should sign up for Abdicators Anonymous. You can never find them. They are very inaccessible. And if you do catch up with them, you can't get much out of them, so the next time you won't even bother. They do their jobs and leave you alone to do yours. Some truly trust the people below them and stay out of the way with the best intentions, but most are just too caught up in their own work or their own careers to spend time with their people.

Ray is a classic example of a compulsive abdicator. He was director of strategic planning for a large division of an aerospace company. Following dips in defense orders, the result of a scaleback of military contracts, the division's leaders decided they needed new strategic plans for the four business units. Ray was appointed to oversee the strategic planning process for each group.

Ray had little prior experience managing others; however, his boss, a senior VP, assured him that his primary role was to provide the four unit managers with strategy expertise and support in the planning process. His boss also made it clear that the four managers were accountable to Ray for their results.

Ray decided that the best thing he could do for the strategy initiative was to learn as much as he could about the business units' various markets and feed that information back to the unit managers. He spent all of his time visiting customers and potential customers and downloading what he learned to the unit heads. He also sent them a variety of strategic planning templates to choose from in formulating their plans.

To the unit heads, Ray's approach looked like total abdication and was extremely frustrating. What Ray failed to realize was that the four managers felt completely overwhelmed by the flood of data he was sending them. They also had no idea how to use the templates he had provided—or which one was best for their particular situation. When it came time to present their strategic plans to the senior VP, all four said they weren't ready—and they blamed Ray for it.

We also hear a lot of stories about 1-4-1 managers. These people tell you what needs to be done in fairly general terms. They leave you alone to handle it. Then they criticize you for not doing it the way they wanted it done. The 1-4-1 cycle is also known as the "leave 'em alone and zap 'em" strategy or the "seagull technique," in which managers swoop in from far away, flap their wings, make a lot of noise, leave some fresh droppings on everybody's windshield, and then fly off again. Whatever you call this pattern in your organization, the result is definitely frustration for the people on the receiving end.

Denise was a manager who had the misfortune of working for a seagull with highly developed swooping skills. She worked in the financial services industry and was head of a technology resource team responsible for equipping a new facility. Her boss, Suzanne, told her that the new location needed to be equipped with state-of-the-art computers that would be quick, accurate, and fault tolerant. Suzanne also stressed that all three criteria needed to be met in order to satisfy their internal customers.

Denise was left alone and proceeded to research possible vendors for this huge order. After three weeks—and little contact with Suzanne—Denise presented her top three choices in priority order. She was careful to delineate the pluses and minuses of each vendor, the result of painstaking research that had taken up a considerable amount of evening and weekend time.

In the middle of Denise's presentation, Suzanne interrupted to point out that two well-known vendors had not made the final cut. Denise started to explain that those vendors had inferior specs compared to the three she had chosen. Suzanne interrupted again to inform her that since both vendors were customers of their firm, one of them would ultimately receive the bid. Suzanne insisted that Denise go back to the drawing board and make one of those vendors her top choice. Denise left the room fuming, angry with Suzanne for dropping this latest bomb, frustrated about the time she had wasted, and wondering which of the two vendors Suzanne wanted her to select.

You may recognize these *frustration* scenarios in your organization because we hear similar stories everywhere we go. You may even be guilty of engaging in one or more of them because most of us stumble from time to time. Fortunately, there are other choices.

EMPOWERMENT

When we ask people to talk with us about the worst managers they have known, we also ask them to talk about the best ones they have worked for or observed. Again, there are striking similarities across a wide variety of industries.

We will show you the percentages in a minute, but, as you did before, take a few minutes to play with this question yourself. This time, think of the best leader you have seen in your organization. In the spaces below, distribute 100 points among the four styles to show how often this leader used each style.

```
┌────────────────────────────────────────────────┐
│  YOUR BEST LEADER                               │
│  ─────────────────────────────                  │
│  PERCENT OF USE                                 │
│  ───────────                                    │
│                                                 │
│  _____   _____   _____   _____             │
│  Style 1  Style 2  Style 3  Style 4             │
└────────────────────────────────────────────────┘
```

Then take a look at the data about best leaders in Figure 11, on page 122.

As you saw with the worst leaders, there are some recurring themes in the data about these best leaders, too. There are some variations in the percentages that different industries assign to each style, but the pattern is quite consistent and the stories that people tell are remarkably similar.

In every type of organization, people tell us that the best leaders mainly use Styles 3 and 4. They give employees lots of responsibility and are available to support them when they need some assistance.

Sometimes the best leaders also use Style 2 as a backup style. Although their preference is to keep decision making in their team members' hands, they are willing to listen to recommendations and step up to the plate to make tough decisions when people need them to.

To a lesser extent, they also use Style 1. The best leaders are good at making sure everyone has clear expectations about what he or she needs to do.

When we ask people to describe their best leaders in words, these stories also present some clear themes. One fascinating lesson for us has been that the best leaders start out just like the worst leaders do. They begin with Style 1, and then they move to Style 4. That's why we told you earlier that there is a high

BEST LEADERS

INDUSTRY	AVERAGES (PERCENT)			
	Style 1	Style 2	Style 3	Style 4
Accounting	6	16	36	42
Financial Services	12	19	36	33
Consulting	15	22	33	30
Technology	11	17	33	39
Energy	18	21	32	29
Manufacturing	14	19	33	34
Pharmaceuticals	12	17	33	38

Figure 11 Best Leader Profiles

probability that the people who work for you perceive you to be using the 1-4 pattern.

That's where the similarity ends. Instead of staying in Style 4 or going back to Style 1 when problems arise, the best leaders move to Style 3. They listen and ask questions to probe for a full understanding of the situation. They want to know their team members' thinking about how to fix the problem, and they help them make up their minds about the best actions to take. When they offer support, it is to help team members with their responsibilities, not to take over and undermine their sense of accountability.

These best leaders are also willing to roll up their sleeves and get their hands dirty. If problems require them to make the decisions, they will shift to Style 2 by taking input from the key people who are involved and making timely decisions that enable their team's work to move forward.

Figure 12 shows you how best leaders use the four styles. The sequence is 1-4-3-2. We call it the *empowerment* cycle because people who experience this sequence of styles consistently report that they feel truly empowered. And if any window is not opened, people say that they don't feel empowered.

To do their best work, people want you to give them complete information, including directions, advice, explanations, and consequences. That's Style 1.

Then, they want you to trust them, delegate meaningful responsibilities to them, and give them the authority they need to do what you hired them to do. That's Style 4.

When they get stuck, as everyone does sooner or later, they want your support to help them think through their own decisions without undercutting their sense of responsibility. This is where Style 3 comes in.

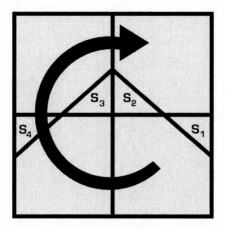

Figure 12 The 1-4-3-2 Empowerment Cycle

And finally, if they are still stuck and need you to step up to the plate, they want you to listen to their ideas and make timely decisions based on their recommendations. This last step is Style 2.

When you use this 1-4-3-2 empowerment cycle, Style 3 is a key pivot point. By listening to people at critical checkpoints, you do two things simultaneously. You help them develop their own problem-solving capabilities while diagnosing problems that you may need to resolve if they cannot.

From the Style 3 window, you give yourself maximum flexibility. You can stay in Style 3 as long as you need to by listening and supporting team members' decision making. You can shift back to Style 4 when the time is right by giving them feedback that they're on the right track and recognition to encourage them to continue assuming responsibility. Or, if you find that problem solving is necessary, you can make a smooth transition to Style 2 because the listening you have done with Style 3 should give you all the input you need to make a well-informed decision.

The Style 3 window helps you keep your leadership options open. Remember, people probably see you moving from Style 1 to Style 4. The critical move comes next. If you go back to Style 1, you are taking over. Even if you do it in a matter-of-fact way, you will be perceived as dominating. If you stay in Style 4 too long, you will be seen as abdicating. If you jump to Style 2, you will be viewed as over-involving. If you keep moving clockwise to Style 3, you have a lot of flexibility.

We want to be very clear. We are not saying that Style 3 is the best style or the style you should use the most. All four styles are critical, all the time, regardless of the main style you are using. And if you want to empower your people, using all four styles in the 1-4-3-2 sequence can make your life and the lives of your employees a lot easier and a lot more productive.

DELEGATING ≠ EMPOWERING

In terms of leadership behavior, Style 4 is the easiest style to use—all you have to do is let go. But if that's all you do, you will be abdicating, not delegating, and people will not feel empowered. If you don't give clear directions at the outset, you will be accused of abdicating. If you leave people on their own too long, you will be accused of abdicating. If you don't provide support when it is needed, you will be accused of abdicating. And if you don't make timely decisions when the ball is in your court, you will be accused of abdicating.

A simple formula to avoid abdicating and to become empowering is $1 + 3 = 4$. The keys to effective delegating are clear directions up front and availability for support as you go forward. It's what you do with Styles 1 and 3 that turns abdicating into delegating. That plus a dash of timely problem solving turns delegation into full *empowerment*. It isn't easy to avoid being accused of abdicating. The only way to be seen as empowering is to use all four styles.

DON'T YOU HAVE TO USE DIFFERENT STYLES IN DIFFERENT SITUATIONS?

Sure. But it's not enough to select the best main style for each situation. Actually, you have to use a different mix of all four styles in every situation. And regardless of which window is open the most, if you open them in the 1-4-3-2 sequence, you are going to be a lot more effective. Consider these two cases.

Joe just started working for you. He's bright and energetic but definitely a rookie. He has limited experience with your technology and no background in your industry, but he is enthusiastic about learning everything.

So what are you going to do? You know that Joe needs a lot of guidance from you. But do you hold his hand all day?

Of course not. You give him an assignment and tell him what he needs to know to get started. That's Style 1.

Then you leave him alone to give it a try. That's Style 4.

After a while, you return, ask him how he's doing, listen to what he says, and look at what he's produced. That's Style 3.

Then you give him feedback and redirect him so he learns the right ways to get the work done. That's Style 2.

You start with a lot of directing, use a little delegating, follow that with some developing, and then move on to a lot of problem solving. Mostly 1 and 2, with a little 4 and 3 in between.

Elizabeth's situation is totally different. She's been working for you for a long time. She's very experienced, knows what she is doing, and is very much in sync with your thoughts about what is important. In all honesty, she knows her job responsibilities a lot better than you do.

So what mix of styles do you use with Elizabeth?

You know that she can operate very independently, so you will delegate a lot of responsibility to her. But when you think of your full range of interactions with her, all four styles come into play.

You take time with her on a regular basis to clarify departmental goals and her individual objectives. And if a new initiative is required in her area, you give her all the information you can so that she understands what needs to be accomplished. That's Style 1.

Most of the time you stay out of her way and let her do her work. You trust her to handle decisions as well as, if not better than, you could. That's Style 4.

Occasionally, you check in with her to see how she's doing and find out if she needs anything from you. And once in a while she seeks you out to ask for some advice or assistance. That's Style 3.

Finally, there are a few times when Elizabeth wants you to get more involved in a sticky situation. She gives you a full briefing but relies on you to get some resolution as quickly as you can. That's Style 2.

With her, you are using a little Style 1, mostly Style 4, periodic Style 3, and occasional Style 2. The amount of each style is very different from the amounts you use with Joe. But the sequence is the same.

You have two very different people in two very different situations and you work with them in very different ways. But the 1-4-3-2 *empowerment* cycle enables each one of them to perform to the best of his or her potential.

With each of them, and with each of the people who work for you, 1-4-3-2 guides you to delegate as much as possible while surrounding the delegation with the right amounts of directing on the front end and developing and problem solving on the rear end. Delegating only results in empowerment if all four windows are opened. The challenge is learning what each person needs in each situation, and it is so easy to find out when you let 1-4-3-2 be your guide.

PREDICTABILITY PLUS FLEXIBILITY

Are we advising you to treat everyone the same way? Instinctively, you probably say, "No, that can't be right."

In one sense that is exactly what we are saying. The 1-4-3-2 *empowerment* cycle gives you and the people who work with you some welcome predictability in an otherwise continuously changing world. If people know that they should be getting clear directions, they are more likely to speak up if they don't know what is expected. If they know that it is normal to need support, they are more likely to ask for what they need and accept it when it is offered. And if you know that both are critical, you are more likely to provide them when they are needed. Team leaders and team members perform better when they have some degree of predictability to guide their interactions.

On the other hand, if you said, "No," you are also right. The 1-4-3-2 cycle also allows for maximum flexibility. Even though it starts the same way in every situation, it can end in three places because you don't always have to go through the full cycle. You only go as far as you have to.

Sometimes you hand off responsibility and that's all you need to do, so you end up at Style 4. Sometimes after you have handed off, you need to provide some support, so you go from Style 1 to Style 4 to Style 3. When support isn't enough and you need to do some problem solving, then and only then do you use the full cycle, ending up at Style 2.

The sequence of styles is predictable, and the first two moves happen almost all of the time. After that, each situation is different.

We recently worked with a young Internet research firm that provided a good example of how this works. This firm was widely regarded in the industry as world class in spotting trends and accurately analyzing shifts in the marketplace. Their success had created such dramatic growth that they had to acquire the space adjacent to their overcrowded warehouse in order to make room for a new cadre of analysts.

Rather than engage in a slow, methodical approach to designing and building the new quarters—the old economy approach—they had a construction crew just tear a hole in the brick wall separating the new and old spaces. They purposely left the passageway unfinished and rough, complete with stray bricks strewn on either side of the entryway—a symbol of their "breakthrough" approach to their work.

When the new analysts arrived, the four team leaders who were responsible for the company's target industries met with each of them and explained that they were hired because they were considered to be state-of-the-art technologists capable of a high level of data analysis. The recruits were given super-powered laptops—the primary tool of their trade—a desk, and their choice of assorted ancillary furniture intended to personalize their private workspace.

As soon as the new analysts got online, they received their initial assignment: to become the world's leading expert on their given industry, prepared to provide the best thinking regarding emerging trends that would help their clients craft a strategic direction. Their managers downloaded everything they had on each industry to make sure each of the eager new charges had the information they needed. And they gave them three weeks to get ready. This was Style 1, directing—in the electronic era.

The managers then left them alone for a few days, enabling them to "get their footing" in their target industries. This was Style 4, delegating.

Then they used some Style 3, developing, and some Style 2, problem solving, to help the analysts get up to warp speed as fast as possible. What varied in their approaches that made it more personalized than formulaic was the nature and duration of time spent in the "3-2" zone.

Some of the new analysts, excited about their new workspace and the opportunity to impact an entire industry, simply needed a periodic visit from their manager. So all they got was a high-level review of the approach they were taking, a quick discussion about next steps, a nod of support, and encouragement to keep moving. These analysts quickly found themselves back on the receiving end of Style 4.

Other analysts were confused about what was required or overwhelmed by the daunting task. Some of them just needed a sounding board to help them think out loud about questions and concerns. Others needed to be redirected from time to time when they were heading down a blind alley. The important point is that their managers used the more engaging approaches of Styles 3 and 2 to give each one what they needed.

As an organization, this Internet consulting firm provided every new hire with predictability—clear expectations, stretch assignments, support as needed, and problem solving when required. They were also flexible enough to let people go as far as they could on their own and only got involved as much as they needed to.

Knowing the 1-4-3-2 sequence is one crucial element of Window Wisdom, but not the whole story. The next piece of Window Wisdom is to be able to anticipate how far you need to go around the 1-4-3-2 cycle. The *development* and *intervention* cycles will help you with that.

DEVELOPING TOP PERFORMERS

One of your most important tasks as a leader is to develop the people who are working for you. Leaders who have the most power are the ones who have people in their departments who can take over their jobs at any time or who can move on to other positions of power in other parts of the organization. Leaders who have little or no power are immobilized, stuck in dead-end jobs because they have never developed anyone in their department who could take over if they moved on.

Development is not just a nice thing to do for your people. It is an important key to organizational strength and an important key to your own career mobility.

When they created Situational Leadership Theory, Paul Hersey and Ken Blanchard (1982) showed managers how leadership styles can be used for development. Development is a pattern of styles that enables you to gradually turn over responsibility to members of your team. It enables your people to take on increasing amounts of responsibility and control as their performance potential steadily increases.

The *development* cycle is shown in Figure 13, on the next page. This pattern for using the four leadership styles helps you understand the main style that you should use with a person over a period of time. It shows you how to gradually make the transition from Style 1 to 2 to 3 to 4 as the individual strengthens his or her potential to perform. As the person's ability to do the work and motivation to take on responsibility increase, you should anticipate following this progression upward through the styles one step at a time.

This cycle makes a lot of sense when you think of a new person entering an unfamiliar job. Initially, you should anticipate giving a lot of directions, complete explanations, a clear picture of the payoffs and pitfalls associated with the job, plenty of advice, and ongoing feedback. The person requires clear assignments and frequent checkpoints from you to get oriented to the job. Basically, you are doing on-the-job training.

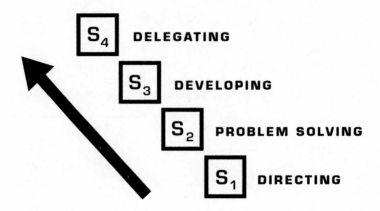

Figure 13 Development Cycle

As the person gains some experience, his or her skills and understanding of job requirements usually start to improve. In addition, the individual usually develops some confidence and becomes willing to own some responsibilities. Consequently, you can begin to ask for input about problems and invite recommendations to your decision making.

In time, as the person gets more experience, you won't have to make as many decisions. You shouldn't leave the person totally alone, but with a little guidance he or she can perform very well.

Eventually, you can delegate the authority to go along with the responsibility. By this time, the person can function independently.

In general, the development cycle advises you to look for opportunities to give increased amounts of responsibility as a person's performance potential gradually increases.

Historically, managers who have learned this concept have often made the mistake of using all Style 1 with every new employee, shifting to all Style 2 at some point, then moving to all Style 3, and eventually using all Style 4 with every experienced member of the team. This approach does not work and is not developmental. To understand how *development* really works, you have to implement these shifts in the context of the 1-4-3-2 *empowerment* cycle.

As depicted in the first step of Figure 14, when you use Style 1 as your main style, you are not handing off significant responsibilities. You may be delegating tasks, but you are holding on to the authority and are still in control. So you aren't doing much developing. What you are doing is on-the-job training—close supervision and frequent feedback to help an individual get up to speed. If you are successful, you will be able to delegate some responsibilities as the next step.

When you are ready to delegate, the second step is to use the full 1-4-3-2 cycle. Start with setting clear expectations, delegate as much as the person is ready to take on, establish times when you will come together to provide support, and anticipate that most of the decisions at critical moments will be their input to your decision making—Style 2. This shift from Style 1 to Style 2 is

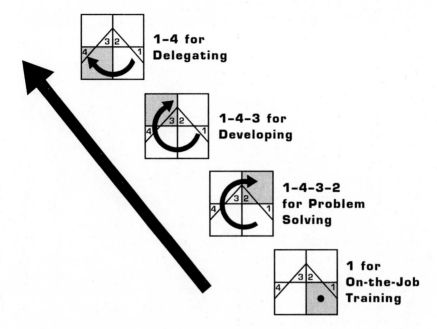

1-4 for
Delegating

1-4-3 for
Developing

1-4-3-2
for Problem
Solving

1 for
On-the-Job
Training

Figure 14 Development Steps

the first step in the development cycle. Development guides you to change the approach you use at key moments. It does not mean moving from all 1 to all 2.

The third step in the development cycle is to use Style 3 with critical decisions. In the context of empowerment, that means directing, delegating, and anticipating the need to provide support at important times—Style 3. As depicted in Figure 14, this does not mean using all Style 3. It means supporting a team member's decision making to help him or her meet the challenges of a stretch assignment that has been delegated.

The final step in the development cycle is to use Style 4 as the main style. To do this, you still have to set the expectations before you hand off and let go. As illustrated in Figure 14, it does not mean letting go 100 percent.

The full set of moves you have to make when you are using the empowerment cycle to develop people is starting with 1 for on-the-job training, using the full 1-4-3-2 cycle to get to problem solving, shifting to 1-4-3 to develop their decision-making skills, and ending with 1-4 for delegating.

GO FLY A KITE

A good analogy for the *development* cycle is flying a kite.

Imagine what would happen if your first step in kite flying was to let out all of the string. The kite would never get off the ground. Now imagine what would happen if you only let out ten feet of string. The only way the kite would fly would be if you ran, and as soon as you stopped, it would come down.

To fly a kite, you do have to run to get the kite launched, but as soon as it gets a little altitude, you let out some string, stabilize the kite, let out some more string, and stabilize it again. And what is your mindset? To let out the kite as far as possible for that kite under those wind conditions.

Development works the same way. You run hard to do the on-the-job training necessary to get an individual launched. Then you use the full 1-4-3-2 cycle until they settle in. You move to a 1-4-3 pattern as soon as possible to get the decisions off of your desk and onto theirs. And eventually you get to the fast-paced 1-4 sequence, when they are ready to work on their own.

Just think of development as gradually letting out the string of a kite. By doing this, you keep people motivated, challenged, and productive. You also build the bench strength that will make your organization more productive and position you to keep advancing your career.

Lenore's is a story of a smooth launching. She was hired as a fact checker by the Internet research firm we just discussed—the one that used the 1-4-3-2 cycle so well. As the analyst division expanded, the volume of work also expanded exponentially, and it became unfeasible for the analysts to check all the facts embedded in their reports. Since the firm charged a high premium to their clients for these reports, recommendations based on accurate data were critical to their credibility in the marketplace. So senior management decided that a new role, the fact checker, needed to be created.

Lenore was a former librarian who had little experience in the Internet world but was believed to be, by those who hired her, a stickler for accuracy. Larry, her supervisor, began Lenore's orientation by giving her a sample report and explaining the importance of accuracy in the document as well as how the documents were used by customers to make marketing and business development decisions. In his initial conversations with her he stressed the importance of full accuracy in the data. He then gave Lenore her first report to check.

Later that afternoon he visited her in her office to ask how things were going and to confirm that she was conducting the appropriate level of fact checking. Lenore had some questions for Larry about how deep to go with her investigating, and he spent the rest of the afternoon reviewing this first report with her, making whatever decisions needed to be made, and teaching her how to decide when to dig deeper and when to move on. Each day that week he gave her another report to work on and continued to work closely with her, asking for her recommendations about what to include but still making the decisions.

The second week, Larry gave Lenore several reports to work on. Having been satisfied with her rigor on the first week's reports, he told her he would still be available to listen to her concerns and offer advice but wanted her to start making the decisions. He still checked in with her each day but was careful to respond to each of her questions with his own question, "What do you think is the best way to go?" Most of the time that was all he needed to do because she was on target. It became increasingly rare that he would have to redirect her and, as the week progressed, he gradually left her alone for longer periods of time.

By the third week, Lenore only had a few questions for him and told him that, aside from a few minor points, she believed she was "getting it." He told her he was confident that she was firmly established in her role and ready to fly solo. From that point on, the analysts began filling her in-box with documents to review whenever they needed them. Occasionally Larry would stick his head in her door to see how she was doing, but as long as she smiled and said everything was fine he left her alone, always reminding her to come see him anytime for any reason.

INTERVENING TO AVOID PROBLEMS

Although the development cycle offers a logical sequence for moving through the four styles of leadership in a gradual way that promotes growth and increased autonomy, not everyone gets off to the kind of start that Lenore had. And these days we hear more and more about people who are parachuted into a job with little or no orientation. We also hear many stories about people who were excellent performers until the expectations for their job got too high. In today's fast-paced world, managers are more frequently confronted with circumstances that demand the opposite of development. We call this the *intervention* cycle.

Intervention is needed whenever it becomes more difficult for a team member to deliver results, a circumstance that can be caused by a variety of factors. When demands such as increased complexity, accelerated change, and increased time pressure reduce a person's ability to perform, you need to respond with *intervention*. You can use this pattern of styles to limit the damage by responding to drops in potential before they cause drops in performance. As you can see in Figure 15, intervention is the flip side of development. Instead of taking place over time, this progression often takes place in a matter of hours or minutes.

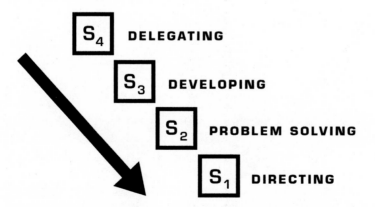

Figure 15 Intervention Cycle

As a leader, sooner or later you have to leave people on their own, whether fron conscious delegation or by default, and when you do that, it is also inevitable that problems will arise that someone can't handle alone. As problems surface, you need to anticipate moving gradually down the styles, one at a time, from Style 4 to 3 to 2 and sometimes to 1.

Some managers use the need for *intervention* as a license to jump from delegating to directing—a guaranteed way to get a reputation as a seagull. Many who have learned some of the older models of leadership mistakenly shift from all Style 4 to all 3 to all 2 or all 1. Neither of these approaches is based on what it really takes for intervention to be successful. As you saw with development, the 1-4-3-2 cycle is the key to making intervention work. Figure 16 illustrates the full set of moves needed for *intervention*.

When their work is progressing normally, team members see you doing a little directing and a lot of delegating. This 1-4 pattern, as depicted in the first step of Figure 16, usually works when you are in a business-as-usual mode.

When circumstances require you to get more involved, you can't start hanging around and listening to people all day. You don't have the time, and you would drive them crazy if you did. What you can and should do is make yourself more available to support a person confronting challenging decisions.

The first step is to help the person be objective about the responsibilities he or she is handling and develop an action plan for turning the situation around. You should use the developing style to ask questions, listen carefully to your team member's analysis of the problem situation, and find out what possible solutions he or she is considering. By doing this, you may discover that all you need to do is listen and sign off on the action plan. You may also find out that other types of support are needed but that, with your support, this person can still handle the responsibilities and solve the problem.

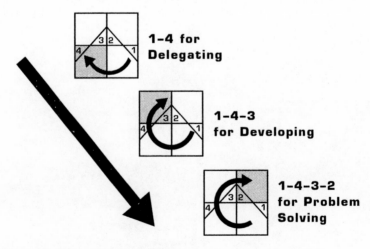

1-4 for Delegating

1-4-3 for Developing

1-4-3-2 for Problem Solving

Figure 16 Intervention Steps

In the context of the *empowerment* cycle, you are taking one step clockwise to use Style 3 at critical moments. Looking at the second step of Figure 16, you can see that the complete mix of styles you are using is 1-4-3.

Sometimes, as you listen to the problem and the alternatives that are being considered, you realize that all the support in the world will not enable this person to solve the problem. When that happens, the next step is to keep moving clockwise through the empowerment cycle to Style 2. As you can see in the third step of Figure 16, you make the decision yourself based on the team member's analysis and recommendations.

If you have listened well in the previous step, you will have received many hints or outright requests (in some cases, demands) that you are the best one to make this decision. So when you do step in, people will usualy be grateful and relieved. By listening, you are intervening with full information and there-fore not simply shooting from the hip. More important, you are not overriding the person who was previously given the responsibility. And by totally includ-ing the team member in your decision-making process, you make it easier for him or her to reclaim the responsibility so that you don't get stuck with it.

Usually, Style 2 is as far as the intervention goes. Once you have asked for input with Style 2, it is hard to go to Style 1 and make a decision without input. And once you are in control with Style 2, it is seldom necessary to become more controlling with Style 1. Unless the ship is literally sinking, you usually don't have to get this direct and are better off using the problem-solving style to take charge while capitalizing on the team member's knowl-edge of the situation.

Intervention does not mean shifting from all Style 4 to all 3 to all 2. The way it really works is moving from the 1-4 pattern, to the 1-4-3 sequence, to the full 1-4-3-2 approach as conditions require you to get increasingly involved.

DON'T LET THE KITE CRASH

As with development, kite flying is a good metaphor for remembering how *intervention* works. Imagine a kite in a strong wind.

What would happen if the kite went into a tailspin and you took no action? The kite would be buffeted in the wind and eventually crash.

What would happen if you pulled really hard on the string? The kite would go into a worse tailspin, or you might snap the string, or you could break the kite itself.

So what have kite flyers learned to do? A gentle tug is all it takes to make the kite right itself. Then they reel in the slack, stabilize the kite, maybe reel in a little more, and stabilize it again. What's their mindset when they are doing this? Let the kite back out as soon as possible.

What they don't do is reel it in all the way and start running. And they don't yell at the kite, "You had your chance; I'm doing the flying now!" They give it the help it needs and let it back out. That's the mindset you need to provide helpful *intervention*.

Harold's case illustrates how this mindset plays out. He was one of the new analysts recruited by the Internet research firm we discussed earlier in this chapter. Harold wasn't just starting a new and very demanding job; he had been transplanted from Britain to the United States and was feeling quite overwhelmed with all the changes happening in both his personal and professional life.

While he was excited about the job, he was also taken aback by the scope of the work and the formidable expectations placed on him to become "the world's foremost expert" in three weeks. Harold had been a newspaper researcher with a strong background in computer science but had never been in the high-powered role of industry analyst before, so he was very intimidated by the directive presented by his boss, Rick, in a Style 1 e-mail.

While he was okay being left alone for a few days to get his bearings, he was very happy when Rick sat down with him on day four and moved into the Style 3 developing mode to ask him how things were going. It didn't take more than a few minutes for both of them to realize that Harold needed more than a sympathetic ear and a little hand holding to achieve the goals set out for him.

Realizing that his gifted new analyst was drowning in a sea of information, Rick shifted to Style 2, problem solving, and spent the next two days helping Harold organize his data and segment his market into industry subsets. After several iterations—and with the help of some of Rick's project management tools—the two of them created a matrix that enabled Harold to move forward in a more structured, orchestrated way.

Eventually Rick was able to become more hands-off in his approach, but he didn't just disappear. He let Harold know that his need for more direction and support than the other analysts was perfectly all right. He also encouraged Harold to ask for support any time he needed it and repeated the firm's belief that the fastest way to develop new skills is to learn as you go while tackling stretch assignments. Rick then shifted into Style 4 with some occasional Style 3 at Harold's request.

Harold was nervous about his initial presentation, but it went extremely well. So did many subsequent ones as he went on to establish an outstanding reputation in the firm. His analysis proved to be uncannily correct most of the time, and his relationship with his boss was one of the strongest in the organization.

WHY IS INTERVENTION NEEDED?

Why would you need to intervene like this? Sometimes personal pressures can impact performance. A person is getting married or divorced. Someone is having a baby or has a parent who is terminally ill. A car accident, a drinking problem, an office romance—there are all sorts of reasons why an individual's motivation might drop off.

More often than not, it is organizational pressures, not personal pressures, that cause you to intervene. In our work with a wide variety of organizations, these four factors are most frequently cited as causes for intervention: change, increased complexity, sudden visibility, and time.

Any major change creates ambiguity, and that affects people's clarity about what they are expected to do as well as their confidence that they can do it. Corporations are downsizing some divisions while investing in others, divesting nonperforming operations while acquiring new divisions with more promise, cannibalizing old businesses and spinning off new ventures, and globalizing their sales forces while moving production to offshore locations. Change is here to stay and so is the pressure that comes with it.

Increased complexity, such as having a wider span of control, expanding your product line, or any other version of "do more with less," also affects people. There are countless examples of excellent performers whose performance has deteriorated when their jobs were automated. You also hear lots of stories about salespeople who went from one product line that they knew well to four or five that they barely understood, or whose territories expanded from one state to half the country. These types of changes often require new knowledge and new skills, not to mention the courage to jump from the frying pan into the fire.

Visibility can also put pressure on people. A major customer starting to complain or senior management starting to look closely at their numbers can easily distract people from their work. Or what about having the auditors show up, or a government regulatory agency? Or suppose the press turns your operation into a cover story? In these circumstances, interpersonal skills and patience get pushed to the limit.

Last, but not least, is time. Imagine that a very capable woman named Mary works for you. An important project has hit your desk and it is due in four weeks. Mary is fully capable of completing the project, so you give her the assignment and use Style 4 to delegate the responsibility to her.

The next day you find out that there will only be three weeks to complete the project. Now you need to use some Style 3 to help Mary think through a new game plan and to support her with some of the tough questions she is confronted with.

Then your boss tells you that the project has become a top priority and you only have two weeks to get it done. Now you need to use some Style 2 to get input from Mary about the other objectives she is handling so you can make decisions about priorities and advise her about how to proceed. She may also want you to get more involved in making some of the tough calls.

Of course, as soon as that is settled, (you guessed it) the customer calls you directly and pleads to have the project done in one week. Now you are in a fire drill. Forget propping up Mary. You have to take charge of it yourself. Assemble your team, tell each person, including Mary, explicitly what he or she can do to help you get the project completed, and coordinate the effort yourself.

The point is that in each scenario Mary is the same person and the project has the same requirements, but the time factor could make any one of the four styles appropriate. Change, complexity, or visibility could affect Mary—or your people—in the same way. Just because people have been performing well with a little directing and a lot of delegating doesn't mean that is all they will need when the bar gets raised.

The one thing you can be confident of in today's workplace is that the bar will always be raised. That's why managers tell us that *development* is nice when you have the time, but *intervention* is a necessity whether or not you have the time. If you don't make the time, you will be doomed.

WINDOW WISDOM

Leadership isn't the style-of-the-month club that some organizations inadvertently promote. And it isn't even the style-per-person-per-situation club that many older leadership models have suggested.

Leadership is more than that. It requires a command of all the styles and a commitment to using them all the time.

Regardless of the main style that is appropriate, you will be most effective if you empower people by following the 1-4-3-2 *empowerment* cycle. Predictability plus flexibility is the name of the game: a predictable sequence of leadership actions plus flexibility in terms of how far you have to go. This piece of Window Wisdom will help you be an outstanding leader as you guide your team to play hardball in the big leagues.

You also have to develop people by gradually opening the windows, 1-2-3-4, and change your general approach in ways that give team members increased responsibilities. The *development* cycle guides you in letting out the kite string.

When people are struggling due to personal or organizational reasons, you also have to intervene, 4-3-2 and sometimes 1, to gradually change your general approach in ways that provide increasing amounts of assistance. The *intervention* cycle guides you in preventing tailspins without trying to turn yourself into a kite.

The development and intervention cycles are guiding principles that can help you anticipate how far around the 1-4-3-2 cycle you need to go. In the next chapter, we will show you how to analyze exactly how far you have to go.

Through the Working Glass: Viewing Followers Through Their Window of Potential

To help you fine-tune your diagnostic skills and develop your effectiveness as a leader, this chapter will show you the *Window of Potential,* a device for assessing each team member's performance potential and a way to determine what main style to use under which circumstances. It is a tool for analyzing how far you need to go around the 1-4-3-2 cycle in any situation—a formula for knowing the right approach to take when important decisions are on the line as well as a guide to empowering your people.

The Window of Potential is based on four characteristics of ability and four characteristics of motivation. The ability factors are technical skills, interpersonal skills, job knowledge, and organizational power. The motivation factors are interest, confidence, willingness, and alignment with organizational goals.

By assessing ability and motivation you can accurately diagnose performance potential and can align your Window of Leadership with each team member's Window of Potential. Once the two windows are aligned, effective leadership is almost guaranteed because if you follow through on your diagnosis, you will be giving the people what they need. Once you establish which window is needed, all you need to do is provide what that window calls for. Just be sure you pay attention to the fact that, as conditions change, any window can suddenly close on you, requiring you to open another one that offers a better view of the new situation.

To diagnose performance potential, you have to understand that it is a task-specific concept. Any job—yours or one of your team members'—is made up of goals for each assignment or responsibility, and each goal has a number of tasks or steps that must be accomplished in order to achieve it.

When you analyze performance potential, you are not focusing on career potential—how far a person is going to rise or how fast he or she is going to get there. You are assessing the ability plus the motivation to accomplish a specific task, knowing that the potential for other tasks may be completely different.

You also need to fully understand the concepts of ability and motivation. Ability is crucial in these rapidly changing times, because if people are in over their heads, they won't reach their full potential without appropriate leadership. Motivation is equally important. Gone are the days when a leader could motivate employees by offering job security and career advancement. Today, employee motivation is based on far more immediate issues than hypothetical opportunities down the road.

Let's take a look at the four ability factors and four motivation factors so that you can get a better understanding of the concept of performance potential.

WHAT IS ABILITY?

When you think about ability, there are four factors to consider. Unfortunately, in most organizations, when leaders think about followers' ability, they only think of the first factor, *technical skills*—a person's education, training, and experience. Then they assume that all of the other ability factors are present.

Assumptions are always dangerous, especially here because the other three factors are equally important.

The second factor is *interpersonal skills*. These include the skills for leading downward with people at lower levels, the skills for leading upward with your boss, as well as the skills for developing effective relationships with peers, vendors, customers, and so on. In sales or service jobs these skills are essential, and the higher a person rises in any organization, the more important these skills become.

The third factor is *job knowledge*. One of your people might have impeccable technical skills and outstanding interpersonal skills, but if that person doesn't know your expectations or doesn't understand customer requirements, he or she really doesn't know what the job is all about. Without that, how can this person be expected to deliver the necessary results?

The fourth factor is *organizational power*. In order to have the power to deliver results, a person also has to understand the back alleyways and hidden channels of the organization. He or she needs to have a network of people to call on in order to cut through the red tape and get things done. This applies to your organization, but also to your customers' organizations. Your people need to know how to get in and out and through these organizations in order to get things done.

WHAT IS MOTIVATION?

There are also four factors to consider when you think about motivation. The first factor is *interest*. This is important because if a team member is not interested in the work itself, then he or she will not be very enthusiastic about it. But in most organizations, interest is monitored in a very superficial way, by focusing on how early people come in, how late they stay, and how willing they are to work on weekends. Interest is important, but motivation is more complicated than the hours your people put in.

The second factor is *confidence*. This is extremely important, especially when organizations and the people in them are facing increasingly difficult challenges. Have you ever worked with people who have great skills but lack the self-confidence to use them? Or have you ever been in a situation where you weren't totally confident of your skills? Without confidence, how motivated will any person be to take on increased responsibility?

The third factor is *willingness to assume responsibility*. Most often, willingness is a function of a person's skills, interest, or confidence, but not always. These days, it is not uncommon for people to be skilled, highly interested, and very confident, but so busy and stressed that they're reluctant to take on new responsibilities. So, if someone is going to motivate them, there is going to have to be a very strong incentive, whether it's a carrot dangled in front of the nose or a stick applied to the rear end, to encourage them to take on new responsibilities.

The fourth factor is *alignment with organizational goals*. If a team member's goals are not consistent with the organization's goals, the result will be frustration and conflict. There are some highly motivated people in every organization who are motivated for all the wrong reasons. They will do anything and will walk over anyone to accomplish their own agenda. If their efforts are not in sync with the organization's values and your department's mission, their commitment may do more harm than good. Alignment is also a critical factor when an organization is going through a major change. If people aren't sure where they fit, where the organization is going, or what management expects, their motivation is hindered. Consequently, they may not be willing to take on as much responsibility or to commit their time and energy without more frequent check-ins to be sure they are on track.

ABILITY + MOTIVATION = THE WINDOW OF POTENTIAL

So what do you do with these factors of ability and motivation? Focusing on a specific task or job responsibility, you use them to assess a team member's ability and motivation as high, moderate, or low. Based on that assessment, you then assign two points if it's high, one point if it's moderate, and zero points if it's low. How do you make that assessment? By thinking about the four factors for ability and the four factors for motivation.

If all four factors for ability are present, give two points for ability. If you have one or two question marks about any factor, give one point. And if you have three or four question marks about these factors, give zero points.

That doesn't mean the individual has no ability. It just means that there are too many question marks to put any points into the equation.

The same assessment takes place for motivation. If there are no problems, give two points for motivation. If there are one or two concerns, give one point. And if you have three or four concerns, give zero points. Again, that doesn't mean there is no motivation, just that the number of concerns doesn't warrant putting any points into the formula.

So, use the four factors to assess ability and motivation as high (2 points), moderate (1 point), or low (0 points). Then, all you do is add those assessments together to determine this person's performance potential for the specific task or action step that you are focusing on. Remember, this is not an overall assessment of a person. It is a diagnosis of a person's ability and motivation to perform certain aspects of his or her job.

As shown in Figure 17, A2 + M2 equals P4. High ability plus high motivation gets you to the highest level of performance potential.

A2 + M1 or A1 + M2 equals P3, the next highest level of potential. In these situations, the team member is very capable, but there's one factor missing from either ability or motivation. It could be anything on the list—technical skills, interpersonal skills, job knowledge, organizational power, interest, confidence, willingness, or alignment. Whatever it is, P3 is still a very high level of performance potential.

There are three ways to get to P2. The most common one is in the middle, A1 + M1, moderate ability and moderate motivation. But the two

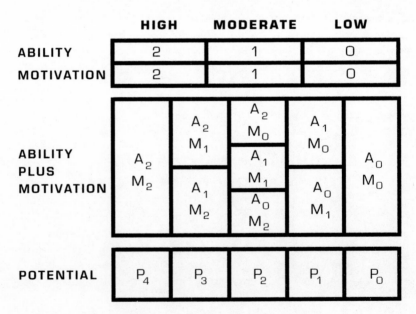

Figure 17 The Window of Potential

extremes also occur at times. One is A2 + M0, when someone is very capable and experienced, but disinterested or burned out. The other is A0 + M2, when a person is new to a job and not very experienced but is overly confident and out to set the world on fire. Both of these cases also add up to P2, a moderate level of performance potential.

Any combination of 1 plus 0 adds up to P1, which is a relatively low level of potential.

The math, when you get down to the end, is very simple. A0 + M0 = P0, the lowest level of potential.

WHAT'S YOUR WINDOW OF POTENTIAL?

Before you try diagnosing your team members' performance potential, it is important to apply this concept to yourself. So take a few minutes to think about your own Window of Potential. As you think about these five levels of performance potential and the nine combinations that make them up, think about how they apply to you. Think about your job, the goals you're accountable for, and the huge range of tasks you have to perform to achieve those goals. Now try to think of some tasks that fit into each level of performance potential.

Can you think of some tasks that are P4? Can you think of some tasks that are P3 or P2? Are there any that are P1 or even P0? Take a few minutes to think about your job and how you'd classify some of the different tasks you have to do.

If you were able to identify some part of your job as P4, high ability and high motivation, that's normal. Everybody has some part of their job that is A2M2. If you didn't have any P4 situations, you probably would have been fired a long time ago.

Did you classify some parts of your job as P3? Most people do. Almost everyone has some P3 tasks where they could use a little help with some aspect of their work.

How about the P2 level? You certainly aren't alone if you have some P2 situations. In a typical department of any organization, about 75 percent of the people have some P2 situations.

What about P1? This category is more common than you may think. It is very normal to have some responsibilities for which you have only a little ability and, consequently, little or no motivation. At least 30 percent of a typical group has some P1 cases.

Did you find any P0 parts of your job? Don't feel alone if you did. It is not unusual to have a task or two that you are lousy at doing and that you avoid like the plague. In a normal group, about 10 percent of the people will admit publicly to having some P0 situations. In reality, we suspect that everyone has some. We certainly do!

The main purpose for asking you these questions is to drive home a very important point. What is normal for you is normal for most people. When most people look at their jobs and the range of tasks that are required, they need to use the full Window of Potential to assess themselves.

It's important to keep this in mind as you think about matching your leadership styles with your team members' potential. Do not get caught in the trap of labeling people as P4, P3, P2, P1, or P0. Instead, always remember that you are assessing their task-specific potential. You're diagnosing situations, not pigeonholing people.

MATCHING YOUR STYLES TO A FOLLOWER'S WINDOW OF POTENTIAL

Figure 18 shows you how to match your Window of Leadership to a team member's Window of Potential. You can see that the five levels of potential are at the bottom and the four leadership styles are at the top. The intersection of the dotted lines with the diagonal shows you which style you use for each level of potential.

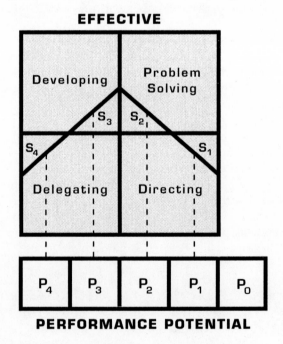

Figure 18 Matching Styles to Potential

Use Delegating in P4 Situations

In a P4 situation, the best style is S4, delegating. The person has the ability and the motivation to accomplish the task. So, in a P4 situation, delegate the responsibility and the authority, and then let the person run with it. Just keep yourself informed so you don't lose your own accountability. In terms of the empowerment cycle, you are following the 1-4 sequence—giving clear directions, handing off responsibility, and staying out of the way.

Use Developing in P3 Situations

In a P3 situation, you should use Style 3, developing. The potential is strong. There are just one or two factors missing in either ability or motivation.

Whatever it is that's missing, your job is to provide support. That could mean technical advice, interpersonal coaching, clarification of job knowledge, or use of your organizational power. Support could also mean prioritizing interests, bolstering confidence, getting people to take on more responsibility, or signing off to ensure alignment with organizational goals. Whatever it is, you're giving people the support they need to succeed with their responsibilities. Within the empowerment cycle, you are using the 1-4-3 sequence—directing, delegating, and on-the-fly developing by making yourself available to provide support.

Use Problem Solving in P2 Situations

In a P2 situation, the best style is S2, problem solving. Remember, there are three forms of P2. The most common is A1M1. When a person has moderate ability and moderate motivation, it's common sense to incorporate his or her thinking into your decision making.

It is also true in the two extremes. With the person who is very capable but turned off, you don't want to lose his or her expertise, so you should structure his or her involvement in your decision making. How about the person who is very green and overconfident? You want to channel that motivation in appropriate directions. Encourage participation but offer frequent advice and feedback. Under these circumstances, you are using the complete 1-4-3-2 cycle—directing, delegating, listening to find out if developing is all that you need to do, and anticipating that what you hear might actually be input to your own problem solving.

Use Directing in P1 Situations

In a P1 situation, the best style is S1, directing. In these situations, you are essentially doing on-the-job training. The people have some ability or they have some motivation, but there are many performance factors that they are lacking. It is important to structure the work in a way that makes them feel challenged without being overwhelmed. You should give them clear directions and complete explanations. Frequent feedback will keep them on the right track while helping them develop the skills and confidence to move into the P2 category as soon as possible. In these situations, you are not delegating responsibility. You are using Style 1 to assign tasks that will prepare the people for taking on responsibilities as soon as they are ready.

What About P0 Situations?

You have probably noticed that we have run out of leadership styles and P0 is still dangling off the end of the chart. This is not an accident. The leadership styles are powerful tools, but they will not solve all of your people problems. As shown in Figure 19, to make The L4 System work, you have to integrate leadership with human-resource management strategies.

In a P0 situation, where people have low ability and low motivation, don't waste your time or exhaust their patience with increasingly detailed directions and increasingly tight supervision. Instead, the best response is human-resource management.

The first human-resource management strategy is training. One efficient way to change a P0 situation is to increase a person's technical skills, interpersonal skills, job knowledge, organizational knowledge, interest, confidence, willingness, and/or alignment through training.

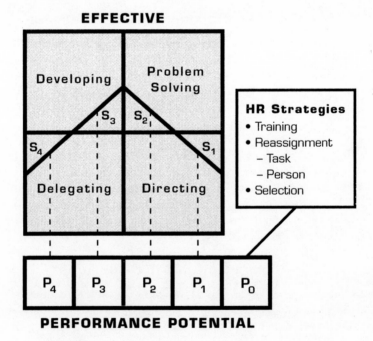

Figure 19 P0 Situations Require Human-Resource Management

The second human-resource management strategy is reassignment. In a P0 situation, a common strategy is to reassign the task to someone who likes it and can do it. It is also common to reassign a person to another job within the department. Job posting is a technique that many organizations use for relocating people to other parts of the company. Sometimes it is necessary to simply cut your losses. We used to call that firing people—now it is called *outplacement*.

The main point in reassignment is to help people find a good fit between their potential and a job description. You are not doing your department or the individual a favor by leaving a person in a job where he or she consistently fails.

The last human-resource strategy is selection. If you have a bad fit, you should be more proactive the next time in selecting the people with the ability and motivation to be top performers.

The main point is this: If you're going to lead a high-performing team, you have to select the right people, assign them to the right jobs, and give them proper training. But all these actions do is put your people onto the playing field. To make sure they perform, you have to use all four styles on an ongoing basis in a way that matches their Window of Potential.

ARE YOU ADDING VALUE?

So what do you get by matching leadership styles to follower potential? The answer is performance! Figure 20 illustrates this point.

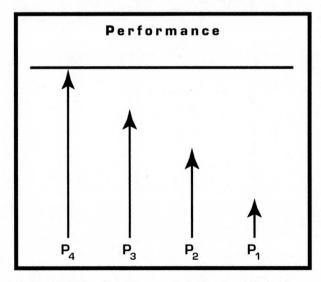

Figure 20 Performance Potential Versus Performance Expectations

Think of the horizontal line as a performance line. It represents the standards for excellence in your organization. The arrows show what would happen at each level of performance potential if the people were left on their own.

In P4 situations, if you leave people alone, they will hit the line. In P3 situations, if you leave people on their own, they will come close to the mark. In P2 situations, people will get about halfway by themselves. In P1 situations, they can just get started.

Figure 21 shows that your job as the leader is to make sure performance is on target. It's your job to make sure that everyone hits the line. To do that, you have to provide the value-added leadership that guarantees performance. It's your role to close the gap between expectations and potential.

That means that, in a P1 situation, your role is to give clear assignments with complete instructions and provide close supervision and frequent feedback. This use of the directing style results in on-the-job training that is needed to achieve the desired performance levels in this type of situation.

In a P2 situation, your job is to listen to a team member's problems, solicit his or her recommendations about what needs to be done, and then make the decisions that will ensure performance. Your use of the problem-solving style takes advantage of the ability and motivation the individual brings to the situation without letting him or her flounder.

In a P3 situation, your job is to provide the type of support that will make this a developmental opportunity. The person has strong performance potential and, with a little help from you, should be able to hit the performance line.

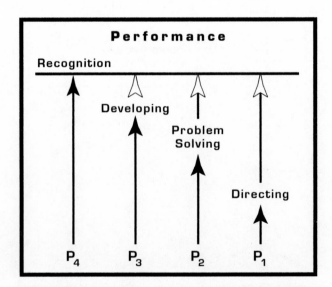

Figure 21 Closing the Expectations–Potential Gap

Just remember that support means different things to different people in different situations.

In a P4 situation, even though the individual is quite capable of hitting the performance line without any help, don't forget to give him or her recognition for outstanding work. If you don't appreciate your top performers for their efforts and the results they produce, they may not be your top performers for long. Either their motivation will drop off or they will start looking around for someone else to work for.

This approach is different from what passes for supervision in most organizations. Typically, employees are lucky to know what the performance standards are. Whether or not they do, they are most likely to be left on their own to try to hit the line. Their managers have their own jobs to do and have limited time to help their employees. Instead, they fill out forms once a year passing judgment on how close their people have come to hitting the mark.

Often, this type of performance management system also claims to reward the best performers and get rid of the worst. In reality, all that happens is that people feel judged and threatened. Under those conditions, who do you think eventually bails out? Of course, the best ones do. They've got the credentials and the confidence to move on. Then the organization is worse off than it was before. Organizational performance drops, then people on the low end are laid off, and a smaller and less talented workforce is left to keep the ship from sinking.

If your organization operates this way, you are probably not getting the most out of your people. And you may be sowing the seeds for disaster. Leaving people alone and then judging them is a far cry from being clear about expectations and then using all four styles on an ongoing basis.

It is much wiser to use the 1-4-3-2 empowerment cycle and go as far as performance potential dictates. Setting the performance bar by giving directions and clarifying expectations is the first step—Style 1. Giving people a chance to see how close they come to hitting the bar is the second step—Style 4. Filling in the gap by using the style that matches their potential—Styles 2, 3, or 4—is all that's left to do. By analyzing each person's Window of Potential and aligning your Window of Leadership with their needs, you raise the probability that all of your team members will hit the performance bar.

RAISING THE PERFORMANCE BAR

In today's competitive business environment, the performance bar never stays in one place for very long. It is always being raised. It could be you raising the bar on your people. It might be your manager raising the bar on you. It could be the competition raising the bar on your product or service, your line of business, or your whole company. And these days, technological developments might be raising the bar on your entire industry.

The one thing you can be sure of is that the performance bar will always go up. To illustrate that, the bar has been raised in Figure 22.

When the bar is raised, you have to be careful to avoid the trap of trying to do it all yourself. Many managers do just that. They come in earlier, stay later, spend every minute of drive-time on their cell phones, stay online at all hours of the night, and try their hardest to fill all of the gaps. They may be able to sustain that for a short time, but over the long run, they can't do it, especially when they are stretched thin.

Reality is that you can't do it all yourself. Your people have to do it. These days most managers know that they have to drive responsibility down into the organization. And every manager who pushes responsibility down talks about empowering his or her employees to handle these new responsibilities. But, in many cases, employees don't feel empowered at all. Instead, they feel buried.

If you drive responsibility down to the members of your team and then leave your people alone with these increased duties, you aren't empowering anyone. You're just unloading the dump truck on their shoulders. When you push responsibility down, you are raising the bar for your people, and you have to anticipate how the performance bar looks from their perspective.

New job requirements often create gaps in an employee's skill set. While a person's ability doesn't deteriorate, a raised bar can bring to the surface question marks about technical skills, interpersonal skills, job knowledge, and even organizational knowledge. It is also very common for a person's motivation

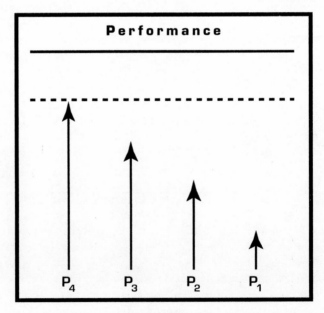

Figure 22 Raising Performance Expectations

to be affected. Interest can wane, confidence can be shaken, willingness to take on responsibility may be reduced, and alignment with organizational goals is almost always uncertain during a time of change.

When the bar goes up, you have to anticipate that performance potential may go down relative to the new expectations. So you have to prepare yourself to do even more leading, as illustrated by Figure 23. In response, you have to anticipate providing more leadership. In a situation that used to be P4, you now should use Style 3, developing, to help people hit the new line with your support. In a previous P3 situation, you now need to use Style 2, problem solving, to listen to their problems and recommendations and then make the tough decisions that they may lack the confidence or alignment to make.

In situations that used to be P2, you may not have the luxury of involving staff in your decision making; you may simply need to use Style 1, directing, to get them pointed in the new direction. And in situations that used to be P1, you probably can't afford to keep up the on-the-job training and should consider human-resource management strategies. Basically, you need to fish or cut bait.

If you are going to fish, training is one option that helps people meet new standards by improving their technical skills, interpersonal skills, job knowledge, interest, confidence, and willingness to assume responsibilities. Organizations that do a good job with change management are usually prepared with training programs designed to help their people handle new and increased responsibilities.

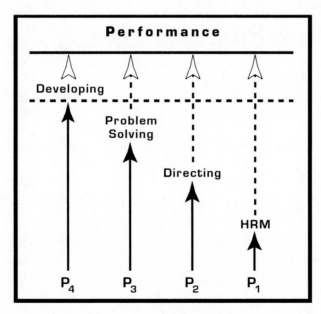

Figure 23 Do More Leading When Expectations Increase

All the training in the world won't save you from the reality that in some cases you may have to cut bait. The leaders of major changes consistently tell us that their greatest challenges come when they have to counsel people into lower-status jobs or out of the organization. It isn't pleasant, but doing it well can make the difference between success and failure.

WATCHING THE KITES THROUGH
THE WINDOW OF POTENTIAL

Remember the discussion in the last chapter about development and intervention? Figure 22 illustrates more than the principle of filling in performance gaps. It is also a good illustration of the *development* cycle. As performance potential gradually increases from right to left, you gradually let out the kite string from directing to delegating. As people's ability and motivation improve, which usually occurs as they gain experience, the styles you use at critical moments shift from 1 to 2 to 3 to 4. As this plays out in terms of the *empowerment* cycle, the full set of moves you make shifts from 1 to 1-4-3-2 to 1-4-3 to 1-4.

Figure 23 is a good illustration of the *intervention* cycle being used when the bar is raised. It shows how you move back one step in the cycle from a main style of 4 to 3 to 2 to 1 to human-resource management. In terms of the empowerment cycle, moving from 1-4 to 1-4-3 to 1-4-3-2 will make life a lot easier and work more productive. And if you have to move back to the Style 1, on-the-job training, approach, in most cases some HR moves aren't far behind. When your company is pushing hard and every manager is stretched thin, you have to have people on your team who can and will take on the responsibilities.

As you look at development and intervention through the Window of Potential, assessing ability and motivation relative to performance expectations can tell you exactly how much string to let out and guide you to reel it back in if the winds are blowing too hard.

HOW GOOD ARE YOU AT MATCHING
STYLES TO POTENTIAL?

Remember the cases you read in chapter 1? The first eight cases involved individuals, and there were two cases for each level of performance potential. In the next four sections, you can see how effective (or ineffective) your responses were at each level of follower potential.

Start with the P1 Situations

Cases 1 and 8 were P1 cases. In each situation, the follower's performance potential was relatively low. Put your answers in the spaces below to see how much of each style you used in these cases.

	Style 1	Style 2	Style 3	Style 4
Case 1	B _____	A _____	D _____	C _____
Case 8	A _____	B _____	C _____	D _____
Totals	_____	_____	_____	_____
Percentages MULTIPLY X 10	_____	_____	_____	_____
Effectiveness MULTIPLY · · X 10 · · · X 5	_____ +	_____		= _____

After adding each column, multiply your totals by 10 to find out what percentage of each style you used in these P1 situations. Then, to calculate your effectiveness score, multiply the totals for the best style by 10 and the next best style by 5, and then add those two products together.

In these P1 cases, the best style is Style 1. By using Style 1, you are directing two people who need instructions and frequent feedback. By providing specific directions, you can keep them focused on achievable tasks. Close supervision should enable them to perform satisfactorily while developing skills and confidence.

If you didn't select Style 1 with Tom, in case 1, you probably weren't recognizing his need for clear directions to help him get oriented to the new assignment. Until he fully understands the job, he won't appreciate your point of view that his skills are all right. And until he knows that, his confidence and willingness will remain low.

With Jenny, in case 8, the situation is quite different but still requires you to step in and take charge. She knows what she has to do and knows that she is not very good at it. The job requires more attention to detail than she has the technical skill or interest for. As a result, she is not willing to accept more responsibility and is more aligned with looking for another job than doing this one. You should encourage her to find another position, but until she can move on, you need to direct her work and monitor her closely so that your department doesn't suffer while she looks.

If you used the next best style, Style 2, you were over-involving these team members. Getting their input may be meeting your needs but is probably not helping them. Right now, Tom needs to get fully oriented to the job at hand. When that has occurred, he might have some meaningful suggestions to make. And since Jenny is a bad fit for her job, her input will not help you much and might delay her moving on. At least you picked the second best choice because Style 2 still leaves you in control, which is important in these two cases.

If you used a lot of Style 3 with these two individuals, you were over-accommodating. You may be trying too hard to give these people developmental opportunities when they are not ready for decision-making responsibilities. They probably view you as friendly and may appreciate your offers of support, but they are not getting enough direction to make them productive.

If you selected Style 4 in these cases, you were definitely abdicating. It is not appropriate to give these people so much responsibility. They need direction and close supervision. Without this, they will flounder, feel discouraged, or direct their efforts to the wrong places.

Look at the P2 Situations

Write your answers to cases 2 and 5 in the spaces, and then complete the calculations.

	Style 1	Style 2	Style 3	Style 4
Case 2	C ____	A ____	B ____	D ____
Case 5	A ____	D ____	B ____	C ____
Totals	____	____	____	____
Percentages MULTIPLY X 10	____	____	____	____
Effectiveness MULTIPLY	____ X 5	+ ____ X 10		= ____

In the P2 cases, Style 2 is the best style. With these two people, your best response is problem solving. They have some ability and some motivation, so it is appropriate to involve them in the decision-making process. By doing this, you are helping them learn the critical issues that affect problem solving in this line of work. You are also benefiting from their skills and/or enthusiasm while making them feel involved and appreciated.

In case 2, Susan has good skills and the confidence to use them. Her performance has suffered because she lacks job knowledge and is out of alignment with the norms of your team. By listening to her ideas, you can make her feel valued; that should make her more likely to listen to your point of view. She also can learn a lot about the job and the organization through these discussions.

Ted, in case 5, has his own narrow perspective of the department's goals.. That, coupled with some rough interpersonal skills, leads to his not performing as well as someone with his skills and experience could. By seeking his input, you can broaden his understanding of the organization while letting him know that you still appreciate what he can offer to the team. Also, by seeing you in action, maybe he will learn some better ways to work with people.

If you selected the next best style in these cases, Style 1, you were too dominating. If you just tell Susan what she needs to do differently without showing respect for what she can do, she may not be receptive to the reorientation she needs. In Ted's case, if you don't acknowledge his capabilities, he may feel too discouraged to keep trying. At least you picked the second best choice by taking charge when you had to.

If you chose Style 3 actions in these cases, you were over-accommodating. Since both individuals have some performance-related problems, you should not leave them in charge of making critical decisions right now. Too much responsibility might make their situations worse than they have been. Take their input for now. If improvement becomes noticeable, you can acknowledge that with increased opportunities.

If you used a lot of Style 4 in these situations, you were guilty of abdicating. These team members do not understand how their actions are affecting organizational performance. Until they do, they should not be left on their own. If they are, they are likely to create some problems for themselves and others.

Look at the P3 Situations

Write your responses to cases 3 and 6 in the spaces, and then complete the calculations.

	Style 1	Style 2	Style 3	Style 4
Case 3	C ____	D ____	A ____	B ____
Case 6	B ____	C ____	D ____	A ____
Totals	____	____	____	____
Percentages MULTIPLY X 10	____	____	____	____
Effectiveness MULTIPLY			____ + X 10	____ = ____ X 5

In the P3 cases, Style 3 was the best style. If you chose Style 3, you were developing. By listening, you are helping these people think through their own decisions in their areas of responsibility. Your support helps them handle challenging assignments while developing their skills and confidence in the process.

In case 3, Joe just needs an orientation period to fully understand how to apply his skills most productively. Unlike Tom, in case 1, Joe is highly motivated and raring to go. A little coaching from you at critical moments should be all he needs.

Martha, in case 6, had all the ability and motivation she needed to handle the original assignment. Some immediate support from you should help her regain her confidence to handle the new time constraint. Some empathy should also reduce her strong reaction so that she can refocus on the organizational need.

If you used a lot of Style 1 in these cases, you were too dominating. If you are directive with these people, they will feel smothered and will be discouraged from taking initiatives. Telling them exactly what to do will undermine their willingness to assume responsibility without giving enough regard to their ability.

If you selected a lot of Style 2 in these cases, you were over-involving yourself in the decision-making process. You should not need to exercise this much control with either Joe or Martha. They are quite capable of making good decisions with a little support from you. At least this style is better than Style 1, since you do get them involved.

If you chose Style 4 in these cases, it was the second best choice but you were abdicating. It is appropriate to give Joe and Martha responsibility so they will feel challenged, but it is too soon to give them authority to make decisions on their own. They might do all right, but they could also make some serious mistakes. To make these situations developmental, you need to talk with them at critical checkpoints to make sure they are in alignment with your expectations and offer some coaching if they are not.

Look at the P4 Situations

Write your responses to cases 4 and 7 in the spaces in the box at the top of page 155, and then complete the calculations.

In the P4 cases, Style 4 is the best style. If you chose Style 4, you were effectively delegating to people who were capable of handling these situations on their own. Since both Jane and Barry are high on ability and high on motivation, it is appropriate to give them the authority to make decisions on their own. In situations like this, team members usually thrive on responsibility and are motivated by the opportunity to take charge.

Jane, in case 4, is performing very well and does not appear to need any support from you. Your only reason for getting involved is to remind her that she still works for you and is not totally independent. Your best way to do that is to give her plenty of appreciation for the good job she is doing without dis-

	Style 1	Style 2	Style 3	Style 4
Case 4	D ____	B ____	C ____	A ____
Case 7	D ____	C ____	A ____	B ____
Totals	____	____	____	____
Percentages MULTIPLY X 10	____	____	____	____
Effectiveness MULTIPLY			____ + X 5	____ = X 10	____

tracting her from her work. With some recognition for the way she handles her responsibilities, Jane will value you as her boss and continue to perform for you.

In Barry's situation, the reason to consider intervening is based on mounting organizational pressure. Often it is good to anticipate that pressures can require some support from above, but you should not make the assumption that Barry cannot handle his responsibilities on his own. He always has, and there is every reason to believe that he will now. Be alert and stay sensitive to his situation, but don't jump in if you don't have to. By waiting, you may discover that all you need to do is give him recognition for a job well done.

If you used the next best style in these situations, Style 3, you were over-accommodating. You would probably come across as helpful and friendly, but your support is not really needed. In fact, you may be slowing these people down by taking them away from their work at a critical moment. At least with this approach, you are not undercutting their sense of responsibility, and listening to them will probably not cause any serious damage.

If you used a lot of Style 2 in these P4 cases, you were over-involving. There is no reason for you to take over responsibility for decision making. If you redirect Jane, you will be over-involving yourself. And in Barry's case, if you get into problem solving, you will be over-involving him. In both situations, you would be taking these top performers away from the tasks they need to complete.

The worst response to these cases is Style 1. If you chose the Style 1 actions, you definitely would come across as dominating. You would be giving specific directions and close supervision to people who have been handling major responsibilities on their own. Instead of smothering these people and frustrating them, you should be giving them praise for their accomplishments and staying out of their way.

HOW EFFECTIVE WERE YOU?

Before you go on, take a minute to look back at all four levels of potential. What were your effectiveness scores for each level? The best score is 100. Anything less than 80 means that you should think about your real cases at that level of potential. Ask yourself if you are making the same mistakes at work that you made with these hypothetical cases. If you are, keep reading. Chapter 10 will give you some more ways to improve.

ARE YOU READY FOR SOME MORE FEEDBACK?

When you responded to the cases, you may or may not have noticed that there were distinctly male and female names in each case. We did that on purpose to let you see if there are differences between the types of leadership you provide to men and women.

To see how you responded to the male and female cases, just look at the last few pages and copy the numbers from the P1, P2, P3, and P4 cases into the matrix on page 157. Then add the numbers in each column and multiply by 5 to see what percentage of each style you used with each gender.

As you look at these scores, you need to take them with a grain of salt. Sometimes when people respond to the questions, they don't even notice the names. Even if you did read the names, one case might have been about a particular problem that made you think of somebody who was, in fact, the opposite sex of the person used in the case. So it is important not to look at this feedback as an absolute statement about you.

Small differences don't mean much. But if you find some significant differences between the styles you used with the two genders, you might want to ask yourself why. Is it the men and women you work with? Are their needs different? Or is it inside you? Might you be giving one group what you think they need instead of what they really need? Or giving them what you want whether they need it or not?

If a clear pattern appears as you look at the two sets of percentages, you should think about it.

For example, in one department of a company we studied, every manager had dramatically different responses to the men and the women. It turned out that their professional staff were all men, and the only women in their department were secretaries. These managers were, in fact, treating those men and women in very different ways, not because they were all discriminating against women, but because the department's norms for recruiting, hiring, and promoting staff were out-of-date and clearly prejudiced. What followed was a very productive discussion about some strategies for correct-

	Style 1	Style 2	Style 3	Style 4
Case 1	B ____	A ____	D ____	C ____
Case 5	A ____	D ____	B ____	C ____
Case 3	C ____	D ____	A ____	B ____
Case 7	D ____	C ____	A ____	B ____
Totals	____	____	____	____
MULTIPLY X 5	____	____	____	____
	Male Percentages			

	Style 1	Style 2	Style 3	Style 4
Case 8	A ____	B ____	C ____	D ____
Case 2	C ____	A ____	B ____	D ____
Case 6	B ____	C ____	D ____	A ____
Case 4	D ____	B ____	C ____	A ____
Totals	____	____	____	____
MULTIPLY X 5	____	____	____	____
	Female Percentages			

ing this organizational inequity, not a discussion about leading men and women differently.

Another interesting case is a general manager who was participating in an L4 training program with several levels of his management team. When he looked at his overall leadership profile, he had 70 percent in Style 3. This man was beaming ear to ear and said he couldn't wait to take his questionnaire home to show his wife, since she frequently accused him of being Attila the Hun. But when he looked at the differences between his male responses and female responses, his smile started to fade. With the men, he had used all four styles and used them pretty much in the right places. But with the women, he had used 100 percent Style 3. Regardless of the situation, he was more driven by his comfort level with women than their needs in task-specific terms.

When he saw the discrepancy, he asked the women who worked for him for some feedback about his interactions with them. They said he was always very friendly and very supportive but not as straight with them about what they were doing wrong. Also, they thought that he didn't trust them as much to call their own shots.

Later, he was still troubled about this and asked us what he could do differently. We said that it was very obvious. He needed to be nicer to his wife so that she would stop calling him Attila the Hun. Then he would be less afraid of getting in trouble with the women at work and could start treating them as individuals instead of as a group to be handled with kid gloves. He thought the advice might be a little hard to swallow but did say that he would consider it.

These two stories are extremes, and you should be cautious about over-interpreting your responses to the eight cases. However, if you see some strong patterns in the scores, think about them.

Do you use the full range of styles at the right levels of performance potential? And are you objective about your people's needs without letting gender or ethnic background get in the way? These are tough but important questions if you are going to be a good leader!

KEEP YOUR WINDOWS OPEN

Remember, the most important point of this entire chapter is that, to be an effective leader, you need to be open to using all four styles all of the time while being as open as possible to recognizing which style is the primary approach to take in each situation.

Creating Windows
of Opportunity
with Your People

CHAPTER 10

As you have been reading the last two chapters, you have probably been thinking about how these concepts apply to you and your real-world problems. By now, you should have a good understanding of the basic concept of matching your Window of Leadership to each team member's Window of Potential. You should also have a good idea of how to adjust your main style as conditions change for better or for worse. And you should have a solid appreciation of the value of using all four styles in the 1-4-3-2 sequence in order to empower the people who work with you.

In this chapter, you can really sink your teeth into these ideas by trying out two simple structures that make it easy to apply The L4 System to any individual on your team. The first structure is called *situational analysis*. The second is *performance contracting*.

These tools guide you in assessing team members' ability and motivation in the context of specific business objectives. They also help you plan your time by showing you how far around the 1-4-3-2 cycle you have to go on each critical task.

As you start using these tools to determine what leadership styles are needed, it is important to realize that there are a variety of factors beyond ability and motivation that influence how you implement these styles. One of those factors is personality, and that will be covered extensively in chapter 11. Other modifying factors are technological changes, generational differences, and new organizational models. Each of these will be addressed in this chapter to help you gain a full understanding of how to apply the leadership styles that the situational analysis and performance contracting structures guide you to use.

SITUATIONAL ANALYSIS: A TOOL FOR CORRECTING PERFORMANCE PROBLEMS

Before starting the situational analysis process, you need to be sure that you really have a performance problem on your hands. Sometimes you may be uncomfortable with a person who is, in actuality, performing quite well. In that type of situation, you should talk to a friend, talk to your boss, talk to your spouse, talk to whomever you want to, but do not start messing up a good situation.

On the other hand, if there is a performance problem, then you should go ahead with a complete analysis of the situation.

Before you read any further, take a minute to think of someone who works for you whose performance does not meet your standards. As you read about the four steps, try applying the process to your own situation. You will see just how easy it is to make these concepts work for you.

Step 1

The first step is to be specific about the goal that is not being met. Then you need to focus on those tasks for which there is a difference between the actual performance and the ideal results that you expect.

1a. What goal is not being accomplished? _____

_____

_____

1b. What tasks or responsibilities are not being achieved satisfactorily?

Task 1 _____

Task 2 _____

Task 3 _____

Task 4 _____

Step 2

Once you are clear about the problem tasks, in Step 2 you need to identify the ideal style for dealing with this situation by diagnosing the team member's task-specific performance potential. To do that, assess ability and motivation as high (2 points), moderate (1 point), or low (0 points). Write the numbers down next to the "A" and the "M" in the following worksheet. Then add them together to calculate the potential.

For example, if ability is high, write down "2". If motivation is moderate, write down "1". When you add them together, you get P3.

The potential tells you which style is theoretically correct. If it's a P1 situation, S1 is usually the best response; P2, S2; P3, S3; P4, S4.

---

2. For each task, identify the main style you need to use by diagnosing this person's performance potential.

	Ability	Motivation	Potential	Style
T1	A _____	+ M _____	= P _____	= S _____
T2	A _____	+ M _____	= P _____	= S _____
T3	A _____	+ M _____	= P _____	= S _____
T4	A _____	+ M _____	= P _____	= S _____

The performance potential checklist below will help you make this diagnosis. Remember, if you think all four factors are okay, assign 2 points. If you have one or two questions, assign 1 point. If you are concerned about three or four factors, assign 0 points.

ABILITY
- Technical skills
- Interpersonal skills
- Job knowledge
- Organizational power

MOTIVATION
- Interest in the task
- Confidence
- Willingness to accept responsibility
- Alignment with organizational goals

Step 3

This step focuses on your role in this situation. Before taking any action, you need to determine the main style you are currently using. This is important because you may be part of the problem and actually making the situation worse than it has to be.

As shown in Figure 24, on the next page, you may be under-managing. Remember that your job is to provide the right amount of direction and support to help team members hit the performance line. If you are not doing that,

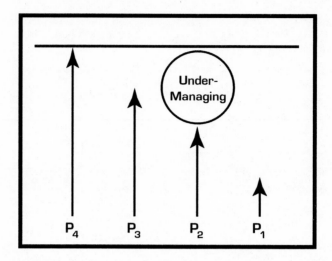

Figure 24 Under-Managing: Failing to Close the Gap

you may be contributing to the performance problem by not getting as involved as you need to.

Or you may be over-managing, as shown in Figure 25. It is possible that you are doing more leading than the situation calls for. In that type of situation, you may be reducing the team member's motivation and actually making performance worse than if you had been less involved.

You can do Step 3 on your own by just thinking about what you typically do with this person. Or you may want to talk with someone who can help you be objective about how you are coming across—your manager, a peer, or a friend. In some cases, you may want to ask for feedback from the person who's having the problem—that's the one person who really knows how you come across.

However you decide to look at your piece of the action, Step 3 is important. The following worksheet will help you work through it.

3. Before taking action, identify the main style you are using. Write the style # in the small space and the label beside it (see box to the right).

T1 S ___ _____

T2 S ___ _____

T3 S ___ _____

T4 S ___ _____

S1 Directing
   Dominating

S2 Problem Solving
   Over-Involving

S3 Developing
   Over-Accommodating

S4 Delegating
   Abdicating

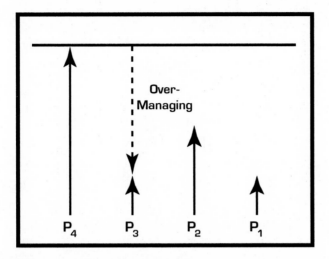

Figure 25 Over-Managing: Widening the Gap by Over-Leading

Step 4

Finally, Step 4 helps you take corrective action. In Step 2, you identified the main style to use for each task. That tells you the style you should be using with this individual at critical checkpoints. Remembering the *development* and *intervention* cycles, if your current style is more than one style away, be sure to go up or down one step at a time. Changing styles too abruptly can make problems worse instead of better.

More important, as you change the style you are using for key decisions, you also need to rethink the situation in terms of the 1-4-3-2 *empowerment* cycle. Did you give this person adequate information up front? Were you clear about the authority that you were delegating and the ways that you wanted to be kept informed? Have you really listened to understand the other person's perspective, and his or her analysis of the situation and ideas for turning it around? If problem solving was necessary, have you made timely decisions when it was clear that you needed to?

Without considering the full 1-4-3-2 cycle, you may not succeed with your action plan. It won't do you much good to shift from Style 4, abdicating, to Style 3, developing, if you were never clear in the first place about what the performance expectations were. Likewise, if you need to shift from Style 1, dominating, to Style 2, problem solving, you need to use the entire 1-4-3-2 cycle. That requires you to explain what you are doing and then give the person an opportunity to follow your directions. And having used some Style 4 to do that, you need to spend some time using some Style 3 by asking questions and listening before you make the shift to Style 2, problem solving. And who knows? A little Style 3 may be all that was really needed. Often when you let go, people surprise you with how much they can do.

4. To change from your current style to the correct main style, use the 1-4-3-2 cycle to identify all of the actions you need to do more of or less of to help this person perform to the best of his or her potential.

S1 = Give information, clarify expectations
S4 = Confirm authority, reward taking responsibility
S3 = Listen, provide support in any area of ability or motivation
S2 = Make decisions based on recommendations

	More of	**Less of**
T1	_____	_____
T2	_____	_____
T3	_____	_____
T4	_____	_____

A CASE WHERE SITUATIONAL ANALYSIS PAID OFF

Sandy was a young supervisor in an accounting firm. She had been with the firm for five years, had been promoted to supervisor after three years, and was hoping to be promoted to manager within the next year. She had supervised many engagement teams on a wide variety of different audits.

Sandy was having a problem with another woman named Jennifer who was one of the staff on her current engagement. An important meeting with a client was coming up, and the manager wanted to meet with Sandy and Jennifer prior to that meeting. The only time they could meet was early in the morning, so Sandy told Jennifer to meet her and the manager at the office at 7:30 A.M. (Meetings of this sort are not unusual in the accounting industry.)

The night before the meeting, Sandy got a phone call at home. It was Jennifer. "Does the meeting have to be at 7:30?"

"Yes. That's the only time the manager can meet with us."

"Well, I have a problem. I get up at 5:30 every morning so that I can run for half an hour, take a shower, make my lunch, and have enough time to drive to the office. If I have to be there at 7:30 I won't have time. What should I do?"

"Why don't you just get up earlier?"

"Well, I already get up at 5:30. I wouldn't want to get up any earlier than that."

"Could you skip the running or run for less time?"

"I can't do that. I have to run half an hour every morning or I'll be worthless all day."

"Okay. Could you make your lunch tonight and put it in the refrigerator?"

"I can't do that. My sandwich would be soggy and leak all over the place."

This went on for some time. Eventually, Sandy had listened long enough and said to Jennifer, "I understand your problem but you will just have to decide for yourself. The meeting cannot be changed from 7:30. I'm sure you'll figure something out."

Of course, the next morning Jennifer arrived twenty minutes late. The manager was furious and Sandy was embarrassed as well as frustrated. But Sandy, Jennifer, and the manager didn't address the problem. They just talked very fast for the ten minutes they had left before the meeting with the client.

After that, Sandy still didn't say anything to Jennifer because she was afraid of being drawn into another lengthy conversation and losing more precious time.

Then, for the rest of the audit, day after day, Jennifer was late for everything.

Some months later, Sandy found out that Jennifer had decided to leave the firm and was clearly not motivated in the way that most staff are in this type of situation. That made the problem more understandable, but Sandy still wanted to know what she could have done differently.

So she used situational analysis.

Step 1

The goal was clear. Jennifer needed to be on time for meetings, work assignments, and deadlines. The critical task was for her to get up in time to take care of her own needs and be prompt for work.

Step 2

Thinking about Jennifer's overall Window of Potential, on the ability side of the equation, she had good technical skills as an accountant, was usually good at communicating with people, understood the requirements of her job very clearly, and did not need much power to complete her areas of the audit. On the motivation side, her interest was waning, she still had confidence in her abilities, she had lost her willingness to take on responsibility, and she was more aligned with her own career changes than accomplishing firm goals. So the general assessment of Jennifer's performance potential was high ability and low motivation, A2M0.

That means that Sandy should have been using Style 2 as the main style with Jennifer.

Jennifer, knowing that she was planning to leave the firm, realized that she had lost her motivation and, in her own way, tried to let Sandy know what she was dealing with. When she called and asked her supervisor to decide for her, Jennifer was inviting Sandy to use Style 2 with her.

Step 3

What was Sandy's piece of the action? She spent a lot of time listening and trying to help Jennifer figure out a way to do everything. She gave Jennifer several options, hoping that one of the ideas would help Jennifer decide. Sandy really wanted to help.

What style was this? Style 3, over-accommodating.

At the end of the telephone conversation, Sandy actually moved to Style 4, abdicating, when she left Jennifer on her own to make the final decision. After the meeting with the manager, Sandy was clearly using Style 4, abdicating, when she failed to confront the late arrival. And she continued in this mode throughout the engagement.

Step 4

What should Sandy have done differently? The main style she needed to use was Style 2, problem solving. Her general approach should have been to anticipate that Jennifer would be able to identify problems and suggest possible solutions but not make good decisions on her own or with support. Sandy needed to call the shots. That would have included being clear about the actions that Jennifer needed to take and also enforcing consequences, like staying late or coming in even earlier the next day, if Jennifer did not take the necessary actions.

Thinking about a complete action plan, Sandy needed to consider all four windows of the 1-4-3-2 cycle. She needed some Style 1 to be crystal clear about expectations, including a specific reprimand about what happened at that first meeting. She needed to use less Style 4, which had her leaving Jennifer alone and hoping that things would get better. She needed more frequent use of Style 3 focused on Jennifer's work. This would provide more critical checkpoints to ensure that the work was getting done in a timely manner and also give Sandy an opportunity to offer praise for doing the right things. Finally, she needed to be more willing to cross over from Style 3 to Style 2 whenever there was any chance of Jennifer's missing a deadline. At these times, Sandy needed to listen to the alternatives, be very decisive and clear about what had to be done and when it was due, and be prepared to enforce consequences if that did not happen.

Now Sandy knew what she should have done. Initially, when she was confronted with this situation, her reaction was that she was faced with an impossible situation. She had tried everything she could think of, had already spent as much time as she could with Jennifer, and was giving up. After the situational analysis, Sandy realized that she was part of the problem, that her actions actually were making a bad situation worse, and that she was not helpless. There were very specific actions she could have taken to turn that problem around.

The next time she had that kind of problem she would know what to do.

ANOTHER SUCCESS STORY

Philippe was a manager in the Canadian operation of an international company that manufactures, installs, and maintains elevators. He had been with the company for ten years and had worked his way up from worker to supervisor to manager.

Philippe's problem was very different from Sandy's. In fact, when he first talked about it, he said, "Here's a situation that doesn't fit into your system. I have a problem that no one can solve."

His problem was with a woman named Marie who worked for him. Marie was extremely capable but kept asking Philippe to make decisions for her that he wanted her to make on her own. Philippe was sure that Marie could do more on her own because whenever he was out of the office for a few days, she handled everything perfectly. Whenever he would call in, she had everything under control and his peers told him how well Marie did in his absence.

The problem was that the minute he would come back to the office, there was Marie with a list of problems for Philippe to deal with.

Philippe really wanted to know how to deal with this situation, and even though he was sure that situational analysis would not help, he agreed to try out the process.

Step 1

What was the goal? Philippe wanted Marie to handle her responsibilities independently. What were the critical tasks? Marie needed to be able to identify problems, consider the alternatives for solving those problems, weigh the pros and cons of each alternative, and make a good decision.

Step 2

What style was most appropriate for each of these tasks? Diagnosing Marie's performance potential for each task, she had high ability and high motivation, A2M2, for the first two tasks, identifying problems and thinking of various ways to solve them. So for those tasks, she was P4, and Style 4, delegating, was the best general approach to take.

For tasks 3 and 4, evaluating the options and making the ultimate decision, even though Marie had the ability to do that, she lacked something on the motivation side of the equation. Maybe she lacked full confidence, or maybe she wanted to be sure her thinking was in alignment with Philippe's, but for one reason or another, she appeared to be happier if she did not have to handle critical decisions alone. So Marie's potential for these tasks was A2M1 and Philippe's response to this P3 situation should have been Style 3, developing.

Step 3

What was Philippe's current leadership style? This is what he would typically do: After a trip, he would come into the office and ask Marie what problems she had for him to deal with. She would explain the problems and he would make the decisions.

In addition, if Marie came across a problem when he was in the office, she would come to him with the information and ask him what he wanted her to do. What do you think Philippe would do? Of course—he would make the decision and tell Marie what to do.

What type of leadership was he providing? Style 2, over-involving. He was inserting himself into these situations more than he wanted to and more than she really needed. Philippe was making decisions in many instances when a little support would have helped Marie develop her confidence and be increasingly sure that she and Philippe were aligned in their thinking.

Step 4

Philippe needed to shift from Style 2, over-involving, to Style 3, developing. Instead of listening to the problems and telling Marie how to solve them, he needed to stay in the listening mode. To do that, he needed to ask more questions like, "How do you think that should be handled?" or "What do you think would happen if we took that course of action?" or "What would you do if I were not here and you had to decide on your own?" These questions would help Marie think out loud, get feedback from Philippe that she is on the right track, and become more confident in handling many of these problems on her own.

There will always be some situations where she wants a supportive ear to help her think through a decision. And there may be occasional problems about which Philippe really does need to make a tough decision. But Marie will learn that most of the time it is all right to decide on her own.

Thinking beyond this general approach, Philippe also used 1-4-3-2 to make a complete action plan for working out this new relationship with Marie.

Rather than just start asking Marie questions and changing the conversational pattern they had developed over the years, he needed to use some Style 1 to give her feedback about his confidence in her abilities and explain that his goal was for her to make most decisions on her own. He also needed to explain that he was willing to support her whenever she felt the need. He might even want to point out some of the positive consequences that might result from this shift, like increased responsibility, good performance reviews, or promotions if those were reasonable expectations.

Then he needed to use more Style 4 to demonstrate his confidence in her. In this case, that meant not walking into the office and asking her what problems she had for him. Unintentionally, Philippe had been sending Marie a message that he wanted her to bring him problems to solve. His new line needed to be something like, "It is so good having someone like you here who can handle everything when I have to be out of the office."

Next, he needed to be very conscious of using Style 3 when Marie would approach him with problems. He had to resist the temptation to just give her his answer. By asking questions and reflecting back her ideas, he would be investing a few minutes with her on each problem in order to gain tremendous amounts of time later on as Marie increased her willingness to handle responsibilities.

Finally, he needed to stop asking her to bring problems to his attention, and he had to be less willing to put the monkey on his own back when she did bring problems to him. It would be better for him and for her if she retained the decision-making responsibility.

MAKE YOUR ASSESSMENTS ACTIONABLE

In the last chapter we introduced the Window of Potential as a task-specific concept and cautioned you against falling into the trap of pigeonholing people as P4, P3, P2, P1, or P0. In addition to warning managers to avoid global assessments of people, we used to teach them not to assess a team member's potential to accomplish a goal or succeed in a job. We always stressed that the analysis could only be effective if it were done at the task level.

Over the years we have learned that, in reality, all of us make broad judgments about people all the time, and nothing we can say will stop that. Our new advice is that if (or, more realistically, when) you make a global assessment about a person that a performance problem exists, don't stop there. Take the assessment down a level and diagnose the ability and motivation to achieve each goal. And when you do an assessment at the goal level, if you find a performance problem, you can't stop there either. To make an actionable game plan for turning the situation around, you need to do the analysis at the task level. That's where the situational analysis tool comes in—when you know performance is not meeting your expectations and you are ready to do something about it.

Linda's situation is a good example of how this works. Linda was a team leader in the research and development department of a Fortune 500 telecommunications company. One of her team members, Jason, was driving her crazy. He had excellent technical skills and was highly valued for his ability to solve complex problems, but his interpersonal skills were terrible, and he was very disruptive to Linda's team. Since solving problems and teamwork were both vital to her organization's success, Linda couldn't make up her mind if she should put Jason up for a promotion or start disciplinary action.

Her real problem was that she was doing only a global assessment of Jason and, at that level, it was hard to know if she should praise or punish him. When Linda took the analysis down a level and thought about Jason's ability and motivation for each goal, it was easy to see that his potential for technical problems was very high and his potential as a team player was equally low. When she did a situational analysis to take the teamwork goal down to the task level, she also discovered that Jason had a high potential for some tasks, moderate for others, and low for only a few. Armed with the analysis, she was able to make an action plan to give him recognition for the tasks he performed well, problem solving for the ones at which he was fair, and training for the few that were outside his skill set.

This case is not uncommon. Even though the situational analysis focused only on those tasks that were blocking achievement of a critical goal, the thought process actually started at a higher and more general level. Global assessments aren't dangerous in and of themselves. They are only a problem if you use them to label people instead of to figure out how to get people to perform.

CHANGING STYLES IN THE ELECTRONIC ERA

Another important learning for us has been how technology can impact the way we are perceived as well as how we go about changing those perceptions for the better. We are frequently reminded that the medium can be as important as the message.

We recently witnessed a phenomenon that is occurring all too often in technology-driven organizations. A manager was displeased with the performance of one of his staff on a particular project. The two people involved were seated in an open workspace with adjoining cubicles. Rather than walk over to his direct report, the manager chose to e-mail his dissatisfaction to the person who was performing below expectations. His curt e-mail stated, "Why haven't I received the analysis that was due yesterday? I'm really disappointed in you—I expected better."

The employee, who had been working diligently on the task but had encountered some unexpected technical problems in the software he was using, became furious that his manager had not chosen to have a conversation with him. He got up from his cubicle, turned to his boss, and said, "Why didn't you just tell me you had a problem with what I was doing? I thought I was making good progress. Why don't you just do it yourself if you don't like the way I'm doing it!" Then he stormed off.

In this case the manager inadvertently intensified the problem he already had. His electronic Style 1 was clearly perceived as over-managing. On top of the other factors that were hindering performance, it created a motivation problem that would have to be dealt with in addition to the initial problem. Whatever style was needed to get the work back on track, the manager was going to have to use some Style 3 to listen to this person's frustration—and all that would do was get him back to ground zero.

While technology can be a powerful tool for communicating information, it can be an alienating and demoralizing force when used in the above fashion. As we have mentioned several times, you want to make sure something is in fact broken before you start fixing it. What the above situation did was break the trust between manager and employee and weaken the person's motivation by diminishing his interest in the task, his confidence, his willingness to accept responsibility, and maybe even his alignment with organizational goals.

While technology can speed things up, it can also slow things down. A rule of thumb when dealing with people problems is the more personal the better. Person to person is best, phone is second best; resort to electronic communication only if necessary. Whichever medium you use, two things are important: an accurate assessment of the situation prior to talking to the other person about the problem, and two-way communication about how to best improve performance. Situational analysis can help you with the first challenge, and face-to-face communication can help you with the second one.

Performance contracting is another tool that makes it easy to have those performance-related conversations.

PERFORMANCE CONTRACTING: AN EVEN MORE POWERFUL TOOL

If you liked situational analysis, you will love *performance contracting*. This structure gives you a simple way to empower the people on your team to tell you what they need. It is also a very useful tool for leading upward so that you can tell your manager when you need support and what kinds of support you need. It is an easy way to put the 1-4-3-2 empowerment cycle into practice with your people while getting for yourself the empowerment you want from your boss.

Unlike situational analysis, which you do on your own by assessing a team member's potential and then changing your styles to match that assessment, performance contracting is not done on your own. This process gets other people 100 percent involved.

Step 1

The first step is to identify goals. Do you ever take it for granted that people know what you want? Have you ever given an assignment, only to find out later that what seemed perfectly clear to you was actually ambiguous to the other person?

If you have had these experiences, then you understand why it is important to do Step 1 and even more important to do it with the person who will be responsible for completing the assignment. Step 1 of the performance contracting process is nothing more than a little bit of common sense that often gets overlooked. Just sit down with each member of your team and clarify expectations. What needs to get done, and when is it due?

Step 2

Have you ever discovered at the last minute that an important step in the process was left out? Have you ever been shocked because a procedure that is second nature to you was totally ignored? Have you ever been amazed that the entire approach to a problem was ill advised? If clarifying goals is sometimes taken for granted, understanding how the work will get done is overlooked even more frequently. And if you don't know how the work will be done, there is a high probability that you and your staff will be out of sync with each other.

So, after you have explained what needs to be done and when it is due, the next step is to be sure that you know how the team member plans to achieve the goal. If the plan is all right, you can sign off on it. If it isn't, you can offer feedback.

In Step 2, you should let the team member take the lead so that you can learn how he/she is going to approach the assignment. Most often this is done in conversation simply by asking how the team member plans to get the job done. Sometimes it may be better to have him or her write down the major tasks that are needed to achieve the goal. Whether you discuss the plan or write it down, the important thing is for the person who owns the contract to tell you the actions he or she plans to take to deliver the desired results in the necessary time frame.

Step 3

Once you understand and approve of the way the work is going to get done, you have to identify the type of leadership that will guarantee your team member's success—Step 3. It is very unlikely that you have had this type of conversation because this topic is almost never discussed up front. If it is talked about, it is usually done behind your back or after the fact when it is too late to do anything other than learn for the next time.

Step 3 should start with the team member's assessment of what he or she needs from you followed by a candid discussion with you about the leadership styles needed for each task. Should you do everything that your people ask you to do? Certainly not! But when you get a proposal, it's important to listen before you react. Then, if you don't agree with the proposal, speak up. If you want more input to certain tasks or want to make a key decision, it's important to say so. Or, conversely, if you want the team member to handle some tasks with less involvement from you, it's all right to say that. The important thing is to reconcile any discrepancies so that you are in sync before the assignment begins.

To determine which leadership style is most appropriate for each task, the first question is, "Is support needed?" If the answer is no, the team member can do that task alone, which means he or she needs Style 4 from you.

If the answer is yes, the team member should tell you the type of support that is needed. Remember, when people ask for support, it can mean anything from the ability and motivation checklists. Support can mean technical advice, interpersonal coaching about a difficult employee or a tough customer, clarifying management expectations or customer requirements, or using organizational contacts or power. Support can also mean prioritizing interests, encouraging confidence, providing incentives (carrots or sticks) to stimulate willingness to take on responsibility, or simply listening and signing off to confirm alignment.

Whenever support is needed, it is also important to clarify who is responsible for making critical decisions. Ambiguity about this question is one of the biggest sources of organizational conflicts. So you have to go on to the second question, "Who is responsible for decision making?" If the team member can make the decision, then Style 3 is needed to provide whatever support is necessary. If you need to make the decision or simply want to make the decision, then Style 2 is needed so that you can make a well-informed decision.

Step 4

This final step is to set critical checkpoints so that you are both clear about when you need to communicate to guarantee adequate support and timely decision making. Perhaps the most important step, this helps the team member and you set milestones and plan your time efficiently. It also helps you avoid last-minute mad dashes to the goal line or being hit with unexpected problems at the eleventh hour.

Paperwork Reduction

Some people have expressed a fear that performance contracts will lead to lots of extra paperwork. We always emphasize to them that *it's not necessary to write a contract for every organizational goal*. In fact, it's not even desirable. If you did, you would probably drive yourself and everyone around you crazy.

Most of the time the questions should just be used as a guide for short conversations about the work that needs to be done. Ten minutes here, fifteen minutes there, to keep you and your team members focused and well coordinated.

Occasionally, if you have a new employee or someone with a performance problem, have had some conflicts with one of your people, or need to coordinate a large project, you might want to use the process more formally. But these are the exceptions, not the rule. Most performance contracts are short discussions at the beginning of an assignment or project. The two people cover the key points, understand who is going to do what, and establish ways to stay in touch with each other as the contract unfolds. It is that simple!

TRY OUT PERFORMANCE CONTRACTING FOR YOURSELF

The best way for you to understand the performance contracting process is from a team member's perspective. If you try out the process on a goal you have to accomplish, it will help you show members of your team how to use it with their goals.

Think about yourself in relation to your manager. Focus on one goal for which you are accountable. The process is most useful if you pick a goal that requires you to get some degree of support from your manager. If you don't need any involvement from him or her, you won't learn much about how the performance contracting process works.

In the spaces below, make some notes about the deliverables and time frames for this area of responsibility.

---

1. Goal What goal needs to be achieved? By when?

Deliverables	Time Frames
_____	_____
_____	_____
_____	_____
_____	_____

Then identify the major tasks you have to accomplish to produce the expected results. Try to list them in chronological order so it will help you view the sequence of events that will enable you to complete the project.

---

2. Tasks What tasks need to be accomplished to achieve this goal?

T1 _____

T2 _____

T3 _____

T4 _____

T5 _____

In Step 3, think about the leadership style that you need from your manager by asking yourself the two questions in the worksheet on the next page. First, is support needed? If not, just check Style 4 and stop.

If support is needed, write down the type of support that you need. The most frequently requested types of support in terms of ability are technical advice, interpersonal coaching, clarifying expectations, or organizational power. In terms of motivation, people most often need prioritizing interests, encouraging confidence, incentives to stimulate willingness, or listening to sign off on alignment. But don't feel limited to these lists. In your own words, note any support thsat you think you need.

Whenever you need some involvement from your manager, go on to the second question to be clear about who should make the key decisions. If it is you with your manager's input, check Style 3. If it is your manager with input from you, check Style 2.

---

3. Leadership Styles If the answer to the support question is NO, check Style 4. If the answer to the support question is YES, write in the type of support that is needed, then answer the responsibility question and check Style 3 or Style 2.

	Is Support Needed?		Who Is Responsible for Decisions?	
	NO = Style 4	YES = What Type?	Team Member = Style 3	Team Leader = Style 2
T1	_____	_____	_____	_____
T2	_____	_____	_____	_____
T3	_____	_____	_____	_____
T4	_____	_____	_____	_____
T5	_____	_____	_____	_____

Finally, in Step 4, identify the critical checkpoints for meeting with your manager to make this contract work.

---

4. Critical Checkpoints What are the key dates for communicating support, making timely decisions, and/or providing recognition for performance?

Key Dates	Actions
_____	_____
_____	_____
_____	_____
_____	_____

WHAT TYPES OF SUPPORT DO YOU NEED?

What types of support did you need to achieve the goal in this exercise? Now think about the rest of your work, the other goals for which you're accountable. What types of support do you need to achieve those goals? Technical advice? Interpersonal coaching? Clarifying expectations? Organizational contacts or power? Prioritizing interests? Encouraging confidence? A carrot or stick to take on responsibility? Listening or sign-offs?

When we ask this question to groups of managers, everyone from first - line supervisors to CEOs says they need support. Almost everyone says that they need advice, expectations, power, prioritizing, and sign-offs. And many people say they need every type of support at one time or another.

It is important to remember this point. Most people say they need support, and their needs are probably not much different from yours.

If your people were reading this chapter, what do you think they would say they need? Even though they might have stronger needs in certain areas, there is a high probability that they would want essentially the same things you do. Remember that the next time you talk with them. If you have these needs, chances are they do, too.

And if your managers were reading this chapter, they would probably say the same thing. So the next time you hesitate to ask your boss for what you need, remember that he or she is just as human as you are. If your manager needs support from time to time, why shouldn't you? And isn't it better to ask for what you need than to pretend that you don't need anything and then fail when you try to do it all yourself?

Sometimes, we mistakenly assume that the goal is for everyone to be able to function on his or her own. We fantasize about hiring a workforce of all P4s so that we can just turn them loose and have everything done to perfection. The reality is that if people could do everything on their own without any support, they would probably be bored. More important, if your organization is doing cutting-edge work and people are being asked to stretch, take risks, and go the extra mile, you have to assume that everyone will need some types of support.

Performance contracting simply acknowledges this reality and makes it legitimate for people at all levels to ask for what they need. It also makes it easy for leaders like you to respond appropriately.

DO MANAGERS REALLY USE PERFORMANCE CONTRACTS?

Sure they do. Many managers tell us that this structure has helped them learn how to clarify goals and roles with those who report to them directly. Others say that even though they have been setting goals for years, performance contracts have enabled them to integrate leadership discussions into the existing planning process.

Here is one example of a manager who has gotten great results from the performance contracting process.

Bob is the director of an organization development department in a Fortune 500 manufacturing company. One of his primary responsibilities is starting and supporting self-directed work teams throughout North America. To achieve his goals, he has to work with lots of people from all over the organization. Most of them report to other people, so when Bob needs their involvement in his projects, he has to be as clear as possible about what he wants and prepared to help these people see the work through to completion.

Recently, Bob asked Dave to help him start a newsletter to keep the teams from different sites around the country up-to-date on new developments. Dave reports to Bob 50 percent of the time and works for two other managers the rest of the time. Needless to say, Dave is in demand and has to do a lot of juggling to keep up with all of his assignments.

Initially, when Bob asked Dave to handle the newsletter project, he just told him that he wanted a newsletter developed and wanted Dave to spearhead the effort. Shortly after that, L4 was introduced to all of the managers who were implementing work teams, and Bob and Dave decided to try out performance contracting to see how it worked.

Step 1 helped both Bob and Dave clarify their understanding of the goal. Initially, Bob had been somewhat vague about what he envisioned the newsletter would look like and when he was hoping to have it distributed. That vagueness had left Dave with the impression that he could develop the concept in whatever way he wanted and that time was not essential on this project. This Step 1 discussion enabled Bob to be much clearer about his expectations, and Dave left the meeting knowing what Bob had in mind in terms of content, format, and timing.

Step 2 was even more illuminating for both of them. Bob had not realized how complex the assignment was until he and Dave listed all of the tasks. Dave had not known exactly how to get started until he thought through the steps with Bob. This discussion actually transformed the assignment for both leader and team member. For Bob, the newsletter changed from a simple request to a complex endeavor. For Dave, it changed from a big and amorphous weight to a sequence of manageable tasks.

Step 3 was also enlightening for them. Bob's original tossing of the ball to Dave was based on the assumption that Style 4 was fine for someone with Dave's level of experience in the company. But when they talked, it became clear that both of them were more comfortable with Bob's using Style 2. In truth, Bob really felt the need to control this first edition. He certainly wanted major input from Dave, but since the whole project was on political thin ice, he needed to protect himself and the project's future. Dave felt the same way. He was happier with Style 2 as the general approach.

After that discussion about who had the final word, they started looking at the specific tasks. Here they found that Bob really only wanted to use Style 2 in the beginning to outline the format and at the end to have final approval of the copy. Other than that, he was willing to use Style 4 and let Dave handle the other steps on his own. Dave was all right with that for most of the tasks, but there was one for which he needed Bob's organizational knowledge about who was involved in successful teams and who might be good contributors to the newsletter.

So after Step 3, instead of using Style 4, abdicating on the whole project, Bob knew that he had to use Style 2 in the beginning and the end, and he knew what support he had to give Dave so he could take responsibility for the other tasks.

Step 4, setting critical checkpoints, also turned out to be important for this particular project. First, it gave Bob and Dave some clear milestones to shoot for. That helped Dave organize his time so that he could manage this project as well as the requests from his other managers. It also enabled Dave to renegotiate the timing on one part of the project when a death in the family slowed him down unexpectedly. Since he and Bob had prescheduled checkpoints, it needed only a routine conversation for them to make an adjustment.

Throughout this entire process, all Bob and Dave wrote down were meeting times in their calendars. The initial meeting took about thirty minutes, and subsequent meeting times varied depending on how the project was moving forward.

Since then, Bob has used performance contracts with several other people. His rule of thumb is not to use the structure for short-term assignments or routine requests. If he has a project that will span a longer time period, especially if he is working with someone new, these up-front meetings have set the stage for clear expectations and open communications throughout the implementation.

A SYSTEMS APPROACH TO PERFORMANCE CONTRACTS

While Bob preferred using the performance contract as an informal conversation guide, some organizations have integrated this process into their formal planning and development structures.

One such organization is the management information services (MIS) of a large insurance company. This entire department, from senior vice president to first-line supervisors, participated in a teambuilding session with L4 as the foundation for the team's development. During the session, each participant formulated at least one performance contract with his or her manager. Participants also identified other initiatives that required more complete discussions back at the office.

After that, all the employees in the department attended an L4 workshop with their supervisors so they would understand the performance contract process and learn the value of leading upward with their supervisors.

This is not uncommon. But what this department did next was remarkable. One of their functions in the company was reducing paperwork by putting procedures and forms onto their computer systems. So they created a personal computer format for performance contracts, the PC version of PCs. Every level of manager then was instructed to clarify goals with each of his or her direct reports and enter the performance contracts into the system by a certain date. That way the department could track who was doing what and systematically provide the support and timely decision making that each contract required.

For the record, that insurance company is one of the most profitable in the world. And the MIS department has played a significant role in keeping that company close to its customers and on the cutting edge of its niche in the industry.

A PC ULTIMATUM

Another Fortune 500 company, this one in the financial services industry, was going through major organizational changes. Some products were no longer competitive, others weren't being marketed as well as they could have been, and the old guard of the company had grown up in a very conservative and risk-averse culture.

Organizational change efforts usually come down to changing some fundamental behaviors on the part of managers. And often that means changing the reward system that has fostered some out-of-date ways of thinking and acting.

In this instance, the executive vice president of a major division had been doing everything he could to get his management team to change. Finally, at one meeting, he said to them, "You know what the problem is? You guys have been getting rewarded for other people's work for too long now. If they perform, your departments meet their goals and you get your bonuses. But no one is stretching and you guys are doing nothing to challenge your people or develop them."

The managers had heard this speech before, so they were just taking it in stride until the EVP added, "So from now on, each of you is required to make performance contracts with every one of your direct reports. The PCs need to set forth challenging goals for every individual, and if your people can handle their objectives without your help, the goals are too easy."

This started to catch their attention. The next line was the kicker. "And from now on, you will be evaluated on the goals you set with your people and how well you support your people's efforts to achieve them. Their input to me will determine your next year's bonuses."

That was the beginning of serious change management.

YOU HAVE TO SPEND TIME TO SAVE TIME

The senior managers of the engineering department of a Fortune 500 aerospace company decided to learn the L4 System because middle managers and supervisors in the department were using the Leader's Window to organize their teams. Michael, the EVP of the department, the SVPs who reported to him, and the VPs who worked for them were all taking the two-day training together. While they all professed an interest in leadership and participated actively in the course, it was also clear that these senior leaders did not want to be there.

In their minds, training was for people at lower levels of the organization who didn't have all the answers yet. Before, during, and after each session, we heard comments like, "We don't have time for this stuff," or "We don't even have time to be here." One SVP put it bluntly: "If you understood our industry, you would know that we don't do this people stuff. Either people perform or we get rid of them."

On the morning of the second day, we taught them about performance contracts and gave them an exercise to practice using the PC process. In this practice session, three of the SVPs, including the blunt one, ended up in a group with their boss, Michael. Afterwards, we asked if anyone had found the structure helpful, and all three of them waved their hands enthusiastically.

Not knowing what they would say and knowing that Michael was the one signing our check, we cautiously worked the other end of the room to make sure there were lots of positive testimonials about the process before the SVPs shared their experiences.

When we finally called on them, all three reported that they got more done with Michael in the five-minute PC discussion than they usually get done in an hour. We asked them what was different, and there were two things. First, before talking to their boss, they spent five minutes thinking about what they could do on their own and what they needed from him. That enabled them to be more focused than usual about what they needed him to do. Second, Michael stayed on their agenda instead of doing what he usually did—talking about his agenda for fifty-nine minutes of their hour together and leaving them one minute for theirs while his secretary dragged them out of his office.

Delighted with what we heard, we turned to Michael and said, "If performance contracts allow you to get more done in five minutes than you usually get done in sixty, we just gave you back fifty-five minutes on the hour. What's that kind of time worth to you?" He smiled and replied, "I guess this means we'll have to pay you now."

THE ONE-SECOND PERFORMANCE CONTRACT

If you want speed, try this technique for negotiating leadership styles that has been perfected by Dick, who is a national director of a large department, and Paul, one of the directors who works for him. Dick and Paul have only worked together for a couple of years but have developed a good rapport and usually see eye-to-eye on most critical issues. Even though they have a close working relationship, they work in a very hierarchical organization that requires the checking and double-checking of most decisions. So Paul needs to get sign-offs from Dick on many issues.

Their performance contracting technique is very simple. Paul walks into Dick's office with a problem that he wants to explain so that Dick can make a well-informed decision. As he reviews the situation and makes his recommendation, he holds up two fingers to indicate that he is just giving input and understands that this is Dick's domain for making decisions.

If Dick is okay with that, he also holds up two fingers. But more often than not, as the explanation unfolds, Dick switches to three fingers to let Paul know that he will offer Paul his input but really prefers that Paul make the decision.

Sometimes, Dick holds up four fingers, and Paul just stops explaining the problem because he knows Dick doesn't want to hear any more about it and Paul has clearance to decide as he sees fit.

And on occasion, Dick holds up one finger. That means that they should both save their breath. It is a done deal from above and there isn't a thing either one of them can do about it.

Then Paul holds up five fingers and they go out for a drink.

INTERNATIONAL PCs

Henry wasn't fast—he was thorough, and extremely effective. When we met him, he was the VP of a worldwide division of a Fortune International 500 company that manufactures industrial building materials. His team was as virtual as they get—he was based in Germany, but only six of his nineteen direct reports worked in the same country. His direct reports, who were responsible for three businesses, included people from Germany, Italy, France, England, Scandinavia, Czechoslovakia, India, Japan, and the United States.

In his previous positions in the United States, Henry had used PCs with great success and even developed a reputation around the company as "the performance contract guy." What did he like about PCs? He said, "They force my directs and me to think hard about what their jobs are. In effect, it results in a thorough job description as we have in-depth discussions about questions like:

- What aspects of the business are you responsible for?

- What can you do to improve the business?

- What is the right priority of the 4-5 goals decided upon?

- What will you need from me to achieve those goals?

- How will we measure results at six- and twelve-month intervals?

- What is my view of high and low performance?

- What achievement will make you the most proud?"

Since Henry's performance contracts were for annual goals, in the first year he spent an average of four to five hours on each one, and a few required as much as seven or eight hours. In subsequent years, the process required little time, even if priorities for the overall businesses changed. At the most, it demanded a bit of rewriting of the previous year's goals. Given the geographic spread, he met with some only once, for the initial meeting, and then completed the PC via e-mail, faxes, and phone calls.

For Henry, the contract was just the beginning. His entire process consisted of preparing the written PC, letting people perform against the contract, coaching them as required, completing mid-term and year-end reviews, and rewarding/recognizing their achievements. It was time-consuming but, to quote Henry, "worth every minute of the time. It creates powerful alignment between my goals and theirs. I have certainty that people know exactly what they will be held accountable for."

Expanding on that, he said, "While seemingly labor intensive, the process actually saves me time. It also fosters an environment of empowerment and enables me to move from S1 to S4 more rapidly. It allows me to focus on expanding people's capabilities by giving me time for coaching and developing people. It also makes performance appraisals so easy as people know exactly how they're doing—they know by October what they'll get in terms of bonus and rating."

Henry also required all of his direct reports to create performance contracts with the people they managed. Why? Henry said, "The initiatives that will have the greatest impact on the business are identified and that ensures achievement of the core goals of our businesses as well as those of the overall enterprise. People know which priorities to focus on the most—it's clear that achieving numbers one and two will be more important than nailing four and five. People know exactly what matters and they can measure incrementally the progress they're making."

His other reason for requiring PCs at the next level was the impact the process had on teamwork. "Performance contracts get people pulling in the same direction. Since many of the same goals appear on most, if not all, of the contracts, it gives everyone a sense of being in it together."

Since his people were from so many different cultural backgrounds, it is not surprising that Henry met with resistance from some of his managers, especially the French ones, who saw the technique as an American approach. Being a true believer, he forged ahead, and gradually even the French managers came around—but only when they saw that their employees liked the process. One of them admitted, "It drove clarity and set priorities. This was refreshing to them as they had been used to numerous and shifting goals from past bosses. It has proven to be a powerful motivator."

PCs AND THE FREE-AGENT ECONOMY

Almost every time we ask a group of managers about the leadership challenges they face, someone will ask, "How do you motivate this new generation?" It wasn't so long ago that the baby boomers (born between WWII and the mid-sixties) were changing the corporate landscape. These days it's Generation X (born between the mid-sixties and late seventies) that we hear about. A new wave, Generation Y, also called Generation Next, has just begun to enter the workforce, and you can be sure that another one isn't far behind.

One way of answering this motivation question is to explain how the generations differ. The following comparisons, compiled by Rene Carew, a Charter Oak consultant who specializes in leading a diverse workforce, highlight the differences between baby boomers and GenXers.

BOOMERS	**GENXERS**
• Loyal to organization	• Loyal to own skills
• Paid dues	• No need to pay dues
• Play by the rules	• Play by their own rules
• Time put in is important	• Results are all-important
• Knowledge of the business	• Knowledge of computers
• Solve problems with experience	• Solve problems with technical skills
• Long-term view	• Short attention span
• Perform tasks thoroughly	• Perform tasks quickly
• One thing at a time	• Multi-task
• Process oriented	• Just-in-time oriented
• Work the hierarchy	• Work their networks

The first four items could apply to any group that is moving into an established culture and are the same things the veterans said about boomers when they were invading the workforce. Beyond those first items, there are some serious differences, but you have to be careful about what you do with them. We know that these differences do not apply to every person in the GenX age bracket—they are generalizations at best. We also know that these descriptors apply to people of all ages who have jumped into the new economy.

These days, people go where their skills are needed and sell their experience to the highest bidder. The old compact between worker and employer is gone. It's no secret that corporations will downsize if they don't need you, and individuals have learned that their only job security is their knowledge and skills. Many have also learned that their pay goes up much faster if they change employers every few years.

What we have now is a "free-agent" workforce, where every organization is struggling with attracting, developing, and retaining talent. This is highly visible in the sports world, where the war for talent has been raging for years. In the business world, it is most prevalent in IT departments, where technical skills are increasingly hard to find.

The dramatic economic growth of the 1990s has accelerated this trend into every aspect of the business world. Like the GenXers, these free agents want to use their technical skills and computer savvy, respond to challenging problems that need a quick solution, and be valued for immediate contributions. They also want flexible working conditions and opportunities to develop new skills.

In exit interviews with departing IT professionals, the five most frequently cited reasons for moving on were (5) location; (4) opportunities to develop skills; (3) new responsibilities; (2) different work schedules. And the number one reason? Their manager. What did they want from a manager?

Most wanted challenging assignments, flexibility to manage their responsibilities, recognition for accomplishments, feedback about problems so they could learn quickly, and a willingness to talk openly about the support they needed for task accomplishment and career development. All the aspects of work that the "performance contract guy" managed so well in the last story.

Doug was a gifted programmer whose story can shed some light on what can happen when a free agent collides with a culture steeped in tradition. Doug was a technical manager working in the HR division of a large consulting company. He had IT responsibilities for the human-resource management function in a firm that had experienced dramatic growth globally. Throughout the 1990s the firm had grown to the point where it had 700 outposts, including ones in every major city plus many remote locations worldwide. The firm was faced with the formidable task of creating human-resource management systems that met the diverse needs of its consulting staff in different parts of the world.

Doug began to experience some disconnects between his view of the world and the organization's from the day he started working there. During his orientation, Doug was introduced to the organization by being told what the "rules" for success were. He was told that his success would be predicated on the extent to which he embraced that which the firm held sacred and the extent to which he fully understood the business they were in. Since Doug was the independent type—typical of many GenXers—he bristled at the thought of "learning the rules" and didn't really understand the emphasis placed on learning the business. He saw himself as a technologist there to do a job.

As the months went by Doug's initial concerns about whether this was the right environment for him continued to grow. His efforts to get new software installed and running—with the intent of working out the kinks along the way—were consistently sabotaged by his boss's insistence that no program be rolled out until it was perfect and free of flaws. His tendency to leave work at 5:00 to pick up his son from daycare was frowned upon—even though he often put in three to four hours of work at home on his laptop after dinner.

He became tired of being on the receiving end of directives from his boss regarding how to spend his time and found his boss's propensity for holding regular staff meetings a distraction from what he considered his real work.

Eventually, Doug left the firm and started his own software company. Working in this freewheeling environment, he was very successful, and two years later he sold his company to a larger IT firm. In an ironic twist of fate, after the acquisition Doug took on his former employer as a client.

As a client, Doug's former employers dealt with him very differently from the way they had treated him as an employee. First, they gave him a specific assignment to work on, with clear deliverables and time frames established.

Then they asked him to lay out a project plan that they signed off on. They also insisted on knowing what roles they needed to play to make sure he hit the milestones in his plan. As he told them what he needed, he also insisted on knowing what decisions he could make on his own, where they wanted to have input, and when they preferred to get his input to their decisions.

Does this sound familiar? It should. Without knowing it, Doug's former employers were following all the steps of the performance contracting process, and these simple steps made Doug feel very different. He could apply his skills to problems that needed immediate solutions, and he had a lot of control over how the work got done and the flexibility to work on his own schedule—all the responsibility without the corporate trappings. This was far more motivational than what he had experienced as an employee, and, as a result, he spent even more of his time helping the company fix its seriously flawed human-resource information systems.

The lesson for the large consulting firm was that if they had dealt with Doug as a unique individual when he was their employee, they would have gotten the long-term benefit of his knowledge and skills at a fraction of the cost. The lesson for all managers who are struggling with attracting, developing, and retaining talent in the free-agent economy is that if PCs work with a virtual, multicultural team operating on three continents, they can also work within one country with people of different generations.

PC DIVERSITY

A footnote to this story is a reminder that all GenXers, and all free agents, are not alike, and it is always important not to stereotype any group of people. Remember the general manager in the last chapter who discovered that he was using 100 percent Style 3 with the women who worked for him? He was treating them all the same way but not dealing with them as people.

Many managers fall into a similar trap. With the best of intentions, they treat a group of people as a class of citizens instead of distinct individuals. We see stereotyping based on profession (accounting, engineering, marketing, clerical), department (manufacturing, sales, finance, IT), level (executive, manager, supervisor, worker), affiliation (core staff, temp, vendor, consultant), and location (home office, field, top floor, basement). We also see people classified according to gender, race, religion, ethnicity, and sexual orientation.

None of this grouping is very helpful. Our strongest caution is to be sensitive to the needs of people who are different from you while treating each person as the unique individual he or she is. The performance contracting process not only will help you manage performance; it is also a tool for working productively with an increasingly diverse workforce.

TRY IT, YOU'LL LIKE IT

The next step is to find your own way to make this process work. With the written structure or without ever writing a single word, with on-the-fly discussions or annual performance plans, the performance contract process can help you be a more effective leader. Just remember the four steps:

- First, you always need to be clear about *what* needs to get done.
- Second, you need to know *how* other people are planning to do it.
- Third, you need to know *who* is going to do what to make sure the plan is completed.
- Fourth, you need to be clear about *when* you need to communicate to ensure performance.

Answering these questions will help you put The L4 System into practice. These questions will also help you implement the 1-4-3-2 empowerment cycle. First, you clarify expectations (Style 1). Then you determine what people can do on their own (Style 4). Then you create a game plan for providing support when it is needed (Style 3) and for making those decisions that you need or want to make (Style 2).

To put it simply, performance contracting takes the guesswork out of working with individuals.

The Personality Prism: Seeing the World Through Other People's Windows

CHAPTER 11

In the last chapter, we talked about the performance contracting process as a structure for implementing the 1-4-3-2 empowerment cycle. It establishes predictability in the way you communicate with the individuals on your team. It is a set of moves that enables you to do what best leaders have been doing for a long time. And it is a process that works in most situations with most people.

Are we telling you to treat all people the same way? In some ways, we are. A predictable pattern of communicating is important. It helps if everyone knows what is expected, what can be done alone, what kind of support is needed, and when you will get together for developing and problem solving.

We also know that everyone is a distinct individual and that the way these predictable steps are played out needs to be adapted to enable team members to work to the best of their potential. How you go about setting expectations, what you do to make people feel supported, even the media you use for communication needs to be personalized if you are going to truly get the best from each person.

People are unique. Even though we know a lot about the basic needs that apply to everyone we work with, we also know that these needs get met in varying ways. We can be scientific about the predictable steps that need to be followed, but we also have to be artistic in the way we implement those steps.

In this chapter, we will explore a powerful way to understand and appreciate individual differences. The *Myers-Briggs Type Indicator* (MBTI®) instrument is one of the most widely used tools around the world and provides a useful framework for looking at human personalities. When used in conjunction with the empowerment cycle, it can help you personalize the way you go about giving directions and providing support.

THE MBTI INSTRUMENT:
A TOOL FOR UNDERSTANDING
DIFFERENT TYPES OF PEOPLE

In their *Introduction to Type* in Organizations* (1998), Hirsh and Kummerow state that "The MBTI provides a useful method for understanding people by look-ing at eight personality preferences that everyone uses at different times." These preferences anchor the four scales or dichotomies of the model: Extraversion (E) versus Introversion (I), Sensing (S) versus Intuition (N), Thinking (T) ver-sus Feeling (F), and Judging (J) versus Perceiving (P).

Most of the literature about type associates these scales with activities of daily life. The E–I preference indicates how you get energized, with Extraverts (E's) turning to people and conversations to recharge their batteries and Introverts (I's) looking inward for some quiet to recharge theirs. The S–N preference is a guide to what you pay attention to. Sensing people (S's) focus on the practical realities of the present, while Intuitive individuals (N) are more interested in imagining possibilities for the future. The T–F preference pertains to the way you make decisions, with Thinking people (T's) employing logic in the objective pursuit of right answers and Feeling people (F's) embrac-ing the personal impact of a decision in order to preserve harmony. Finally, the J–P preference has to do with lifestyle, with Judging individuals (J's) choos-ing an orderly and structured existence and Perceiving people (P's) being more inclined to take things as they come.

We have found that these four sets of preferences have more meaning for managers when they are linked to the process of identifying and solving prob-lems or discovering and planning for opportunities. E's and I's have different ways of engaging with problems or opportunities. S's and N's take different approaches to diagnosing a current situation and analyzing the options for going forward. T's and F's have different ways of evaluating alternatives and deciding which ones will lead to the best solution. J's and P's employ different tactics for implementing decisions and monitoring progress.

As you use the performance contracting process to empower the people who work for you, it can be extremely helpful to know something about a team member's preferences. This is helpful on the front end of the process when you are setting direction, and on the back end when you are trying to provide support. What other people need to get launched may not be the same as what you need, and what is supportive for you may actually be a dis-traction for someone else. In fact, disconnects abound when you find your-self and someone you are trying to lead at opposite ends of any of the four scales. Customizing your approach to the 1-4-3-2 process will dramatically increase your effectiveness in working with people.

WHAT DOES IT MEAN
TO HAVE A PREFERENCE?

It is important to know that while each of us has a preference on all four scales—E–I, S–N, T–F, and J–P—some preferences are strong and others are moderate. In addition, even strong preferences are not absolutes. Most of us behave in ways that are associated with all eight preferences, and all of us can learn how to act in non-preferred ways.

It is useful to think of each preference as the equivalent of a dominant hand. Most of us are right-handed or left-handed, and signing our name or moving a cursor with our preferred hand is an effortless activity. But try signing your name or aligning your computer's cursor with your other hand—or hitting a tennis ball, throwing a pitch, drawing a picture, or even brushing your teeth. It feels awkward and uncomfortable. You have to be very deliberate and focus your thoughts. It takes longer and the results aren't as good. That's why you have learned to use your dominant hand.

The same is true for each scale. It's as if you have four dominant hands. When it comes to problem solving, you have a preference for the way you become aware of problems in your environment. You have a preference for the way you go about analyzing problems or opportunities and generating alternatives for solving the problems or pursuing the opportunities. You have a preference for the way you evaluate those alternatives and make a choice about the best solution. And you have a preference for the way you go about implementing the solution you have chosen.

When you are in a situation that allows you to use your preferences, you work as effortlessly as when signing your name with your dominant hand. When forced to operate in your non-dominant mode, it is just as challenging as using your other hand. When you are with people whose preferences are different from yours, it is easy to wonder what's wrong with them and make judgments about their deficiencies. It is also common to put yourself down and label yourself as inadequate.

Acceptance is better than condemnation. The truth is that you can do lots of things with your non-dominant hand. If you were to break your dominant hand you would learn quickly, developing skill and agility with the hand that has been underutilized for so many years. You could do it, but it would take some time and effort. In a work world that prizes efficiency, most of us don't take the time to overcome the pitfalls of our personalities. We focus instead on short-term results. In a work world that is concerned about retaining talent, developing people's full capabilities, and producing long-term results, it is imperative that we make the effort to develop our weaker hands and learn how to work with people outside our comfort zones.

WHAT IS TYPE?

Your preferences on the E–I, S–N, T–F, and J–P scales create one of sixteen possible four-letter combinations (like ESTJ or INFP) that are referred to as types. There is a wealth of wonderful published material describing the types as well as their strengths and weaknesses. One that we use frequently with our clients is *Introduction to Type in Organizations* (Hirsh and Kummerow 1998), which describes each type in terms of contributions to the organization, leadership style, learning style, problem-solving approach, preferred work environment, pitfalls, and suggestions for development. It is amazing how accurate these descriptions can be.

The best way to start learning about your type is to take the MBTI instrument. It can help you clarify your preference on each of the four scales and determine your four-letter type. Remember that the instrument is exactly what it claims to be, an *indicator* and not the ultimate measure of type. Professionals who work with type always caution people not to rely exclusively on the instrument to validate their type. For many people, especially those who have moderate preferences on one or more scales, it can take a lot of time to do that.

If it is hard to determine your own type, imagine how difficult it is to figure out everyone else's. And even if you know everyone's type, it is also hard to remember what each of the sixteen types is all about. It is too much information for most managers to keep straight, much less use in their day-to-day interactions.

For these reasons, we keep our focus on the preferences themselves. Realizing that you are caught in an E–I misunderstanding, an S–N debate, a T–F disagreement, or a J–P struggle can help you turn tension into teamwork and conflict into collaboration. Knowing these differences can also help you anticipate other people's needs and communicate with them in ways that work for them. This is particularly useful when you are doing performance contracting with team members. It is also very helpful when you are leading upward with your own manager.

Before we show you how to integrate preferences with the performance contracting process, it will help you to understand the MBTI scales and preferences more completely.

THE E–I PREFERENCE: ENGAGING WITH PROBLEMS/OPPORTUNITIES

Externally oriented people, or Extraverts (E's), become aware of problems in their environment by talking with other people, being actively involved in discussions, and generally being conscious of what is going on outside of them. They like to keep their eye on the horizon so they find out about issues as soon as they come up. When problems or opportunities arise, they like to get out and talk to people to find out what's there. They are likely to get all the stakeholders together to hear everyone's point of view, and they will be actively involved in the discussions as a way of discovering their own ideas. Extraverts are the type of people who take in information through talking.

Internally oriented people, or Introverts (I's), become aware of problems by being aware of their own thoughts and feelings. They may pick up the same cues as Extraverts, but instead of going out and talking to people to find out what's going on, they are more likely to wait for the problem to come to them. And when it does find them, they will want to think about it, study it, and analyze it before they start to talk about it. Introverts absorb information quietly.

One of the ways in which E's and I's polarize concerns how much they seemingly care about organizational problems. Since I's don't talk until they have a solution in mind, E's will often accuse them of not getting involved and not wanting to find out about problems or actively pursue opportunities. Conversely, since E's start talking to discover the parameters of the situation, I's will accuse them of overreacting, calling too many meetings, and not doing their homework before they propose solutions.

If there is mutual understanding and appreciation, everyone benefits from having people with their ears (and mouths) close to the ground and having other people who will weigh all the issues and make a reflective response. If there is no such atmosphere, the likely result is finger-pointing and missed opportunities.

Silent Strategy

Joann had worked her way up to vice president of marketing through an unusual channel. She had been a plant manager and, deciding she wanted a career change, shifted into marketing. This occurred after two years of school and a lot of sweat equity. Unlike many of her colleagues in marketing, Joann was an Introvert. Surrounded by Extraverts, she often found herself listening as others spoke.

Joann and four of her direct reports were sitting at a conference table discussing the strategic direction their marketing department would take in the coming year. During this particular meeting she noticed that each of her four managers seemed to be advocating a different position for the future of the group. After witnessing her usually cooperative charges sparring with one another for over an hour, she called a time-out for a process check.

What she found was quite revealing for all of them. The four managers were taking different positions in an effort to find "the one" that would resonate with their boss. They each assumed that her silence during the meeting reflected her dissatisfaction with their thinking. They also assumed that when someone landed on the right strategy she would let them know.

To the four Extraverts, Joann's silence was deafening. In reality she was doing what Introverts do—listening before speaking. In fact, she found merit in all of her managers' ideas and was spending her time thinking about how to integrate each of their ideas into a coherent plan rather than wasting her breath telling them what she thought about the positions they were advancing.

THE S–N PREFERENCE: ANALYZING PROBLEMS/OPPORTUNITIES

The Sensing–Intuition preference has to do with the way you analyze a situation and generate alternatives for solving a problem or pursuing an opportunity. If your preference is Sensing (S), you do this with your five senses, relying mostly on what you can see, hear, or personally experience. When you analyze a situation, you are very careful to focus on the facts, the details, what is going on now—the current reality—and you are conscious of what the history has been. You usually proceed in a step-by-step manner, and your solutions are always realistic and practical.

If you prefer Intuition (N), you tend to rely on your sixth sense. You trust your instincts and feel more comfortable with a broad understanding than a detailed one. Too many facts can overload you. Your focus is not on the past or the present—you prefer the future and home in on the opportunities. You think about the way things could be and about the possibilities for change. You seek opportunities to do new things that will force you to learn and often identify alternatives that are very creative and outside the box.

Strong N's and S's will often butt heads over generating alternatives. Since N's like opportunities and not only embrace change but like to create it, S's will often accuse them of pie-in-the-sky thinking, stirring up the pot, making change for change's sake, and being unrealistic. S's pride themselves on being down to earth, realistic, and pragmatic, but since they are more likely to focus on refining what's already in the box, N's will accuse them of being stuck in the mud, holding on to the past, hugging the trees, and resisting the winds of change.

With mutual respect, S's and N's can complement each other nicely. Successful organizations need people who can push the limits, test the boundaries, and break the mold. They also need people who are grounded and can turn ideas into practical solutions. What they don't need is people arguing about who's right and who's wrong.

Success Takes All the Senses

Howard was a visionary. His capacity to develop software ideas had helped him create a new company that was the envy of his programming peers.

Howard's secret weapon was Lawrence, who loved detail. Without being consciously aware of the Sensing–Intuition preference, the two of them had managed to harness the power of their differences and leverage them into a thriving business.

In the beginning, Howard started his company alone. He tapped into his formidable idea bank to lure venture capitalists into backing him. Soon after setting up shop Howard became decidedly concerned about his capacity to deliver on his promises. While he was long on ideas, he was short on the discipline to bring any of them to fruition.

He decided he needed some help, and he found that help in Lawrence. While not the creative sort, Lawrence was extremely good at writing code and finding simple, practical ways for resolving complex programming dilemmas. Together, they developed a formula that led to dramatic success for them both. Each time Howard came up with a good idea, he and Lawrence would sit down to discuss it, making sure they both fully understood the parameters of the particular piece of software, including all the required functionality and the accompanying bells and whistles that made their products unique. Lawrence would then go off and breathe life into Howard's vision. Howard would go back into the clouds to discover the next brainchild.

Howard tapped his Intuition to envision new creations. Lawrence used Sensing to turn those ideas into reality. It was a match made in heaven.

THE T–F PREFERENCE: EVALUATING ALTERNATIVES AND MAKING DECISIONS

The Thinking–Feeling preference has to do with the way you evaluate alternatives and make tough decisions. If you have a preference for Thinking (T), you decide with your head, objectively looking for the right answer based on logic. You operate from the premise that there is a right answer to every question, and you are probably a perfectionist—always open to critiquing the way things are in order to make them better. When you make an important decision you always take the broad perspective. You try to be fair by weighing historical precedents and considering the precedents that your decision will establish.

If your preference is Feeling (F), you decide with your heart, based on your feelings and the way the decision will make other people feel. Your decision making is driven by a desire to be kind and to maintain harmony. You are more concerned with doing what's right by people than getting the right answer. When you make an important decision, you take a very personal perspective and consider the immediate impact on yourself and the other people who are affected.

T's and F's can be equally good decision makers. T's don't ignore all feelings but instead include them as one factor as they weigh the pros and cons.

F's don't ignore all reason. In fact, many of their feelings are connected to strongly held beliefs about right and wrong. But they personalize beliefs in terms of human values. By making everybody comfortable, a Feeling person can be as decisive as a Thinking individual who is trying to make everything better. The two types just approach the decision from different perspectives.

As with the other preferences, strong T's and F's can get embroiled in conflicts. T's often accuse F's of being too close to a situation, personalizing decisions, and being fuzzy-minded bleeding hearts. F's in turn describe T's as too removed, impersonal, cold, and calculating. It is easy to see how both perspectives are important. You need people who can be objective and cool in a crisis, but it is just as important to have those who understand the impact of "tough business decisions" on people.

Letting Go Is Hard to Do

We recently observed the impact of integrating the Thinking and Feeling perspectives in one of the more difficult aspects of corporate life. The circumstance was one that many of us have witnessed or been a part of in the volatile global marketplace of the twenty-first century.

The case involved an insurance industry giant that had made the difficult decision to shut down a redundant unit that was the result of a recent merger. The decision to close the unit resulted in the downsizing of a hundred employees.

The senior vice president in charge of the decision was a strong T and concerned about potential sabotage that might occur during the departure of the targeted employees. On the basis of this concern, he planned to assemble the hundred people in an auditorium, announce the decision, and escort them out of the building to their cars. This "act of containment," as he called it, would prevent any sabotage since the people would have no access to their workstations.

The HR manager of this business unit was a strong F and concerned about the emotional impact this "herding" approach would have on these employees, as well as the impact such a "cold" gesture would have on the morale of remaining employees. At the same time, he understood the VP's concern for security and knew that the issue must be addressed. He made a few calls to the IT department and learned that it would be possible to put a lock on the computers of the hundred employees so that they would be denied access beyond a certain point in time. He then approached the VP with a plan that would enable the departing employees to return to their workspaces to gather their personal possessions and say good-bye to co-workers while preserving the security of the department's records.

While it was a difficult situation for all, the balance of Thinking and Feeling considerations left most people believing that it was handled as well as possible for both the departing employees and the organization.

THE J–P PREFERENCE:
IMPLEMENTING DECISIONS

The Judging–Perceiving preference focuses on the way you implement decisions—the conditions that enable you to do your most productive work. If you have a preference for Judging (J), you work best in a structured and organized way. You like objectives, goals, plans, milestones, checklists, and checkpoints. Once you have made a decision, that judgment will drive you forward in a very systematic and deliberate manner. You like closure, and you go into a planning process with the mindset of narrowing down the options and making decisions. Having made those decisions, you will then push forward to implement them, regardless of what comes into your path.

If your preference is Perceiving (P), you will implement a decision more flexibly. You focus on whatever is in the foreground of your perception. You enter the planning process exploring all the options, and you are comfortable keeping the options open, waiting to see what new information enters your perceptual field. As a result, you implement decisions with far greater flexibility than those who prefer Judging. You may arrive at the same goal, but you will pause to deal with other issues you perceive along the way. You are not less precise than a J individual; you are just more likely to focus on several different goals, while the J's focus all their energy on one at a time.

When J's and P's get stuck, they can drive each other crazy. The J's often accuse the P's of being disorganized, messy, unfocused, and not goal-driven, flitting from one thing to the next. P's accuse J's of being controlling, inflexible, unwilling to change direction, unable to work without a plan, and hung up on process instead of getting things done. There is a need for people who can plan, organize, and deliver against goals, but there is also a need for people who can be flexible, adapt, and be responsive to an ever-changing marketplace.

Most organizations have Judging cultures that value structure, order, plans, and predictability. Many tout the virtue of being customer focused and market driven but tend to be more enamored of their internal processes. In contrast, the speedy and more entrepreneurial Internet start-ups are often populated by P's who left or were rejected by the big corporations. No wonder they are quicker and more readily adaptable to a world of constant change.

Minding Your P's in a J World

We recently found ourselves working in a corporation that was typical of the structured, orderly, and planful Judging approach mentioned above. The company, a successful manufacturer of construction equipment, had embarked recently on expanding into the Internet marketplace to grow the "click and mortar" side of the business. To that end, it had launched two initiatives that inadvertently ended up working at cross-purposes.

The first initiative was a drive to become an "employer of choice" for new IT professionals, an effort to recruit and retain the best and the brightest in an increasingly competitive marketplace. While the company did many things right, like offer competitive compensation, state-of-the-art technology, and attractive benefits packages, it did one thing that had a negative impact on getting and keeping some of the people it had targeted.

This had to do with the second initiative, a quality program targeted at streamlining the offices throughout the organization. Beginning immediately, all offices were required to adhere to a set of standards concerning the type and amount of furniture and accessories allowed in individual offices. In effect, all offices would be furnished with the same items, and there would be little room for personalization of one's space.

In addition, some new procedures were instituted, of which the most disconcerting was a new practice designed to create order and minimize a "chaotic frame of mind" within the corporate walls. To that end, the custodial staff started moving through the offices every evening and cleaning off all the desks. Anything left on any desk and not properly filed away was thrown in the trash.

While many of the Judging recruits thought the plan was a bit extreme, it made sense to them, and they were willing to comply. For them, cleaning off their desk at the end of the day was a common practice, and uniformly providing them with the best tools to get the work done was very logical.

For the Perceiving recruits, the quality initiative was anathema. They could not imagine being restricted regarding what they could have in their offices. The idea of cleaning off their desks every night was inconceivable. And the notion that they could not choose new tools with which to do their work convinced them that their new employer was a dinosaur unworthy of their talents. So most of them left and the company found itself in a recruiting and retention crisis that resulted from insensitivity to the need of many of their new employees for openness and flexibility in the way they do their work.

USING PREFERENCES WHEN PROVIDING DIRECTION

The first step in performance contracting is to make sure the team member who is taking on a responsibility is clear about expectations. He or she needs to know what the deliverables are and when they are due. In most instances, these are straightforward conversations, but we have all had times when the message we intended was not clearly received. Often this is the result of communicating in our preferred ways with someone whose preferences are very different. In our experience, these breakdowns are usually linked to one of the scales, but occasionally several scales are involved. In those situations, the manager needs to be very deliberate in setting the stage and monitoring the tone of the conversation. Here are some simple guidelines for working with each preference.

Delegating to E's and I's

Strong Extraverts like talking. They learn through interactive discussions and take in information as they talk. Conversation helps them understand the parameters of the problem/opportunity and increases the likelihood that they will take ownership of the initiative. So when you are giving direction to Extraverts, don't do all the talking. Let them ask questions. Encourage them to think out loud about the issues. And expect to go immediately from explaining what you need to an initial conversation about how they plan to get it done. Even though you own *what* gets done and they need to own *how* it gets done, you should both be involved in discussing the whats and the hows.

Strong Introverts like to think before they speak. They will want a chance to consider the problem or opportunity, find out some background on it, do their homework, and/or analyze the situation before talking about it. If you can give them some notice before you talk about it, that is best. If the situation comes up first in conversation, give them some time to go off and think about it before asking them what their game plan is. It may even be important to allow some thought time to make sure they have a full grasp of the situation. They may also need something in writing. If so, you can put your expectations in writing, or you can ask them to write down their understanding. They are also likely to send you their action plan before discussing it with you. If they do, read it and think about it before signing off—for an Introvert, that is a sign of respect.

Joe was manager of engineering for a small division of a large manufacturing company and a strong Introvert. Many of the engineers reporting to him were also Introverts, and Joe often found delegating to his best engineers to be a simple, straightforward task. He would e-mail them an assignment and suggest that if they had any questions they e-mail back, and he would respond. Rarely did one of his staff need more than this.

Tom was new to the department and quite different from his peers—and his boss. He was a strong Extravert and often wanted to talk through his assignments with his boss before starting on them. Initially Joe was concerned that Tom was in over his head because he asked so many questions, and Tom was frustrated with what seemed to be his boss's disinterest in his work.

During a teambuilding session in which team members were sharing their MBTI scores with one another, Tom's difference stood out. He was the only Extravert in a sea of Introverts. Once this difference became evident, Joe and Tom were able to have a conversation about Tom's need to talk things through. The two of them worked out a plan for how they would deal with each other's needs in relation to delegation. Joe became less concerned about

Tom's competence, and Tom became less concerned about Joe's interest. Moreover, they both continued to work together very productively.

People near the midpoint of the E–I scale often have a set of needs that are different from the needs of those with strong preferences. Typically, they need to have an initial conversation to understand the parameters of the situation. They won't understand the perspective of key stakeholders on their own without some dialogue. But they usually won't commit to a plan of attack immediately. They will want to step back, think about it, reflect on the issues and possibilities, and then come back with a recommendation. Sometimes with moderate Extraverts and Introverts, it takes several iterations of talking and reflecting before they are ready to go.

Getting S's and N's Started

Team members with a strong preference for Sensing like facts, figures, numbers, and details. The first thing they focus on is the current situation—what's going on right now. Then they focus on the past—how we got here. They like to preserve the things that are already working. They hate to throw out the baby with the bath water and don't like starting over from scratch. This could affect the type of responsibilities you ask them to take on. They are best at solving problems and fixing what's broken. And when you give them an assignment, be sure to give them details about what the problems are and how they came about. If you have data, show it to them. If you have numerical targets, give the figures to them. The more concrete you can be, the more they will be focused.

Team members who strongly prefer Intuition like a broad picture of the possibilities. They have limited interest in the present and almost no use for the past. Their focus is the future—where we want to go. They like to use their imaginations, be inventive, and create something new. They love beginning with a clean sheet of paper, doing blue-sky thinking, and starting green-field ventures. They will be most motivated if those are the kinds of assignments they get. When getting them started, be careful not to overload them with detail. Start with the conclusion first and give the background only if they ask for it. Paint a broad picture of where you want to end up and leave them a lot of room to be creative about how to get there. If you have to give them data, limit it to a graph that shows a pattern or trend line, but you might do well to just give them the concept of where you want them to go.

A recent experience with a client points out the different ways S's and N's get things started. The experience had to do with the need to strengthen the coaching skills of a group of sixty senior executives.

After conducting a 360-degree feedback process with these executives, we consolidated their individual data to see what collective development needs the members of the group had. We knew that they were weak in the kinds of skills we typically teach in our coaching skills classes. The VP of HR, a strong

N responsible for providing development opportunities for this group, shared our intuition and needed no convincing. She was ready to roll out the program.

In contrast, the executives who needed the training were strong S's, the kind of people who "eat data for breakfast." Fortunately for us, we had the data to support our intuition. When the collective results from the feedback were tabulated, 95 percent of the respondents were weak in providing feedback to others, 90 percent were weak in teaching and guiding others, and 100 percent were weak in empowerment.

In order to engage the participants in our training program, the first thing we did was present these data. We not only showed them graphs of the 90, 95, and 100 percent results. We also pointed out that the results came from questionnaires completed on all sixty executives by ten respondents each, a total of six hundred people. With fifty items in the questionnaire, we were looking at a total of 30,000 data points! The participants found these data compelling and were a captive audience for the entire two-day program.

People near the midpoint of the S–N scale are different from people at either end of the spectrum. For strong S's, the facts speak for themselves, and for strong N's a vision tells the whole story. People in the middle need both. They usually like to start with the big picture but then need it filled in with plenty of details. If all they get is the data, they aren't sure what they mean, and if all they get is the desired outcome, they don't understand where it came from. As a result, it can take more time to brief a moderate Sensing or Intuitive team member, and you need to anticipate this.

Giving Responsibility to T's and F's

Team members with a strong preference for Thinking are logical. They want answers to be right and expect decisions to make sense. They are perfectionists by nature and critical of things that aren't done properly. They focus on the long-term impact of decisions with the best interests of the company in mind. ST's are particularly good at keeping the trains running on time, while NT's are adept at creating systems for smooth operations. When giving assignments to strong T's, let them know that something isn't working right and get them charged up about eliminating inefficiency (ST's) or creating more effective systems (NT's). If there is a better way to do it, the T's will uncover it, and they will be highly objective about pursuing alternatives even if pain must be endured to produce long-term results.

Team members who strongly prefer Feeling are considerate. They are tuned in to their own feelings and the feelings of others. They like to establish and maintain harmony, will avoid conflict, and work to reduce tensions. They focus on the immediate impact of a decision on people's motivation and often look at change from more of a personal perspective than an organizational one. When you ask strong F's to take on a responsibility, it is a good idea to ask how they feel about the assignment. Encourage them to talk about the people who will be affected and to speak openly about any concerns they have. Help them understand that their role will be to make things better for people, whether it means doing a better job of listening to customers or helping employees cope with some unpleasant changes. And be sure to let them know how much you value their willingness to help out—they thrive on being appreciated.

We recently worked with a small consulting firm with a tendency to launch projects that failed to come to fruition. In exploring the problem with organizational members, we discovered that the make-up of the group was decidedly skewed toward the Feeling preference. The senior members in the firm, it turned out, were strong T's who would create task teams on any and all ideas that seemed to them to be good business opportunities.

After a short investigation it became clear to us that the only projects that succeeded were those for which someone in the organization had some passion—and that ideas that lacked a champion languished. A leader with the personal drive to accomplish the results was the necessary ingredient.

We suggested a simple solution to the firm's leaders. Find out, when launching a new initiative, if there is anyone who has a passion for the subject. If no one does, we suggested, abandon the project. While reluctant to accept that there are limitations to what they can get people to do, the leaders found that this new operating principle led to more completed projects and fewer false starts.

People near the midpoint of the T–F scale are different from people with strong preferences. When it comes to making tough decisions, strong T's go to their heads and draw logical conclusions, while strong F's look into their hearts and do the right things for people. People in the middle often have the most difficulty making tough decisions. First they think about it, then they check their feelings, and then they think some more, working back and forth until sometimes they are paralyzed with indecision. So when sending moderate T's or F's off on a difficult assignment, make sure they know that you will be available to support them with the hard calls. Without this they may feel overwhelmed from the start.

Handing Off to J's and P's

Team members with a strong preference for Judging are organized. They work best with goals, plans, checklists, and checkpoints. Their need for closure drives them to limit the options they want to consider and to let decisions stand once they have been made. They work best when they can focus on one thing at a time, and nothing gives them more satisfaction than checking things off their to-do lists. When giving strong J's an assignment, make sure they know what has to be done and when it is due. Let them take control of the plan for how the work will get done and get out of their way so they can "just do it." If a variety of options are still being considered, make sure that is understood so the J's don't start implementing too soon—they get very frustrated if they are halfway to closure only to find out that others haven't even committed to the path they are going down.

Team members who strongly prefer Perceiving are flexible. They work best with limited structures and controls, adapt well to unexpected circumstances, and thrive in a troubleshooting environment. Planning gets in their way and blocks them from diving into the fray. Starting too soon can also cause them to fritter away their time on nonproductive activity. They are at their best with last-minute rushes and often don't get into gear until the deadline gets close. J's often see P's as procrastinating, but their reality is that to start too soon would be a waste of time. Since most organizations have Judging cultures and most managers are J's, P's are often forced to conform to planning processes, adhere to interim milestones, and provide regular progress reports. To be effective in launching strong P's, it is best to let them go at it in their own way, at their own pace, and on their own timetable. It is also wise to give them assignments that appear to have impossible deadlines—these people have an amazing capacity to jump in and get things done before the strong J can even make a plan.

We recently witnessed the turmoil that can exist when J's are thrust into P situations and vice versa. The scenario involved the technology planning team for a large financial services company that was erecting a new building in a major city. The project leader was chosen in part because he had demonstrated the capacity to be flexible. He had a strong preference for Perceiving.

Most of the people he had chosen for his implementation team were strong J's—people who perform best with a clear plan to follow. The turmoil arose because the nature of the project required the planning team to construct "what if" scenarios that were based on a variety of paths that might be taken in the course of developing the facility. The project leader, being a P, was quite comfortable with the notion of "what if" scenarios. His charges, however, were quite uncomfortable and resistant to completing any project plans until they knew that the "right" path had been determined.

To complicate things further, the team leader's manager was a strong J who had great interest in seeing the plans for the "what if" scenarios completed. Consequently, the team leader spent most of his time convincing his team to complete their plans even though they were "what if" plans and the rest of his time encouraging his boss to get definitive answers from his superiors regarding the direction of the project. It was quite a dance, and one that only a true P could pull off.

People near the midpoint of the J–P scale are unlike their colleagues with stronger preferences. They like to have clear structures and milestones, but they also need some room for flexibility. They often make plans but ignore them, make checklists but lose them, and have checkpoints but change them.

With these people, you can help them make a plan, but don't push them to make it too detailed. All they need is a broad outline, and they will adapt it from there.

USING PREFERENCES WHEN PROVIDING SUPPORT

The performance contracting process guides you to use Styles 1 and 4 to hand off meaningful responsibilities. It also sets the wheels in motion for using Styles 3 and 2 to support a team member's decision making or get his or her input on a decision you will make. If preferences are useful on the front end of this process when you are giving direction, they are extremely helpful on the back end when you are providing support. What feels like support to you may not come across as supportive to a person with different preferences.

Giving Support to E's and I's

Strong Extraverts will feel the most supported if you can meet with them face to face, but a telephone call is okay if need be. The important point for them is that they learn through conversation. When you are in a conversation with strong E's, it is important to let them do a lot of the talking. You probably won't have to do much to get the meeting going. Extraverts enjoy dialogue and are stimulated by interaction, so don't make the conversation totally one sided. Just try to understand the situation as they see it. Often, that's all the E's need, anyway—just an opportunity to think out loud.

Strong Introverts are likely to have a solution in mind before coming to you. They will often give you a report to read or send you an e-mail prior to the meeting so that you will have time to reflect before giving them a response. And they will feel more supported if you think about their ideas before responding. If you want to have a conversation with I's, you may need to draw them out by asking questions and encouraging them to elaborate on their thinking. Just know that the meeting may be for your need and not theirs—an e-mail response might be more to their liking.

Dave is an executive who had a disconnect along the E–I continuum with a manager who reported to him. Very happy with the progress this manager was making on a particular project, Dave decided he was going to show support by sending the manager daily e-mails reinforcing that he was on the right track.

Dave was blindsided one day when the manager scheduled a meeting with him to discuss what was not going right. Startled by the request, he asked the manager what led him to believe there was anything wrong. The manager pointed out that while the two of them were in the same building complex, just floors apart, Dave had not spoken to him for several weeks. He interpreted this lack of face-to-face contact as dissatisfaction.

The lack of face-to-face contact actually represented a difference in preference. The executive was a strong Introvert whose e-mails were a stretch for him. The manager, in contrast, was a strong Extravert who interpreted the lack of face-to-face contact as a clear message that he was in trouble.

For moderate Extraverts and Introverts, support may mean a combination of e-mails and conversations. And when you meet with them, don't be surprised if they go away from the discussion, think about the key points, and come back for further discussion.

How to Help S's and N's

When you need to support strong S's, expect them to come loaded with facts and figures. Whether they communicate in writing or in person, they will likely want to review what has been done in order to bring you up to speed. Often they will go back to square one to review the background of the situation, but they almost always will go over the steps they have taken to fix it. They will often discuss their activities and want your reaction to what has been done or your input about the immediate next steps.

Strong N's are less likely to focus on the past or the present. They will want help with the possibilities. That may mean brainstorming (EN's) or exchanging ideas (IN's) about the alternatives that should be under consideration. It could involve weighing the pros and cons of various options to help them decide which ones to pursue. It could also include a discussion about the best ways to implement a decision that has already been made. Whether it is face to face or in writing, the conversation will need to focus on the big picture and be forward moving to feel satisfying to the strong N.

A good example of managers not getting the support they need is the case of a company president who frequently butted heads with several of his senior vice presidents. Mike, the president, was a strong S whose claim to fame was bringing the company "down to earth" after several years of freewheeling investments in capital equipment and new product development. The result was financial success based on expense reduction tactics.

Several of Mike's senior management team were strong N's who respected what Mike had accomplished but feared that the company would ultimately go under due to lack of innovation. Frequently, they would come to him with ideas for entering new markets, acquiring new technologies, or developing new strategies.

Full of enthusiasm for creating the future, they would hit a brick wall with Mike. He would listen only halfheartedly to their ideas and then ask them for reams of data to document the validity of each proposal. And while he had their attention, he would invariably haul out a spreadsheet indicating some problem in their area and ask what they intended to do about it.

One frustrated N after another would leave his office. They came in looking for support for pursuing a new opportunity and instead got refocused on fixing an operational problem.

For moderate S's and N's, critical checkpoints can be time-consuming. They will want to review the past, fill you in on the current status, and involve you in thinking about where the initiative is heading. It is hard for them to just focus on next steps without making sure you are on the same page, and it would be frustrating for them to only bring you up to speed and not talk about what's coming up. They need to do both in order to feel that they have your full attention.

Being There for T's and F's

Strong T's will come to you to hone their thinking. They know that their analysis of the current situation and/or the possibilities can always be improved, and the people who add value to them are those who can find a flaw and help them overcome it. T's look to others to help them find the best answer, so they invite criticism and actually feel disappointed if their thinking doesn't get pushed to a new level. With TJ's you have to be careful not to overdo it. If they have heard your critique, incorporated it into their thinking, and reached closure, they will expect you to admire the new and improved version and will feel frustrated if the criticism continues. TP's, on the other hand, enjoy keeping the options open and can stay in a continuous improvement dialogue ad infinitum.

Strong F's often feel hurt by the criticism their Thinking counterparts thrive on. More than anything, they need appreciation for their efforts. They also like to talk about how they are feeling about the assignment. Since T's often see F's as fuzzy thinkers, it is very common for them to give F's the opposite of what they need. Instead of providing validation and encouragement, they point out the flaws in the Feeling people's thinking, which actually undermines their confidence. At critical checkpoints, the most important thing you can do for strong F's is make them feel valued. Support them on motivational factors first: interest, confidence, willingness, and alignment. Then move on to the ability factors when they are ready. And before you offer any criticism or advice, ask them to share their ideas—if they are feeling confident enough to trust their instincts, what you hear will be very solid.

We recently worked with the director of nursing of a medium-sized hospital who had the unenviable job of setting guidelines for the nursing staff about boundaries related to patient care. Experiencing ongoing slashes in her budget, she found herself continually in the position of relegating to aides tasks that were previously performed by nurses. She was quickly developing a reputation as being an unfeeling witch who was insensitive to patient needs.

The president of the hospital knew she was a strong T capable of making the tough decisions. The director of nursing, believing that her job was to find creative ways to address client care issues while staying within the increasingly stringent budget required to keep the hospital afloat, went to the president for help. She was feeling overwhelmed by the task and maligned by the reputation her circumstances had created.

The president, recognizing that he was dealing with a person who felt attacked but knowing that she was a T, conveyed his appreciation for the difficulty of her situation and then moved quickly to problem solving. The result of their meeting was the establishment of some official guidelines that would emanate from the president's office, thus taking some of the heat off the director of nursing. They also decided that she would chair a task force to look for alternative funding to support continued excellence in nursing care.

The director of nursing walked out of her boss's office feeling truly supported—in large part because her boss treated her as a T by supporting her problem solving rather than simply offering the empathy and appreciation that would satisfy an F.

Moderate T's and F's often need help with making tough decisions. They get caught between their heads and their hearts and can agonize over the options they are considering. Unlike strong T's, who rely on clear principles to choose, and strong F's, who trust their values to make choices, those in the middle flip-flop between ideas that make sense and the feelings that they spawn. Help them lay out the full picture. Often, as they talk, their conclusion becomes obvious to you long before it does to them. Reflecting back what you are hearing is usually all they need to get to a resolution. If it's not, you should be prepared to take their input and make the decision.

Touching Base with J's and P's

When J's come for support, it is usually because they have hit a milestone and want to share the joy of checking something off their list. A check-in like this is an update (usually pre-scheduled) to make sure you know where they are in their action plans. Acknowledge their accomplishment, appreciate them for the progress they have made, and let them get going on the next item. Sometimes J's need support because they are having trouble getting closure on a task or goal. Often that is because they bit off more than they could chew. Help them articulate what they have completed and get them to identify a plan for going forward—one that has smaller steps and opportunities for checking off some accomplishments.

P's come for support on a more irregular basis. They are unlikely to schedule checkpoints; and if you schedule them for a Perceiving team member, expect them to be ignored or avoided. P's focus on whatever is in their perception and deal with what requires immediate attention, so if you need an update, let them know it, and they will focus on your agenda. Left to their own designs, they may not get started until the deadline approaches. Strong J's often use the tactic of giving P's a plan with pre-set deadlines under the assumption that it will help them organize their time. In reality, the deadlines just hang over their heads. It is better to let them go at their own pace, anticipating that as the real deadline approaches, if they need help it will be on the spur of the moment. Try to respond on the fly; then step back and let them keep churning.

Jay and Nate were co-owners of a small business, and they drove each other crazy. Jay was a strong J, and Nate was a strong P. When Jay would take the lead on a new development, he would tell Nate when he would have something to show him and work diligently to meet that deadline. At the appointed time, he would present a nearly finished product to Nate so that his partner could add his perspective before the job was completed. Nate would give Jay a few ideas, and Jay would thank him. Then he would make the changes and show the finished product to Nate, who would find a few more good ideas for Jay. Jay would grit his teeth, pretend to appreciate the additional suggestions, make the new changes, and return to show Nate the final, final version. Of course, Nate would come up with more options to consider and Jay would hit the roof. Desperate to get closure on his work, Jay could never get satisfaction from showing anything to Nate, who would always want to stay open to new possibilities.

The converse was also true. When Nate was in charge of an initiative, he would never commit to a deadline and would never bring anything for Jay to look at. When Jay would initiate a meeting, Nate would be able to talk in broad terms about the options he was considering in hopes that Jay would join him in a brainstorming session. Jay, seeing that nothing real had been done yet, wouldn't want to waste his time. Instead he would push Nate to have something for him to look at the next time and would set a date for their next meeting in order to give Nate a target to focus on. Unable to get some help with exploring the possibilities, Nate would still have nothing to show at the next meeting and be increasingly frustrated with Jay for expecting closure on a project that hadn't really gotten started.

Moderate J's and P's are sometimes their own worst enemies since they like to make plans but then ignore them. At a check-in, they may feel the need to talk about the plan as well as explain what has happened that knocked them off course. Don't get caught up trying to teach them to stay on plan (if you are a J) or convincing them to stop wasting their time making plans they don't intend to follow (if you are a P). Just support them as they recalibrate their plan and encourage them not to worry if they can't stick to it.

PREFERENCES AND PROBLEM SOLVING

It is so important to consider personality when trying to lead. If the way you are leading is not perceived as "user-friendly," you will encounter resistance and possibly outright rejection of your leadership efforts. That's what happened to Simon when he tried to use Style 2, problem solving, with Martine, who was having difficulty achieving work goals because of poor time management.

Simon had a strong preference for Intuition, relying heavily on his "sixth sense" when problem solving. When he first broached the subject with Martine, he said, "I get the impression you are not doing a very good job managing your time. You seem easily distracted. I have a sense you could get a lot more done if you didn't waste so much time focusing on things that don't concern you."

Martine had a strong preference for Sensing, so phrases like "I get the impression," "you seem," and "I have a sense" didn't mean much to her. Since S's rely on facts, details, and specifics for taking in information, Simon would have communicated more effectively if he had said something like "I noticed in the past two weeks that you attended six meetings in other departments and your last three reports were submitted late. Let's talk about what your priorities should be and determine what you can do to stay on schedule."

Simon's miscommunication with Martine was compounded by the fact that he had a strong preference for Judging while she had an equally strong preference for Perceiving. His advice to her was: "At the beginning of the week, I make a list of my top priorities, make sure I have all the resources I will need to accomplish them, and set up a schedule so I know what I have to get done each day. If you did that, you would be a lot more organized."

To Martine, this advice sounded like it came from another planet. The idea of planning everything in advance and adhering to a schedule was stifling. If she worked that way, she wouldn't get anything done. The keys to maintaining her momentum were her abilities to juggle multiple tasks simultaneously and to shift from one task to another when she started to get bored or lose interest. The problem was that she got so interested in the diversions that sometimes she lost track of her own priorities.

Simon's attempt at problem solving was also hindered by the fact that he was an Introvert and Martine was an Extravert. Remember, I's tend to rely on internal thought processes, work with ideas, and reflect before they act. E's prefer to interact with others, learn through conversation, and act quickly. So when Simon advised Martine to research a variety of products and consider them carefully before choosing one that would help her manage her time more independently, she cringed at the thought. As an Extravert, Martine would have been more likely to find the right organizer by talking to other people to find out what planning tools they were using and the pluses and minuses of each system.

The final straw in this case was that Simon had a strong preference for Thinking while Martine had a moderate preference for Feeling. As a T, Simon wanted to find a logical solution that would help Martine be a more efficient member of his team. As an F, Martine was more concerned about her relationship with her manager and needing reassurance that her he still liked her. Unfortunately, despite Simon's intention to be helpful, their S–N differences left Martine with a vague understanding of the problem, their J–P and E–I differences left her with advice she couldn't use, and their T–F difference left her feeling criticized instead of helped. Martine felt thoroughly frustrated by their conversation, avoided bringing up the subject again, and reassured herself by talking to her colleagues about how stiff and demanding Simon was.

This story may seem extreme since the two people are polarized on all four scales—the leader is an INTJ and the employee is an ESFP. Usually the differences are not so far-reaching, but there are countless scenarios you may encounter when you are out of sync with the person you are trying to lead in terms of any of the four dichotomies. It's important to remember that whatever the gap, you can bridge it by paying attention to personality preferences and making the effort to walk in the other person's shoes. Doing this can save you from inadvertently stumbling on the path to effective leadership.

WORKING WITH DIFFERENT
TYPES OF PEOPLE

It won't help you to try to plan the best way to work with each member of every team you lead. There probably aren't enough hours in the day to do that, and even people who work very closely with the MBTI assessment can't always determine what a person's type is. And knowing a person's type doesn't always tell you the full story. Often people with the same preference find themselves in conflict because one has a moderate preference and the other has a much stronger preference. Also, while the MBTI tool covers many of the dimensions of personality, factors such as family history, ethnicity, and social status come into play when determining an individual's responses to the world.

The best thing to do is be yourself. Use your preferences, employ your dominant hand, and do what you normally do. When you find yourself having difficulty working with another person—feeling awkward, having to be conscious of what you say and do, going slowly, or struggling to get results—step back and explore what the source of the conflict might be. Often it is related to personality type. If you can figure out which scale you and the other person are polarized on, it will help you figure out how to relate to your colleague differently.

Better yet, if you and the other person can talk openly about the differences, it can often help the two of you develop respect for each other's strengths. If both of you can listen better, appreciate the other's perspective, or defer to the other when that person's preference makes him or her better equipped to respond, you will both be much more productive in the long run. You and the other person will feel better about working with each other, and you will be far more likely to be the kind of leader that others want to follow.

Creating Positive Group Dynamics: An Underused Window of Opportunity

CHAPTER 1 2

In chapters 8 through 11 we focused on the keys for working effectively with individuals. Avoiding frustration, using all four styles to facilitate empowerment, changing main styles to encourage development or provide intervention, and viewing team members through their Window of Potential are powerful tools for working with individuals. When leaders put these tools into action by creating performance contracts in ways that work with each team member's personality, the results are very positive.

However, for most leaders, transforming a group of individuals, even a group of talented and motivated individuals, into a high-performing team is a more challenging task. In this chapter, you will learn how to lead the group dynamics that can make or break a team. You will learn the predictable needs of groups and how they manifest themselves. You will learn how to use the leadership styles to respond to those needs—a set of moves we call the *group development* cycle, which can help any team achieve results. You will also get some suggestions about adapting those moves to the chemistry that makes every team unique.

WHY TEAMS FAIL

One reason teams fail is the fierce individualism present in many cultures. For example, getting ahead in America has always meant competing with others. In fact, this rugged individualism is considered by many to be a hallmark of the "American way." And all too often, that means beating your peers to the next promotion instead of collaborating with them to beat the real competition. Getting these competitive individuals to participate in a group effort proved to be a challenge that produced far more failures than successes in the 1980s and 1990s, both in the United States and in many other cultures around the world.

As we enter the twenty-first century this challenge continues to be formidable. The business landscape is littered with dot-com start-ups and reinvented organizations with "click and mortar" spinoffs. The young and not-so-young professionals who populate these enterprises are aggressively competing with one another for the best jobs. Most of them fancy themselves as troubleshooters who can single-handedly use their technical prowess to solve their organization's problems. They are no more likely to subordinate their own success for the good of the group than were their more traditional counterparts. And as long as organizations continue to reward and recognize individual efforts over group efforts the situation is unlikely to change.

Another cause of teamwork problems is that most attempts at building teams have come under the aegis of some special companywide initiative that is not integrated with the day-to-day workplace. Most companies have some experience with quality circles, employee involvement groups, or continuous improvement programs. The problem is that typically these initiatives simply inject isolated techniques that some would call gimmicks into current organizational structures that don't support teamwork. People go off to a quality meeting, sit around a table, and try to get the group to agree on something (anything!). Then they return to business as usual in the office or on the shop floor, where there is no way that their colleagues are going to "waste their time" like that.

A new emphasis in many organizations has been on teamwork software that is supposed to somehow miraculously create a team without really paying attention to the needs of the people on the team. Too often, at the end of the day, nothing changes because little attention has been paid to the group dynamics necessary to build commitment to creating change or to mobilize a team and position it for success. The critical ingredient for team success is the human factor, and it has been virtually ignored by many.

Finally, much of the training that does focus on teams has perpetuated some distortions about group development that actually make it harder for teams to succeed. If the teamwork revolution that has taken the corporate world by storm is to succeed—and many believe that economic prosperity depends on it—then those charged with leading teams need to learn the skills necessary for making teams work.

The individual skills we have already discussed are critical, but leaders also need a road map of what happens in the course of a group's journey and a compass for navigating that course. In this chapter, that's exactly what you will get.

In the next chapter, you will see how to integrate these group skills with the individual skills you have already learned. When these two sets of skills are put together in the right way, they will provide you with a template for building and sustaining high-performing teams.

A GROUP IS NOT THE SAME AS A TEAM

When we talk about leading a high-performing team, it is important to be clear that a group is not the same as a team. Working together in the same department or having the same reporting relationship automatically makes you a member of an organizational group, but it does not necessarily make you a member of a team.

A bus is a good analogy for thinking about the difference between teams and groups. If you think of ten people riding on a city bus, they meet the technical definition of a group. They're all in one place, heading in the same direction at the same time, at the same speed, under the direction of one leader.

However, each of them is a distinct individual with his or her own purpose. All get on and off the bus at their own stops, and while they're on the bus, they usually go out of their way to avoid contact with the others. Occasionally, a couple of people will develop a camaraderie of the trenches and establish a passing friendship.

In contrast, if you think about a team bus, all the players get on and off at the same time. They have a clear mission, interrelated goals, clear roles and responsibilities, and strategies with contingency plans. They have practiced and developed systems and learned how to coordinate their individual efforts. On the way to the game, they get one another pumped up and motivated. After the game, if they won, they talk about who made the extra effort or the exceptional play that led to victory. If they lost, the conversation focuses on the extra effort that would have made the difference between winning and losing. In either case they are looking back at what helped them achieve success or hindered them.

TEAM = INDIVIDUALS + GROUP DYNAMICS

A team is different from a group. It is also more than the sum of the individual parts. We think of it as the individuals plus the group dynamics that bond those people together. Figure 26 illustrates this concept by depicting four individual contributors plus a circle that represents the group dynamics that are created when they come together as a team.

Think of a team this way. When you lead a team of four individuals, you also have to manage a fifth entity, the group. The group has a life of its own. Its needs must be understood very differently from the way you understand individual needs. To lead a team, then, you need to know how to diagnose group needs, you need to know how to use the leadership styles with groups,

Figure 26 Team = Individuals + Group Dynamics

and you need to understand how to use the power of groups to enhance the performance of individuals.

A DISTORTED VIEW OF
GROUP DEVELOPMENT

If you are going to lead a group effort, you have to understand the predictable stages of development that groups go through. Unfortunately, the conventional wisdom taught in most corporate training programs is the Forming-Storming-Norming-Performing model of group development. This model, developed by Bruce Tuckman back in 1965, was based on a literature review dominated by research with therapy groups, T-groups, and other non-task-oriented groups. Despite this, Tuckman's model has been popular for several reasons. The terms are simple, it is comforting to believe that Storming is natural, nice to think that storms will turn into productive norms, and reassuring to believe that the endpoint will be Performing.

Tuckman's model has been very useful, especially for groups that are embroiled in conflict. But as a guide to team development it provides a distorted view of the realities of groups and has perpetuated several harmful conclusions about what it takes to have a productive team. First, many managers have come to believe that Forming consists of simply meeting everyone on the team. In reality, a team orientation requires a lot more than that. It means clarifying the team's mission, defining goals and roles, and establishing procedures for getting the work done. At the outset, the group needs to form around a clear purpose and then get focused on the best ways to accomplish that purpose.

The second distortion is the idea that Storming is inevitable. In reality, lots of groups get focused and productive without storms. There are countless examples of groups that came together, clarified what they had to do, and got on with the job of doing it. In our research on high-performing teams, almost every exceptional team started that way. They all had open discussions and candid exploration of opinions and ideas, but not conflicts. While Storming often does occur, it is not a required stage of group development. Of course, if you believe it is supposed to happen, that belief may become a self-fulfilling prophecy.

The third distortion is the illusion that Storming automatically turns into Norming. We have met too many team leaders and facilitators who are convinced that dwelling on conflicts is the best way to get the group ready to perform. In reality, storms occur because the group is not focused. The mission and goals are ambiguous. Roles are confusing. Operating procedures are dysfunctional. These problems don't go away by themselves or disappear by arguing. To focus a group requires a concerted effort to answer these questions: What are we expected to do? And how are we going to coordinate our efforts to get it done?

The final distortion is that Performing is the endpoint of a group's development. In our experience, groups often move beyond Performing and level off—becoming complacent, burnt out, or defensive. These symptoms will arise if the group is put on auto-pilot once it hits the Performing stage. But, if you don't assume that Performing is the endpoint, leveling can be countered by refocusing and revitalizing the group.

PRACTICAL STAGES OF
GROUP DEVELOPMENT

To overcome these misleading notions, a team of Charter Oak consultants has created a new, business-oriented, reality-based model of group development. We call the four stages Forming, Focusing, Performing, and Leveling. In the next section, you will learn how to recognize these stages. After that, we will show you how to use the leadership styles to create positive group dynamics in the teams you lead.

Figure 27 depicts what we call the *group development curve*. It illustrates the four stages of development for teams that are expected to produce results.

When people come together, as they do in a team effort, the group will usually progress from forming to focusing, then to performing, and finally to leveling unless they take a time-out to identify problems and find ways to increase performance. As groups pass through these stages, they look and feel very different, so it is important to know the visible indicators that are typical of each stage as well as the group needs that cause those indicators to appear.

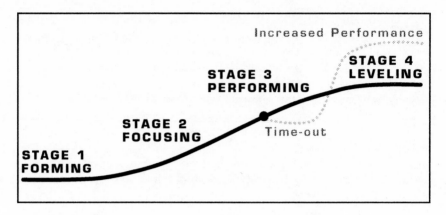

Figure 27 Stages of Group Development

If you are leading a group of people at work or in your personal life, you will find it more interesting if you keep that group in mind as you read this material. If you are not leading a group right now, you might want to think of a group that you are a member of. As you read, think of the visible indicators you are aware of and try to identify the underlying needs that are causing them. If you can do that, it should be easy to diagnose your group's stage of development.

Figure 28 summarizes what you are most likely to experience from a group that is at each stage of development. In Stage 1, Forming, the visible indicators are individuality and cautious, polite communication. People are guarded about the demands that the group may place on them and are more focused on the goals they are already trying to accomplish. There is dependency on the leader as people wait to be told what needs to get done. In essence, the group is looking for a clear definition of the boundaries.

Stage 2, Focusing, usually begins with questioning to test how open the leader will be. It is important to anticipate this and accept it as a part of the process that enables team members to buy into and gain ownership of the group's mission. In Stage 2, there will also be some exploration, which is healthy but can lead to false starts. You may also experience conflicts that can develop into power struggles if the questions don't get voiced, the answers aren't helpful, or suggestions are ignored. In essence, as soon as you establish the boundaries in Stage 1, the group will question and test them to see if there is room for them on your team.

When the Stage 2 questions are answered and team members' input is heard, the group is ready to move into Stage 3, Performing, which is typified by productivity, shared responsibility, and a clear sense of purpose. Group members are confident in themselves and trust each other. There is open communication and interdependence, and members' commitment to the group's mission leads to mutual support. In Stage 1, the group is looking for

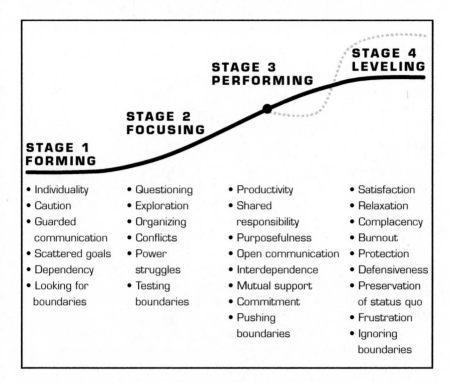

Figure 28 Indicators of Group Development

boundaries. In Stage 2, members challenge and reshape the boundaries. In Stage 3, they accept the boundaries and work to do the most they can within those constraints.

Stage 4, Leveling, is next. One result of all the achievement in Stage 3 is a sense of satisfaction, relaxation, and, eventually, complacency. Some people will burn out or become lethargic. Others will try to preserve the status quo and get protective or defensive in the face of any changes. And some group members will eventually feel frustrated and angry. In essence, the group starts ignoring the boundaries.

Look at Figure 28 and ask yourself where your team is on this curve. What indicators are telling you that the group dynamics of your team fall into one stage or another?

It is also valuable to understand the underlying needs that cause these symptoms to be present. Those needs are sumarized in Figure 29. If you know what is driving certain behaviors, it is much easier to address them in constructive ways. If you do not understand those drivers, you may misinterpret some statements as distracting the group from its work.

In Stage 1, the Forming stage, the primary needs are to understand what the group's mission is and how each person can contribute to accomplishing

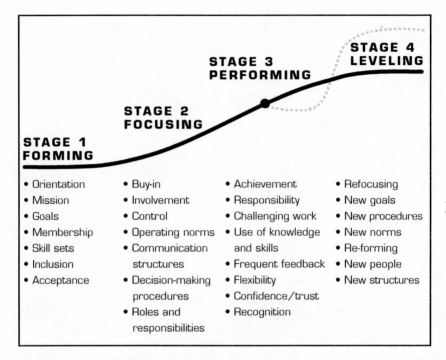

Figure 29 Group Development Needs

that mission. Team members are also looking for inclusion into the group and acceptance as a needed and respected member. The basic questions on their mind are: "Who are these people? Why have we been brought together? And what do you expect from us?"

The underlying needs in Stage 2, the Focusing stage, are buy-in, involvement, and organizing the work. Team members want to know what their specific roles and responsibilities will be and how they will coordinate their efforts: The group needs operating procedures for getting the work done, identifying and solving problems, involving one another in decision making, communicating within the group and with other key stakeholders, measuring progress, and valuing accomplishments.

The underlying needs at Stage 3, the Performing stage, have to do with getting the work done. Team members want achievement, responsibility, and an opportunity to use their knowledge and skills. They want spontaneous feedback and the flexibility to take quick responsive actions. They want to feel trusted by their teammates and be confident in each other. They want to identify and solve problems, discover and go after opportunities. And, as always, they want recognition for their efforts and their accomplishments.

In Stage 4, the Leveling stage, the underlying need is to take stock of how the team is working—what's going well and what needs improvement. Sometimes, members just need time out to relax, have some fun, connect with one another as people, celebrate a success, or debrief a difficult situation. Often there is a need to get refocused on new goals or new procedures or norms for utilizing the group's resources. Occasionally, the group needs to re-form, which means adding or subtracting members or restructuring a large group into small groups or several small groups into one large group. Sometimes the group needs to disband because its real reason for being has ceased to exist. In Stage 4 something needs to be done as a catalyst for change.

As you did with Figure 28, try to identify your group's needs and corresponding stage of development in Figure 29.

WHERE IS YOUR GROUP?

Before you reach a definite conclusion about the group dynamics of your team, consider some complexities that often cloud people's perceptions. If you can avoid those traps and determine your group's true stage, you will be better equipped to provide the leadership your team members need.

Often managers make the mistake of assuming that if work is getting done, their group must be in the Performing stage. That isn't necessarily true. All groups get some work done. Some do it with ease, but in other groups everything is a struggle. To diagnose a group's stage of development, you have to observe the interactions and listen to what people are saying in the spaces between getting work accomplished.

The group is in the Forming stage when you are hearing questions like "What do they really expect from us?" or comments like "I'll say this to you but I won't say it in the meeting." In the Focusing stage, you hear discussions about who should do what or complaints like "They'll never give us the resources or time to get this done right." The Performing stage produces conversations about the work—status reports, updates, ideas about how to solve problems or go after new opportunities. In the Leveling stage, people complain about being stretched thin and burned out, or they want to take time out to talk about better ways to get the current work done or to reorganize to pursue new opportunities.

Many managers also say that they aren't sure about their group's stage because individuals or subgroups are in different stages. It is critical to differentiate the needs of the group from the needs of individuals. When you are diagnosing a group's stage of development you have to step back from the group to be objective. If you were a thousand feet above the ground, it would be impossible to distinguish one person's voice from another's and sounds would seem to be coming from the group as a whole. That's how objective you have to be. Every action on the part of any member needs to be seen as an indicator of the group's stage and a product of the group's underlying needs.

Whenever the visible indicators suggest more than one stage, a group that is ramping up needs to pay attention to the lowest stage. If any individual is making forming noises, the group needs mission, vision, and purpose.

Whenever there are focusing sounds, the group needs help with roles and responsibilities or the structures and procedures for getting tasks accomplished. When the choir is singing performing songs, the needs center around coordinating the work, identifying and solving problems, or uncovering and pursuing opportunities. But as soon as any indicators of leveling start to surface, attention needs to be paid to clarification of goals, roles, and operating principles as well as to finding ways to revitalize everyone's energy or to focus on new opportunities. Stage 1 takes priority over Stage 2, which takes precedence over Stage 3; but as soon as Stage 4 starts to interfere with performance, it becomes the most pressing need.

With that in mind, where is your group? Forming? Focusing? Performing? Leveling? There is no right answer to this question. Don't feel that your group should be in any one stage of development. It is normal to find groups at all four stages. Typically, if we ask this question in any group of managers, about equal numbers will say that they have worked with groups at each stage.

LEADING PRODUCTIVE GROUP DYNAMICS

Once you understand the four stages of development, and you know where your team is, the question that usually comes to mind is "How do I lead groups through each stage?"

That's where the leadership styles come in. Leading a group is different from leading an individual. We have been preaching that you need all four styles with individuals, starting with Style 1 and rotating clockwise to Style 4, then Style 3, and finally Style 2. To orchestrate the group dynamics, you only use Styles 1, 2, and 3. The *group development* cycle starts with Style 1, but this time you move counterclockwise, to Style 2 and then to Style 3. Then you move back clockwise from Style 3 to Style 2 to Style 1 when the group starts leveling. Groups are more complex than individuals but easy to manage if you have the right mindset and know what to do at each stage.

When a group is in Stage 1, the Forming stage, you start the *group development* cycle with Style 1, the directing style, to reduce the ambiguity that is present at the start of any new venture. Provide the group with information using clear directions and complete explanations, and point out consequences. Clarify the group's mission—why you have brought them together and what the group is expected to accomplish. Identify individual roles. Explain why each person has been invited to join the team and give everyone a chance to talk about his or her skill sets and the contributions he or she expects to make. In addition, you also need to make people feel wanted, needed, and welcomed. Let them know that the team can't succeed without each and every one of them.

You can see in Figure 30 that the communication is mostly downward in Stage 1. That doesn't mean that the leader is the only one who gets to talk. In fact, a healthy dialogue is often the best way to ensure proper flow of information. More important, in order to manage the inclusion process and make sure that everyone feels welcome, you need to encourage considerable communication among the team members as well as between them and you. The downward arrows simply indicate that after all is said and done, the bottom line in Stage 1 is for the team to understand your expectations. The big questions on their minds are "What does this group need to do? And what do you want from me?" If they get answered, you have managed the forming process well.

When a group is in Stage 2, the Focusing stage, you need to use Style 2, the problem-solving style, to help people buy in and get organized. Encourage their questions about mission and goals as well as their ideas about how they can contribute. Respond openly and try to foster open communication among the team members. Before you make assignments, you need to know who has the ability and/or the motivation for each responsibility, who is willing to lead each aspect of the team's work, and who else wants to be involved. So you should invite members' input about who wants to do what and how their responsibilities will be interconnected. You should also involve them in establishing structures and guidelines for coordinating everyone's efforts. And since exploration is natural and valuable, you should anticipate providing lots of feedback to channel the discussion in the right direction. Involvement is the key to Stage 2—it enables team members to buy in, and it shifts ownership for the group's mission from the leader's responsibility to shared responsibility.

STAGE 1: FORMING

Figure 30 Forming Requires Giving Information to the Team

In Figure 31, you can see that the arrows are directed upward from the team members toward the leader. Again, this does not mean that communication is one-way from the bottom up. In Stage 2, in order to guarantee adequate problem solving about the best ways to organize and operate the team, you need to facilitate an open discussion to be sure that team members' ideas are listened to and the concerns are heard. The arrows point up to remind you that in Stage 2 the most important issue is involving the members in determining the best ways to work together. The surface questions for Focusing are "What am I responsible for? What am I taking the lead on? What support do I need? When and how do I need to support others? And how will the right hand know what the left hand is doing?" The underlying question is "Are you calling all the shots or are we in this together?" If you are doing most of the talking, these questions will never get answered, the group will not get focused, and storms will start to brew. With full involvement, the team will help you find the answers and will be ready to start performing.

When the group progresses to Stage 3, the Performing stage, the *group development* cycle moves to Style 3, the developing style. There are two dimensions to using Style 3 with the group. The first is to make sure each team member is empowered to pursue his or her responsibilities and has the full support of the group in implementing them.

To accomplish this, you need to have the right mindset, and that requires seeing the world from the team members' perspective. When you are using Style 3, each team member is responsible for making decisions on behalf of the group. Your role is to support each individual and make sure that other team

STAGE 2: FOCUSING

Figure 31 Focusing Requires Inviting Input from the Team

members as well as key stakeholders outside the team do the same. From their perspective, this looks like Style 2 because it is input to their decision making—input from you, from other team members, and/or from other stakeholders. You are using Style 3 to support them, and the group is using Style 3 to support them, but from their perspective they are now using Style 2.

With this in mind, for you to be effective using Style 3 to lead the Performing stage, think of it as distributed Style 2—or D2—for team members. With the D2 mindset, someone is always empowered to make decisions with team input. When the group moves from focusing to performing, the dynamics change from input to one leader to input to lots of leaders. Team members are taking on leadership responsibilities on behalf of the team, and your role is to support their problem-solving and leadership efforts. To do that, you need to do a lot of active listening with individual team members and facilitate open communication outside team meetings.

The second dimension of using Style 3 to lead Stage 3 is to bring the team members together to coordinate their respective efforts. You need to have periodic team meetings for updates and mutual support. These may be face-to-face meetings, but they are just as likely to happen via conference call, video conference, or some online structure. Regardless of the medium, the purpose of these meetings is open communication about the work itself. That may include status reports, progress checks against goals, problem identification and problem solving, opportunity identification and planning to pursue opportunities. This is a critical role for the team leader that often gets overlooked as other team members take on leadership responsibilities.

Your role in these meetings is to make it safe for each individual to put information and issues on the table without being afraid of their being taken over by the group. You have to be vigilant to steer the communication toward the individuals who have been empowered to lead. Do not let the loudest or most persistent voices take over, and be careful not to let the team lapse into group decision making. For D2 to work, the group needs active listening from you when it comes together. And the more you listen to them, the more they will listen to each other and to you.

You also need to remember to give people plenty of recognition and praise for their accomplishments. Using their knowledge and skills to achieve results is fun, but even that wears thin if people don't feel appreciated for their efforts. In Figure 32, you can see that arrows are directed to members of the team. When Stage 3 is handled well, all members are empowered to make decisions on the basis of input from others. As illustrated in the figure, they may get input from other team members, from you, or from key people outside the team. The important thing for you to remember is that, from their perspective, this looks like Style 2, since they are deciding with input. In your role as the leader, you need to use Style 3 as a facilitator who steers communication in the right directions and supports your team members with their decision making.

STAGE 3: PERFORMING

Figure 32 Performing Requires Steering Information to Team Members

This is very different from saying that it is the group's responsibility to decide. If it is the group's decision, then it is no one's decision. Asking the group to decide is one of the biggest traps for leaders who try to make teams work. It usually results in endless discussions, pointless debates, frustration, and wasted time. True, there are some examples of teams that work through the frustration and perform very well. But the vast majority of teams that strive for group consensus end up with "groupthink" or worse. And that is one of the main reasons so many companies keep talking about teams but do business as usual.

Remember this picture. This is what D2 looks like: Distributed Style 2. Shared responsibility. Clearly empowered team members. Clarity about who else will be involved in the decisions. And a leader who actively facilitates communication to build the trust that will make this work.

While the group is in the Performing stage, you also need to legitimize activities that will keep the group's spirits high and help the team identify strategies for continuous improvement. Encourage some socializing by visiting over meals, having drinks together on occasion, bringing in food if you all have to work late, or just taking a few minutes to show that you care about each other as people. Celebrate from time to time, especially if you have reached a milestone. And, most important, call time-outs on a regular basis to get team members to share developments in their respective assignments, identify current or anticipated problems, organize to pursue new opportunities, and/or bring up ideas for improving the way the work gets done.

Think of these actions as "managed leveling"—operational time-outs while the group is still in the Performing stage that enable team members to coordinate the work and feel connected to one another. If you don't make these key interventions while the team is rolling, you will begin to see some of the Stage 4 symptoms emerging. Burnout takes over if people never get a chance to renew the team spirit.

If your group is already in Stage 4, the Leveling stage, you should not use Style 4. In fact, a leader's use of Style 4 is one of the most common causes for leveling. How do you use Style 4 with a group? It's easy—don't bring the team members together. If you never bring your group together, you are part of the problem because you are abdicating the needs of the group.

If you delegate to the group, you are also creating problems because that will invite competition and power struggles as the group tries to get refocused without the help of a leader. Besides, not much is likely to get done because if it's the group's responsibility, it's no one's responsibility.

If you can't be present with the group, don't leave the group on its own—if you do, you will be abdicating. If you can't be there to lead, delegate to an individual team member and empower him or her to lead the group. Or, if you want to be more egalitarian, you can delegate to several team members by empowering them to lead specific areas of responsibility. But be careful because if you do that and disappear for too long, the group will still see you as abdicating.

Groups like to have someone in charge. If no one is, a new leader will emerge, or competing leaders will get into conflicts, or the group will start to come apart out of apathy. If you are not leading the group, then an informal leader will take over and most likely steer the group in a different direction. So for Stage 4, the *group development* cycle does not go to Style 4; it requires the intervention cycle.

To intervene with a group, you need to first use Style 3 to diagnose the situation by asking individuals and subgroups questions to find out their perceptions and to enlist them as contributors to the solution. Next, you should use Style 2 by bringing the group together to share your diagnosis and involve them in problem solving. This type of meeting is one step deeper than operational time-outs. These are developmental time-outs that go beyond working the task. Revitalizing the group may include strategic planning to redefine the mission or create a long-term vision, training to strengthen leadership or customer service skills, team building to improve communications or decision making, or process re-engineering to develop better ways to organize work flows, measure results, or monitor customer satisfaction. It may also include more complete celebrations of success such as sales recognition events or year-end outings. These refocusing activities should get team members involved in managing and implementing necessary changes.

If that is not enough to get the group back to the Performing stage, you need to move to Style 1 to re-form the group. The simplest and most common way to do that is to bring a new person in—good leaders are always looking for new talent to revitalize their teams. Another common action is to move someone out of the group—good leaders are also willing to step up to performance problems. They also keep their eyes open for opportunities for their best people to move ahead in the organization and will often move people out before they start to burn out or get bored. A third tactic is to reorganize the existing membership—break up a large team into subgroups, put two groups together under one leader, or shuffle several players to form new subgroups.

Whatever moves you make to re-form the group, it is important to recognize that you now have a new group, and it is critical to go back to Stage 1 to clarify the mission, reestablish the individual roles, and make people feel like they're part of the team. If you don't manage this transition, new people will learn the norms by the water fountain or in the cafeteria. Informal leaders will emerge, everyone except you will be determining the future of your group, and you will lose the benefit of bringing new blood in or moving deadwood out. If you go to all the trouble of reorganizing and you don't take the time to form and focus the new group, you have failed to manage the change.

LEADING THE GROUP + THE INDIVIDUALS

When you lead a team, you have to lead each individual with the right mix of leadership styles for his or her potential. Usually, that means using the 1-4-3-2 empowerment cycle, and from all of our data about best leaders and ideal leaders, we know that means using mostly S3 and S4 with individuals.

Simultaneously, you have to lead the development of positive group dynamics. Even if you could use mostly Style 4 with every individual, you still would need to form the group with S1 and get the group focused with S2 before you could move to S3 to facilitate high-performing, D2, distributed leadership, and shared-responsibility team effort. Figure 33 illustrates that the strategy for leading groups is completely different from the strategy for leading individuals.

In the beginning, team members want to know if you know where you're going and have a passion for getting there. They want to know if anyone is driving the bus, and your use of Style 1 is the answer.

Next they want to know if you are willing to listen and involve them in organizing to achieve the team's mission. By using Style 2, you turn your assignment into a shared mission.

Then they want to know if you are smart enough to divide up the work so that each person owns a piece of the puzzle and knows how he or she is linked to others. Distributed Style 2 answers this question.

Team members also want to know if you will bring the group together to coordinate their individual efforts and call time-outs so people can let their hair down—relax, celebrate, have some fun—but also continuously ask if there are better ways to get the work done. Your use of Style 3 should accomplish these objectives.

Periodically, they will want to know if you have the wisdom to step back and ask if the team is doing the right work in the best ways. This brings you back to Style 2.

Finally, they want to know if you are always looking for ways to reenergize the group with new people—new talent, skills, and experiences—plus encouraging people who are ready for another challenge to move on before they drag the team down with them. If you do, you have to go back to Style 1 to start over with a new group.

The full *group development* cycle for leading positive and productive group dynamics is 1-2-D2-3-2-1. Unlike leading individuals who thrive on predominant use of Styles 3 and 4 with a little 1 at the beginning and 2 at the end, leading the group requires predominant use of Styles 1 and 2 with a little 3 in the middle to keep the wheels turning smoothly.

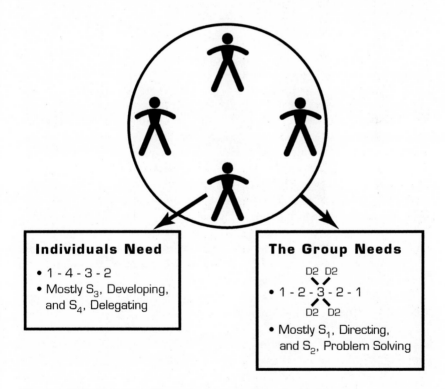

Individuals Need

- 1 - 4 - 3 - 2
- Mostly S_3, Developing, and S_4, Delegating

The Group Needs

- D2 D2
- 1 - 2 - 3 - 2 - 1
- D2 D2
- Mostly S_1, Directing, and S_2, Problem Solving

Figure 33 Leading Groups ≠ Leading Individuals

WHAT LEADERSHIP STYLES
DO YOU USE WITH GROUPS?

Remember the cases you read in chapter 1? You already know what leader-ship styles you used with the eight individual cases. Now you can see what responses you chose in the last two cases, which focused on group situations.

Write your answers in the spaces in the chart below to see how much of each style you used in these cases. After adding each column, multiply your totals by 10 to find out what percentage of each style you used in these situations.

	Style 1	Style 2	Style 3	Style 4
Case 9	C ____	D ____	A ____	B ____
Case 10	B ____	C ____	D ____	A ____
Totals	____	____	____	____
Percentages MULTIPLY X 10	____	____	____	____

These group cases presented you with two very different situations. Case 9 had to do with a new team made up of people from different departments meeting for the first time. Case 10 dealt with an existing team that had per-formed well over time but was starting to show signs of burnout.

Even so, cases 9 and 10 have some things in common. Both cases have to do with groups of people trying to work together as a team. Neither case calls for the use of Style 4, which would come across as abdicating, since any effective group requires some degree of involvement from its leader. Both cases also require the use of multiple leadership styles, which reflects the fact that groups tend to be quite complex, with stages of development shifting on an ongoing basis.

Case 9 involves a new cross-functional team organized for the purpose of improving quality in your department. Since this is a new group made up of people who know each other professionally but may not have worked together on a focused team effort, this group would start at Stage 1, Forming, and require some Style 1, directing, to get it started.

As the leader, you would want to thank everyone for committing his or her time and effort and let everyone know how critical his or her involvement will be to the success of this group. You should also explain your perception of this team's mission, its goals and the time frames, and the roles you envision for yourself and the other members of the team.

If that were all you did at the beginning, however, it would not be enough. To get the team members properly focused, you would then need to use some Style 2, problem solving, to solicit their input, their points of view, and their analysis of the current situation. You would also want to ask for their ideas about specific roles and responsibilities, and, most important, what it would take to make this team achieve results and work smoothly together.

In case 9, if you selected a balance of Style 1 and Style 2, you would be effective. Your use of Style 1 would ensure that the team gets the complete information it needs. Your use of Style 2 would orchestrate the buy-in process that is necessary to give the team a shared mission and an open climate in which every member of the team can contribute to the team's success.

If you used only Style 1, however, you would come across as dominating. The group would have a clear understanding of your expectations, but, without the opportunity to buy into a shared mission and a common set of objectives, they would see the team as yours instead of theirs. If they agreed with your assessment and recommendations, you might succeed. However, since it is unlikely that everyone would agree, using only Style 1 could put you in the position of leading with nobody following.

If you selected only Style 2 in this case, you might be all right in the long run because Style 2 leaves you in charge while being open to questions and suggestions from the team. Over time, the key members would ask all the questions that were needed in order to get clarity about the team's mission, goals, time frames, roles, and so on. However, in terms of efficiency, you might be slowing down the forming process as well as delaying the focusing process by failing to give people as much information as possible at the outset.

Furthermore, if you were to start with Style 2, you might not come across as strongly as you need to at the outset. The other leaders who were asked to attend this meeting would want to know, "Why am I here? What's the purpose? What is this team all about? What do you expect of me?" If you were to start with good answers to those questions, they would see you as credible and the use of their time as being valuable. If they had to drag them out of you, they would be less likely to see that their time was being well spent.

If you selected Style 3 for this case, you would be coming across as overaccommodating. Later on with this group, after specific goals have been identified, areas of responsibility have been assigned, and members of the team have been empowered to take the lead on particular tasks, Style 3 would be quite appropriate for orchestrating the group's productivity. In fact, it is the ideal way to help team members keep one another up to date, stay in close communication with one another, and get emerging problems out on the table. However, at this point, when the group is new and just trying to get its feet on the ground, you would come across as the kind of leader who could waste a lot of precious time with limited chances of obtaining results.

Particularly since this group is composed of other leaders, it is important to be strong at the outset. Often leaders of this type of team make the mistake of assuming that since all the members are high-powered leaders in their own right, they won't allow anybody to lead the team very forcefully. As a result, the leaders over-accommodate and lose the respect of the other members of the team. Then these high-powered leaders are quite likely to take the group over. They will get impatient and impose their own structure, which will then lead to more confusion, chaos, power struggles, and so on.

If you selected Style 4 for this situation, you would be abdicating. Your efforts to get other members of the team to take the lead in defining the team's mission and identifying what the team needs to do would produce one of two results. If they thought the group had value, team members would compete with one another and with you in their attempts to take control of the group. If they didn't think the group was important, they would simply check out. You would find them missing meetings, coming late, leaving early, withdrawing, and going off to do something else that they considered a more productive use of their time.

Case 10 presents a very different kind of group situation. The group in this case is a functional work group that has been together for a number of years and has been a very productive team. Individuals on the team have performed well and have worked smoothly in collaboration with one another. In many organizations, the only reward for successful teamwork is more work. The result after a while is burnout, which is what's happening right now in this case.

The best response in this type of situation would be the intervention cycle, starting first with Style 3, which could be done with one-on-one interviews or by bringing the group together for an open discussion. In either format, your role would be to ask questions, listen, and try to fully understand the different team members' points of view on what's going on in the department, what's working well, what's not working well, and what kinds of changes can be made to improve the situation.

Sometimes those discussions are sufficient to clear the air, get the team refocused, and recharge people's energy. However, if burnout has settled in, you would need to take the next step and use some Style 2, problem solving. With this approach, you would direct the group's attention to the most critical issues that surfaced in the prior discussions and then engage in some very focused problem solving in which members of the team would give you input about the causes of the problem and potential solutions. Together you would think through the alternatives and consider the costs and benefits of each. Ultimately you, as the leader, must decide what action plans will be pursued as a result of these meetings. So, if you selected a balance of Style 3 and Style 2, you would be leading this group through the intervention cycle in an effective way.

If you selected only Style 3, you could come across as over-accommodating by listening to everybody's point of view and then going nowhere as a result of those discussions. In fact, you could make the problem worse by bringing it to the surface and then taking no action.

If you used only Style 2, you run the risk of over-involving yourself too quickly. Often leaders who do this are guilty of pursuing quick-fix solutions without fully understanding the underlying causes and without getting the entire team's buy-in to the actions required to fix the problems. Consequently, these leaders often come across as going through the motions of having a meeting, getting the input, getting a quick solution, and saying that's that. Unfortunately, nothing really changes as a result.

If you selected Style 1 in this situation, you were overreacting by putting the responsibility entirely on your own shoulders for solving a problem that is better dealt with by the group. If the solutions you impose are good ones, you may get away with it and even earn some short-term respect from your colleagues, but you are probably sowing the seeds of future resistance as well as setting yourself up to be blindsided by future problems. No leader is good enough to anticipate all the issues that will surface in a group; therefore, you need to establish norms that encourage team members to bring problems to your attention and to always be thinking about ways of working together, smarter and better. Furthermore, if the solutions you impose are not well received or don't work, then you will definitely be perceived as dominating.

If you selected Style 4 in this situation, you would come across as abdicating. Occasionally problems will go away all by themselves, but generally problems on the surface are indicators of underlying issues that need to be addressed. If you don't ask for team members' thoughts and don't encourage open dialogue about the problems and potential solutions, the group will quickly lose faith in you as a leader. That does not mean they will stop talking about the problems and what needs to be done to fix them; it simply means that they won't talk to *you* about them anymore. Instead they will bitch and moan to one another. In time, the focus of that complaining may very well redirect itself toward you. Instead of talking about the issues and how to fix them, they may equate you with the problems and talk about you and your lack of effectiveness as a leader.

Now that you have thought about your responses to these hypothetical cases, here are two real cases that make these points even more dramatically.

A CONSENSUS FOR CHAOS

Denise was hired as the new general manager for a microelectronics firm by Joe, the founder and CEO. A technically talented, ambitious entrepreneur, Joe had watched his company grow from a start-up with six employees to an organization with a staff of sixty. Knowing that he was too hands-on to be effective in what had become an increasingly diversified organization, he realized that he no longer had the ability (or the inclination) to manage the day-to-day operations of his shop. In hiring Denise he chose someone he believed had the skills to run a multifaceted company that required far more coordination of disparate functions than his limited high-control style allowed for.

While just out of graduate school, Denise was an expert in "high-performance systems," an approach to management designed to enhance a company's performance through the use of teamwork. She had expertise, Joe was led to believe, in transforming traditional hierarchical organizations into more streamlined, horizontal, participatory models. In making his decision to hire Denise, Joe was particularly impressed with her insight into the problems that entrepreneurs have when their companies grow beyond the reach of one person's hands-on control. "I want you to turn us into a high-class teamwork operation," was his charge to her. "And I don't care what it takes to do it. The ball is in your hands."

Denise, exhilarated at the opportunity to apply all her hard-learned theory, set out to do the job she was hired to do. She immediately called a "community meeting" at which she announced that Joe, the CEO, had hired her to change the way things were done in the organization.

The decision-making process in the company, she announced, was about to change dramatically. She instituted a model she had studied in school called PPBS, which stood for Planning, Programming, and Budgeting System. The central focus of the system was on consensual decision making. This new approach meant that from that point on all the decisions would be made in an open forum. There would be frequent scheduled meetings of the entire employee group at which anyone could have a say about anything. Furthermore, she proclaimed that any member could call an additional unscheduled meeting of the entire community to address unanticipated issues as they emerged.

Since the group was so large she also added a structure within which the large group would work. At the first full employee meeting she instructed people to form six teams of ten. Each team was made up of as diverse a group of employees as possible to avoid clustering with people who were in the same department or performed the same function. These teams, Denise explained, would help in managing the size of the overall group. When an issue was brought up, each team's members would spend some time talking about it among themselves for a brief period to give everyone a chance to have input. Then the community would reconvene as a whole, each team would report on its conversation, and after the reports the overall group would attempt to gain consensus on whatever the issue happened to be.

While Joe was a little disconcerted over the thought of giving over so much power to so many people, Denise had come highly recommended and he decided, for the moment, to give her the benefit of the doubt. As time went on, however, Joe's doubts grew, and the possibility of any benefit coming from Denise's approach diminished rapidly. From the outset there was a great deal of confusion. People were excited about the possibility of having some say in how the organization was run but doubted whether Joe was really going to give up control. They also had a lot of fears, most of which went unspoken except during private conversations in the washroom, about what kinds of negative repercussions would follow if anyone took a position that differed from Joe's. In the past, Joe, like many entrepreneurial founders of organizations, had shown little tolerance for any ideas that were divergent from his. While people had heard from Denise that decision making was now in their hands, no one really believed that was true.

During the first few community meetings, people asked Denise many questions about how she intended to manage the day-to-day operations and any changes she would make. Her response to them was, "My philosophy is that we will make all important decisions in this forum." When asked more probing questions, she would most often turn the tables on the questioner and ask, "What do you think about that?"

Within a month of Denise's taking charge, things began to unravel. Some people started showing up late to the meetings, reading newspapers during the meetings, and avoiding any real substantive conversation, while others kept bringing up issues for discussion that had little or no real consequence, like whether to use powder or liquid soap in the washrooms. Joe noticed that there was a lot of conversation buzzing in the hallways, most of it negative, about the new scenario. When he asked Denise what she thought was going on, she replied that it takes time to build a high-performing organization and people need time to get acclimated to operating in new ways. Within two weeks of that conversation Joe asked Denise for her resignation.

What happened in this scenario is being played out in corporations of all sizes all over the world. In an effort to reinvent their companies by restructuring and reshaping the way they operate, shifting from traditional pyramid-like organizations to more streamlined, horizontal, participatory approaches, organizational leaders and would-be organizational leaders are making the same mistakes Denise made.

One of her biggest mistakes was not paying attention to the stages of group development as she was trying to craft her new organization into a team-driven system. By trying to force a consensus approach right out of the starting gate, she virtually ignored the first two stages of group development. She tried to tap into the kind of shared responsibility that can occur only in a situation where the team has genuinely built itself up into the Performing stage.

What Denise should have done was realized that her new organization and its respective teams were in the Forming stage, and that they needed a lot of direction from her. She should have formed an alliance with Joe, and together they should have crafted a new vision for the organization and clearly articulated what that vision was to the troops.

Next she should have orchestrated and encouraged discussion of what the new way of doing things would mean, allowing people to express their concerns and figure out how they could best succeed in the new organization. Then she should have focused on the functional work teams instead of the community, helping them use their time to develop operating systems that would work for them. She also should have established rewards for team performance to really send the message that what mattered was producing team results, not whether or not Joe liked what you had to say. These efforts would have helped her move the teams through the Focusing stage.

Had she carefully moved the work teams through the first two stages, Denise would have had a much better chance of creating the kind of collaborative organization she had hoped to create and avoiding the kind of chaotic one she was forced to leave.

MAKING A GOOD TEAM EVEN BETTER

Now that you've seen how not to manage teams, we'd like to tell you about a team in which the group dynamics were managed extraordinarily well.

The team involved Karen, who was the head of a strategic planning department at a large manufacturer of building supplies. Karen and her team of six managers and four support staff were known throughout the organization as a high-performing team. Her bosses often used her group as an example of a model team, her department was designated as an important rotational assignment for new recruits with leadership potential, and other fast trackers were often assigned to her team to learn about teamwork. The team had a reputation for working extraordinarily hard, often putting in long hours, working evenings and weekends, and achieving extraordinary results. Members were all committed to quality and to making sure that the work they did was the best it could possibly be.

Karen had done a good initial job of building her team. They had a clear mission, and all the members had bought into the goals of the group. Stages 1 and 2 of the *group development* cycle, Forming and Focusing, had been managed very well, and high performance was now the norm. These people really cranked out the work and it was always top quality.

When we first met Karen, her team was beginning a transition process that would significantly affect their work. Rumblings were beginning to surface that some people were growing tired of the relentless pace that their high performance had wrought. For example, one member said, "I don't mind putting in long hours once in a while, but it never ends." Some people observed that there seemed to be nothing but peaks in the way they worked, while others complained that they never seemed to take time to celebrate their successes. Conflicts began to emerge and it became increasingly clear that the team was heading toward serious burnout.

Without thinking per se about the stages of group development, Karen knew intuitively that her team was approaching the Leveling stage and needed some refocusing. She also knew that making that shift required her to rethink what her team was all about and how it operated.

As she talked to some of her customers, Karen began to question whether the team was really utilizing its resources to the fullest extent and meeting the needs of the customers in the best possible way. In further discussions, she and her boss agreed that the department could offer a lot more to the future of the corporation if some changes were made.

With that in mind, Karen began the process of moving some people out of the department and recruiting replacements who could add a different kind of value to the team. In addition, she decided that some formal teambuilding might help the new team get started on the right foot.

As soon as all of the new people were onboard, an off-site session was held for the purpose of getting the team properly formed and focused. There were two agendas for that meeting. The first was to facilitate the re-forming of the group by giving people an opportunity to really get to know one another. The second was to reexamine the mission and operating norms of the team to see if they could be improved upon, so that high-quality work could be sustained without burning people out.

Even though most of the team members had been together for a few years, their incredible work pace had not left them much time to know each other as people. And with three brand-new team members, it was critical for the group to deal with the inclusion aspect of forming. The off-site teambuilding gave them a way to do that in a relaxed and safe environment that invited them to let their hair down and really get connected.

As soon as the people started to feel like a solid group, the conversation shifted to rethinking the team's mission and each person's role. That started with Karen's sharing of her perspective, which included input from her boss and the customers she had spoken to. After that, the group moved headlong into refocusing.

Initially, the discussion was about the team's mission and people's ideas about how to add more value by providing different services to a broader customer base. There was a lot of excitement about that. The conversation got stickier as everyone started thinking through what changes they would have to make to achieve the new mission.

An example of the type of issue that was addressed was the way Karen parceled out the work. Her style in the past had been to look at an assignment and determine who would be best for that assignment, sometimes based on the person's expertise in that area, but just as often based on her judgment that the project would stretch him or her developmentally. Then she would assign responsibilities on a one-to-one basis.

As the refocusing stage proceeded, one of the changes made was to have Karen present projects to the group before giving them to anyone and get more input from the team as to the best way to proceed. This shift would enable Karen to solicit the team members' thoughts on who might be interested in or skilled for a particular assignment, who might work well together, what might be a developmental opportunity for someone, and so on.

As the team members began to work in this new way, they got energized. They also expressed the belief that, if this were truly the way they would now work together, they could accomplish even more than they had in the past and be assured that they were adding the most value to the organization as well. And as they talked they created for themselves what we've been calling the distributed leadership approach.

Talk about buy-in! People started saying things like, "I want to be the lead person on that project," "I think I can make a contribution as a support person on this project," and "I'm willing to do that, but only if she agrees to help me with this." People started taking responsibility for all sorts of things that had previously been considered part of someone else's domain, including Karen's. She still retained her leadership position and her power in the group, but she strongly embraced this new way of operating. She realized that utilizing everyone on the team to refocus the way members operated had gotten their buy-in. She also recognized that it would bring them to a new level of performance that would be even more effective than in the past.

Perhaps the most important lesson in this case is the fact that even high-performing teams can get into trouble. The first thing a team leader needs to do is make sure he or she moves the team through the Forming and Focusing stages in a way that positions the team for high performance. Karen did that very well. The next thing a team leader needs to keep in mind is that the stages of group development are not static, but rather dynamic and ongoing.

Karen could have made the mistake of assuming, as many team leaders do, that her high-performing team was at its best and was destined to stay in high performance forever. She didn't. She understood that unless a leader intervenes, a high-performing team is destined to fall into leveling. Karen responded to the leveling signals her team was sending her and did the right thing. She got input from her customers, brought in new talent, and got assistance with re-forming and refocusing the group. The result was that she, with the team's help, transformed her department into an even higher-performing team than it had been.

DO GROUPS HAVE PERSONALITIES?

In the last chapter, we talked about the way personality type can influence the way you manage the performance contracting process with different individuals. We are often asked if groups also have personalities. We don't think they do per se, but the interplay of team members' personalities certainly gives each group its own chemistry.

How can you use this to increase your effectiveness as a team leader? One way is to consider the predominant preferences of the team members and customize the communications to work best for them. Another is to make sure that team members with non-dominant preferences don't get ignored or frustrated. A third is to balance the varying preferences and take advantage of each person's strengths.

The Soft-Spoken and the Outspoken

Consider a team of mostly Extraverts (E's). For them, the Forming and Focusing stages will work best if they can be done in person, but other approaches will work as long as there is plenty of time for discussion. Don't expect that after you introduce members to one another, announce the team's objectives, and explain how each person fits on the team, members will be ready for you to give out assignments. They will have lots of questions about who, what, where, when, and why, and they will have something to say about each one. Remember, Extraverts take in information with their mouths moving.

In the Performing and Leveling stages, you also need to find ways for an Extraverted group to have lots of conversation. Since members learn from hearing their own thoughts as well as others', problem solving and team planning will be more effective through interaction. Strategic planning and team-building won't work well if people don't come together. And don't even think about celebrating success by e-mailing everyone a gift certificate.

In contrast, a team composed primarily of Introverts (I's) might listen to your forming speech with members just nodding their heads. Until they have had some time to think about the issues, they won't have a lot of questions or recommendations. If you want to get them more involved in focusing, try sending them some material to read in advance and giving them some questions to think about before they come. When you get them together, you might want to start by having them talk in pairs to break the ice. Whenever you want their ideas, give them a few minutes to make some notes to themselves about the topic before launching into a discussion.

In the Performing and Leveling stages, an Introverted group will not need to come together very often, nor will the team members want meetings to last very long. They may prefer to keep each other updated via e-mail or voice mail and may float new ideas to the group in the same way. Planning and re-focusing activities will be most effective if you talk to members individually first so that you can start the meeting with a summary of the key issues. Or better yet, send them the summary ahead of time so they can think about the issues before the meeting. With a heavily Introverted group, you don't need to plan a lot of celebrations—time off for good behavior will be more appreciated than having to spend additional time with the group.

In a predominantly Extraverted group, make sure the Introverts don't get distracted by too many meetings. In the meetings they do attend, invite them to share their thoughts and try to get the Extraverts to reflect before they respond.

In a heavily Introverted group, make sure some meetings are scheduled. In those meetings, give the Extraverts some opportunities to think out loud without having done their "homework" or send out a proposal in advance and get the Introverts to respond in ways that encourage exploration.

In a balanced group, let the Extraverts get the conversations started but be careful not to let them dominate the airtime. Extraverts start talking to explore the parameters of a problem or opportunity and Introverts sit back, take in the information, and speak when they have a solution in mind. To use the strengths of both preferences, encourage the Extraverts to jump-start the analysis of the situation and summarize their points so they feel heard, and then ask the Introverts to share their thoughts about possible courses of action.

This is much better than having the Introverts accuse the Extraverts of talking to hear their own voices or not thinking before they speak. And you don't want the Extraverts accusing the Introverts of not caring enough to open their mouths or wanting to study everything to death.

The Dreamers and the Doers

In a group that is predominantly made up of Sensing (S) team members, the Forming and Focusing stages need to include facts, figures, numbers, and details. To get their arms around a situation, S's want to know the background—what's going on now and how did it get this way? Since they need to know with some degree of precision, you have to be prepared for some very probing questions. ES's will get oriented through discussions, especially ones that focus on taking immediate action. IS's will prefer to read spreadsheets and supporting documents, especially if they focus on ways to keep things running smoothly. What these S's have in common is the need for detail about the current reality and the history behind it—information that will help them get grounded.

When a Sensing team comes together in the Performing and Leveling stages, they will feel most productive if they focus on what has been done. Updates will often include a rehash of the problem situation and the plan for fixing it, as well as a review of the steps that have been taken. Presentations will be filled with data, and numbers will abound. Speakers will offer facts and build to a conclusion or expect the audience to draw their own conclusions. Leveling meetings will focus on ways to improve productivity and may be dominated by fish bones, why charts, and statistical processes.

For a team of Intuitive (N) people, focusing on the past and present is like being stuck in the mud. They prefer to be bubbling over with excitement about the future. Forming and focusing take place at a high level as N's look at the possibilities from a broad perspective. They like pictures, charts, images, and models but feel overloaded if you bore them with too many details. EN's love to brainstorm—nothing gets them more motivated than throwing around ideas, especially ones for creating structural or system-wide changes. IN's are more likely to present a well-conceived idea—a model, a concept, or a vision—something that brings a different perspective. The important thing for a group of N's is having a chance to be innovative and use their creativity.

When an Intuitive team has Performing meetings, the conversation focuses on where they are going, not where they have been. Progress reports explore the options and focus on the next steps that are most likely to produce the desired future. Presentations include charts and pictures and may be vague or inaccurate about factual matters. Speakers start with conclusions and only provide backup detail if they have to. Leveling meetings are also future oriented and tend to focus on vision, values, models, concepts, and whole-system changes.

Since most teams have both Sensing and Intuitive members, it is usually possible to use both sets of skills. Encourage the S's to diagnose the current situation and the N's to envision the future. Invite the N's to imagine new possibilities and ask the S's to make sure plans are realistic. Let the Sensing members monitor the team's activities while making sure the Intuitive members keep the vision alive.

In a predominantly Sensing group, it is important to give the Intuitive members room to dream and explore the future. Conversely, in a heavily Intuitive group, you need to allow the Sensing members to keep things practical and realistic. In a mixed group, you have to maintain enough mutual respect so that the N's don't accuse the S's of hanging on to the past and defending the status quo, and the S's don't accuse the N's of needlessly stirring up the pot and promoting change for change's sake.

Sense and Sensitivity

For a team of Thinking (T) members, forming and focusing need to be based on logic. T's want to hear a dispassionate, matter-of-fact presentation of the problem or opportunity. They expect an objective analysis of the historical precedents that inform the current situation—strategies and policies and the rationale behind them, structures and systems and the reasons they exist. To get focused, NT's need to think about and/or debate the long-term impacts of the team's actions—the pros and cons, the costs and benefits, and the logical outcome of what they plan to do. ST's are more concerned about short-term fixes but still want to think about why the trains aren't running on time and what it will take to correct the problem. What all T's have in common is the need to think that what they are going to do will make their world a little better than it would be if they don't proceed.

For a group of Feeling (F) individuals, forming and focusing need to touch members' emotions. F's respond best to a personalization of the problem or opportunity. They like to know how people are being affected in the current situation and how problems are manifesting in people's behavior and what people are saying about them. To get focused, SF's need to identify some concrete activities that will increase harmony—a party, a take-a-customer-to-lunch campaign, or an employee recognition program. NF's are more likely to focus on ways to tap into human potential, such as with teambuilding sessions, leadership development activities, or career counseling systems. What all F's have in common is the need to feel like they are making a positive impact on how people interact with one another and the way they feel about their work.

Most corporate environments are predominantly made up of T's, but many smaller organizations are populated with F's, and most workplaces have some of each. As a team leader, you should make use of both preferences. Encourage the Feeling team members to talk about the human factors involved in any organizational change—those that are present and those that are desired. Invite the Thinking members to discuss the strategies, structures, and systems—how they cause dysfunction and ways they can be improved. Organizational improvements require behavioral and structural changes that require both an analytical and an empathic point of view.

In a group that has mostly Ts, you have to get them to acknowledge and appreciate the sensitivities of the F's as well as their empathy for the feelings of others. In a Feeling-dominated group, you need to encourage a respect for the objectivity, logic, and long-range perspective of the Thinking members. These strengths will be wasted if the T's accuse the F's of being fuzzy-minded bleeding hearts or the F's accuse the T's of being cold-blooded and heartless.

Go with the Flow or Make the Flow Go

Imagine a team of Judging (J) people. For them, the Forming and Focusing stages will be incomplete until a plan is in place. Since J's thrive on goals, tasks, checklists, and checkpoints, they are in their element with focusing. Because they are also driven toward closure, they may not spend enough time on forming and may develop project plans without understanding the team's mission, knowing who the players are, or learning what each one brings to the party. They are more likely to go through the Forming process if you list the steps that are involved and check off each one as they complete it. Judging teams do very well with complex assignments—they just need enough time to create a complete plan, because they will not perform efficiently without one.

In the Performing stage, J's prefer scheduled meeting times. They like brief check-ins to compare actual progress against the plan, and whenever they can check something off, members will be pleased. When they cannot, they will make a new plan. Leveling meetings also need to be structured for Judging team members to participate comfortably. If you can get them to sit still long enough, they can plan for improved teamwork as readily as they can organize for an assignment.

In contrast, a team of Perceiving (P) members will be stifled by a project plan. Their approach to forming and focusing is to explore the options. They like to know what the team has to do but prefer to stay open about how to get the work done. They also like to know what the other team members can contribute, but, instead of defining roles, they work better if the relationships emerge as the work demands. Unlike J's, they will enjoy the Forming process but will resist attempts to get organized and structured in the Focusing stage. Since P's do their best work at the last minute and are exceptional troubleshooters, they do best with assignments that require an immediate response and have no time for careful planning.

In the Performing stage, a Perceiving team will come together when it needs to. Schedule meetings if you must, but assume that some team members will always have good reasons for missing some. When you do get together, don't waste your time planning an agenda because it won't be followed—you will do better to find out what needs to be addressed when you get there. If leveling meetings are needed, a Perceiving group will respond as they do to any other topic: as long as they perceive the team's issues as the most pressing, they will consider all possible ways to make improvements. Don't expect definitive actions for going forward, but changes will occur in bits and pieces over time.

If you have a predominantly Judging group, you need to make sure the Perceiving team members don't get stifled by all the planning and that the Judging members appreciate how flexible and responsive the Perceiving members can be if they let them run. Most large corporations have Judging cultures and have been weeding out the P's for years but are in need of their skills for increased customer responsiveness and to reinvent themselves faster than the competition.

In a group dominated by Perceiving members, you need to help them accept that structure is needed at times and encourage them to let the Judging members provide it. In even the most spontaneous and creative organizations in the dot-com economy, employees still want clear expectations, structures for salary and benefits, and guidelines for acceptable behavior. And while customers are clamoring for increased responsiveness and flexibility, they still expect to get clear proposals, well-managed projects, and timely and accurate invoices.

If you can take advantage of the best of both preferences, your team will be a lot more successful than if the J's throw the P's out the door for being unpredictable, irresponsible flakes, or the P's escape the corporate confines because the J's are micromanaging, process-driven control freaks.

In their *Introduction to Type in Organizations,* Hirsh and Kummerow suggest that it is "wise for you to consult others of opposite preferences when making important decisions." That is not an easy thing to do, especially when you are pressed for time and stretched thin. It is easier to make decisions in your preferred mode. But that's what the power of teamwork is all about. Decisions may be slower but will usually be better if you can develop norms of mutual respect and include everyone's unique contributions in the Forming and Focusing stages of group development. If you do that, you will have many hands—and brains—working together to achieve results in the Performing stage and willing to push to higher levels of performance in the Leveling stage.

The Secrets of The Leader's Window: Making Teams Work

As we emphasized in the last chapter, one of the main reasons teams don't work is an inadequate understanding of what leaders have do to orchestrate the group dynamics that occur when team members come together. Without the leadership skills required for building and maintaining group synergy, all the programs, projects, and structures in the world won't help them make teams successful. But as you saw in the case of Denise, bringing the whole group together for decision making can also lead to disaster.

The challenge of leading a team is combining what you know about leading group dynamics with what you know about leading individuals. That's what The Leader's Window does, and that's what this chapter is all about. It will show you how to put together the *group development* cycle and the *empowerment* cycle in a simple but sophisticated way that guarantees results while helping you avoid the traps that have plagued unsuccessful teams.

TEAMS DON'T ALWAYS WORK

The view through The Leader's Window is not what most managers see when they look at teams. Here are a few examples.

Jim, the director of organization development for a medium-sized electronics company, was working overtime to eliminate the "invisible boundaries" that existed between divisions. In his determination to "unleash the company's full potential," he had established cross-functional teams designed to create a new kind of organization that thrives on consensus. Despite Jim's all-out effort to promote teamwork across functions, the only outcomes were endless meetings and few results. The managers who were involved were praying that "this too shall pass" so they could get back to their "real jobs."

Robert, the president of a major chemical company, wanted his senior VPs to facilitate team meetings that would involve employees in transforming the company. They were reluctant, and, as their resistance increased, Bob asked us to find out why they were unwilling to "take the leap of faith" required to shift from "fire fighting to fire prevention." "We're too busy putting out fires," was what we heard from every VP.

Mary, a partner in a large accounting firm, had encouraged her managers to improve teamwork by empowering their staffs. "How can we empower anyone when we have no real power ourselves?" asked one manager. "We're merely the conduit for pushing work down the organization. Teamwork here means telling him to do this and her to do that."

These are common complaints from corporations around the world. In their attempts to keep up with the dramatic changes of the past decade, executives have groped for new ways to manage their organizations. Unfortunately, not every new idea is grounded in reality.

SEVEN MYTHS OF TEAMWORK

While teamwork is an essential ingredient of the brave new world, the conventional wisdom about teams is ancient history that fails to deal with the complexity of what it takes to create and sustain a high-performing team. Here are seven deadly myths about teamwork that can actually prevent teams from realizing their full potential. Each myth is followed by a new reality—bits of Window Wisdom for today's fast-paced organizations.

Myth #1: Being a team player is more important than being an individual contributor. In reality, team success requires bringing the right individuals together and getting them to do the right things at the right times.

Myth #2: Assembling a group of highly talented individuals is all it takes to have a high-performing team. In reality, working in cooperation with others can be challenging for high-powered individuals who are used to operating as "lone rangers."

Myth #3: It takes a long time to get teams up and running. In reality, there are many ways a leader can get a team "off to a running start."

Myth #4: Teams have to work through conflicts before they can be productive. In reality, conflicts can tear a team apart and can be avoided if the group's needs are dealt with.

Myth #5: Teamwork means consensus decision making. In reality, while consensus can be useful on the rare occasion when you need full and unequivocal agreement, it most often has a paralyzing and debilitating impact on a team's performance.

Myth #6: Accountability on a team means that everyone is responsible for everything. In reality, if it's the group's responsibility, it's no one's responsibility. Individual team members need to be accountable for specific decisions.

Myth #7: Teams work better if everyone is equal—no leaders or followers. In reality, high-performing teams have strong, passionate leaders who find ways to distribute leadership among the team members. Everyone leads and everyone follows.

This last myth is one of the most dangerous. Some organizations have even experimented with what Brian Dumaine calls "the breakthrough of the 1990's . . . self-managed teams, cross-functional teams, high-performance teams, or, to coin a phrase, super teams" (Dumaine 1990). These attempts at self-direction create structures that support teamwork, and while a few of these initiatives have succeeded, most of them have failed. Why? Because of these myths about teamwork and the misconceptions they perpetuate about the real leadership that is needed to get people to work together.

Jack Orsburn, the lead author of *Self-Directed Work Teams* (1991), the book regarded by most people as the definitive work on the self-management phenomenon, is a strong proponent of integrating leadership training and coaching into any team development process. In Jack's work with his clients, whenever a team starts down the path toward higher levels of employee involvement, one of the first things he does is teach them The L4 System. He used to teach situational leadership primarily as a way to get the team members and their supervisors to start thinking about a range of leadership options, but when Jack discovered The L4 System, he realized that the behavioral descriptions of the styles made it much easier for leaders to learn how to implement each style. He thought that the 1-4-3-2 empowerment cycle would be very helpful to supervisors as they handed off responsibilities to team members, and he thought the 1-2-D2-3-2-1 *group development* cycle would give them a road map for bringing the players together.

Most significant, when Jack saw the four secrets of The Leader's Window, he looked at them, sat back, thought for a minute, and then said, "Yeah, that's it. On this one piece of paper, I can tell you what went right with every team that succeeded. And I can pinpoint what went wrong with every team that failed."

WHAT DOES A HIGH-PERFORMING
TEAM LOOK LIKE?

Have you ever been on a team where everyone was motivated, energized, focused, purposeful, and willing to go the extra mile? If you have, take a minute to think about your experience. What were the circumstances that produced this situation? Who was involved? What did they do—as individuals and as a group? And what role did the leader play in making this a high-energy experience?

These are questions that we have asked managers from all sorts and sizes of organizations—private, public, manufacturing, service, big, medium-sized, and small. As we have listened to their stories, we have found striking similarities across people's experiences. In most cases, the team's mission had the potential for high impact with customers, or it was highly visible in the organization, or both. There was also time pressure—a small window of opportunity to produce results.

Beyond these external factors over which the people had little or no control, there were internal factors over which the team or the team's leader had significant influence. First, the team members were very talented and had the skill sets to get the job done. They also knew why they and their colleagues were on the team.

The leader was passionate about the team's goals, strongly committed to delivering results, and actively involved with the team members. The leader set high expectations and presented the assignment as a challenge, sometimes even a "mission impossible" situation, and an opportunity for each team member to stretch, learn, and take risks. The leader and the team members adopted a can-do attitude, but this aggressive stance was balanced by availability and support from the leader and from other teammates.

Initial meetings got everyone focused on the team's mission and his or her role in achieving it. Team members had clear assignments and knew how their responsibilities were linked to others'. They felt trusted to do what they needed to do on behalf of the team. And they knew they could go to others for help when they needed it.

Ongoing meetings ensured that the communication channels were wide open, with everyone talking to whomever they needed to. As a result, people got information quickly, problems surfaced rapidly, and there was lots of problem solving when the effort hit a snag. They also responded vigorously when new opportunities arose.

One last factor was typical of most of these teams. They found ways to develop a team spirit and often had a lot of fun. They had positive, productive group dynamics. Members felt energized by their involvement with the team. They were focused on what they had to do to make the team succeed and upbeat about the way everyone on the team worked together. These teams were able to accomplish significant results in remarkably short times. They also found ways to celebrate their successes.

REALITY FOR REAL-WORLD TEAMS

The stories we have heard about high-performing teams have given us a reality-based view of what it takes to make teams work—a new perspective that challenges the myths of the past. This perspective is the foundation for The Leader's Window—a comprehensive view of how to make effective team leadership work for you.

As you move through this chapter, you will learn the four secrets of The Leader's Window. Secret 1 focuses on using Styles 1 and 2 with the group to provide the team members with the information they need to get started and, most important, to get the group's buy-in to achieving the team's mission. Secret 2 focuses on using Styles 1 and 4 with individuals to give them the directions they need so you can delegate meaningful responsibilities to them. Secret 3 focuses on using Styles 3 and 4 to give individuals the independence they need to feel empowered and the support they need to guarantee results. Finally, Secret 4 focuses on using Styles 2 and 3 to provide the group with a way to maintain communication, share responsibility, and focus on continuous improvements.

As the secrets unfold and you learn to open and close the different parts of The Leader's Window, you will gain a clear view of how to manage a team and its members simultaneously. When you look at your world through this window, you will see how to unlock the mysteries of high-performance leadership in a way that leads to clarity of focus and commitment of purpose for the teams that you lead.

THE LEADER'S BOX

In chapter 8, we brought up the subject of reality to help you understand why the 1-4-3-2 empowerment cycle works with individuals. Now that we have explained the difference between leading individuals and leading groups, and have shown you how to be an effective leader of a team's group dynamics, we need to return to the subject of reality.

We never said that organizations make it easy for you to be a successful leader. In fact, since most hierarchies have room at the top for only a few people, those who get there often make it as hard as possible for their successors to dethrone them. Not that they do it intentionally. It's just that they become the newest senders of pressure-packed messages that make it difficult for people at lower levels to fully succeed.

With that in mind, try this question on for size. Have you ever felt like you were caught in the middle between conflicting pressures from above and below? We certainly have, and from what we've heard from managers all over the world, it happens to almost everyone who tries to lead in a complex organization. We call this dilemma The Leader's Box since the competing pressures usually make you feel boxed in. Looking at Figure 34, on the next page, can help you visualize and understand this dilemma.

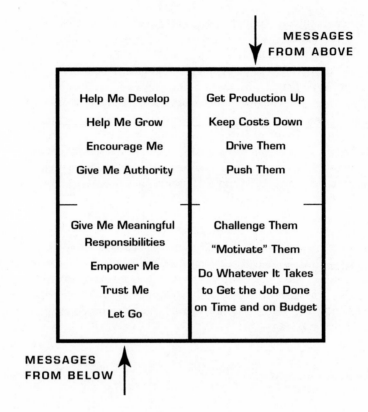

Figure 34 The Leader's Box

On the right in the figure you can see the messages that typically descend from on high. In most organizations, management wants production up and costs down. They expect you to do more with fewer resources. They tell you to challenge your people, drive them, push them, and motivate them. In other words, do whatever it takes to get the job done on time and on budget. Basically, those are Style 1 or Style 2 messages: take charge, be a driver, make things happen, and produce results.

On the left in the figure you can see the messages that tend to bubble up from below. Team members want their managers to let go. They say, "Empower me, trust me, give me responsibility and the authority to go with it." At the same time, they don't want to be out on a limb by themselves, so they also say, "Encourage me, support me, help me grow my ability to do my current job, and help me develop the skills that will open up new career opportunities." These are basically Style 3 and Style 4 messages: give your people opportunities to take charge and help them learn from the experience.

WHO IS RIGHT?

Now, here's a tough question for you. Who is right? Which messages do you listen to—the ones from above or those from below?

When we pose this question to groups of managers, some agree with each point of view. Those who agree with the messages from above say things like "Who signs your paycheck?" and "They're the bosses." Those who agree with the messages from below make comments like "The only way you can get the results management wants is to follow the advice from below."

Some will argue that you have to pay attention to both messages. They say that you should be a buffer by paying lip service to the messages from above while really acting on the messages from below. Their coping strategy is to try to keep both sides happy.

Others who think you have to do both will contend that the situation determines which one you listen to. They say that you should pay attention to the messages from below as long as you have the time to do it and it is working. But if you get caught in a crunch, you have to follow the advice from above. With this strategy, each side gets a little attention, but neither is truly happy.

We are convinced that you can't win if you pick one side or the other. We are also skeptical that you can please everyone. And we are equally reluctant to endorse a strategy of being supportive when you can but sticking it to people when you have to.

In contrast, we are strongly convinced that there is truth in both sets of messages and both need to be delivered all the time. We also believe that if you get these two messages in the right places, you can be a very effective leader. To do that, all you need to do is remember what we talked about in the preceding chapter: To lead a high-performing team, you have to lead the group as well as the individuals. And they have different needs that require different combinations of leadership styles.

When managers say drive them, push them, challenge them, the essential word is *them*. They are talking about the group and may not even recognize them as individuals. And they are right; groups work best when a leader is clearly in charge, using Styles 1 and 2.

When team members say trust me, empower me, help me grow, help me develop, the critical word is *me*. They're talking about themselves as individuals, and they are also right. Individuals work best when they have responsibility with Styles 3 and 4.

HOW DO YOU GET OUT OF THE BOX?

As shown in Figure 35, on the next page, best leaders, instinctively or through learning, deliver these messages to the right places. They use Styles 1 and 2 to

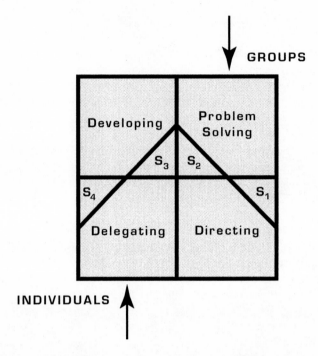

**Figure 35 Use Mostly S₁ and S₂ with Groups,
Mostly S₃ and S₄ with Individuals**

take charge of the group by challenging the team, pushing the group to give its all, and encouraging everyone to take risks and stretch. Simultaneously, they use Styles 3 and 4 to *empower individual team members* by giving them significant responsibilities, letting them know that they are counting on them to deliver top-quality results, and being available to provide support as it is needed.

The worst leaders usually get these messages backward. First they use Style 4 or 3 with the group. They abdicate with the group by never bringing the team members together, or they over-accommodate the group by trying to get complete agreement about every decision that has to be made. Then when the group flounders and things go wrong, they use Styles 1 and 2 with the individuals. They dominate the individuals by criticizing their efforts, barking orders, and undercutting any attempts to take responsibility, or they over-involve themselves by listening a little before they take over.

The way to avoid getting trapped by The Leader's Box is to use mostly directing and problem solving with groups and mostly delegating and developing with individuals.

WORKING SMARTER

In Figure 36, we have added the 1-4-3-2 cycle to the preceding diagram. This picture is a guide for working smarter instead of harder. It shows you how to use the power of the group at the beginning and at the end of the empowerment cycle.

Instead of having separate meetings with individuals to explain their responsibilities, the idea is to meet with them as a group. This saves you time while ensuring that each team member not only knows his or her responsibilities but also is aware of what everyone else is doing. Reviewing assignments as a group can also help you build commitment to the team and establish some peer pressure for individual performance.

After getting the group started, you use mostly delegating and developing with the individuals. This allows them the freedom to work as trusted and respected employees while providing them with the support they need whenever they get stuck.

Finally, instead of doing problem solving with each individual in separate one-on-one meetings, you can again save yourself time by meeting with the

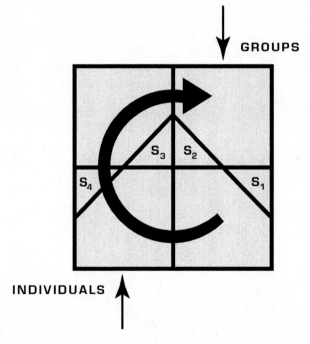

Figure 36 Working Smarter: Use Groups at the
Beginning and End of 1-4-3-2

entire group. This also keeps team members updated about progress toward team objectives as well as informed about problems that are surfacing in other people's areas of responsibility.

Often, the team members can make your job easier and your team's efforts more productive by sharing their experiences with one another. When problem solving is needed, your brain is not the only one engaged in the process. More important, when everyone is stumped or your team is confronting cutting-edge territory, the synergy that emerges from group interaction can lead to quantum leaps in everyone's thinking and breakthrough strategies for the team.

DON'T FORGET WHAT IT TAKES
TO START A GROUP

In order to make this strategy work with a new team, you have to remember to form and focus the group. To get the group properly launched, you start with Style 1 to clarify the team's mission, introduce the team members, and explain what each one brings to the party. Then you need to move up to Style 2 with the group to get the members' buy-in, define responsibilities, and organize the team's processes. The third step is to empower each team member to get the team's work done. That brings you back down to intersect with the individual 1-4-3-2 cycle, as shown in Figure 37.

Now the picture is complete. This is *The Leader's Window*.

Within this picture, there are four distinct phases of teamwork, each requiring the use of two leadership styles. There is a secret for each of these phases, and if you know these secrets, you will be halfway to your goal of

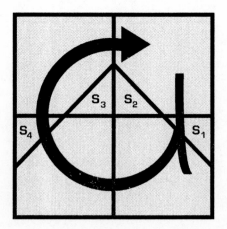

Figure 37 The Leader's Window

being a fantastic leader. The other half is remembering to apply each secret at the right time.

Secret 1

Phase 1, shown in Figure 38, is the *team orientation* phase. In this phase, the team needs to go through the Forming and Focusing stages of group development. This is especially important when you are creating a new team. It is also important when you are adding people to an existing team or losing some experienced team members. Even if the team is staying intact but is taking on new responsibilities or being given a new mission, this team orientation phase cannot be overlooked.

Remembering the stages of group development, you know that all members need to understand the team's mission, learn what they can contribute to accomplishing that mission, and believe that they are absolutely essential to the team's success. You also know that the group needs to buy into the mission and share your commitment to the team's goals. Members need a chance to ask questions, voice their concerns, take on specific assignments, and share their ideas about the best ways to organize the team to work effectively.

The secret to leading this team orientation phase is to use a balance of Styles 1 and 2. You need the directing style to take charge of the group, light a fire under everyone, and give members the information they need. Then you need to use the problem-solving style to get the team involved in identifying the scope of the project, the timing of critical events, the roles that each team member will play, and the ways that you will interact together. This also establishes a team norm for problem solving that will be needed later, when the team is rolling at full steam.

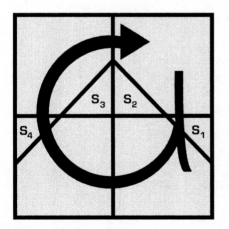

Start with S_1 to orient the group by explaining the team's mission and the members' roles on the team.

Then use S_2 to get the group's buy-in by involving members in identifying the best ways to work together.

Figure 38 Phase 1: Team Orientation

Secret 2

Phase 2, shown in Figure 39, focuses on *individual assignments*. Once the group is formed and focused in Phase 1 and everyone is clear about the overall team mission, its processes, and the responsibilities of each team member, the main question on each individual's mind is, "What do I need to do to deliver results in my areas of responsibility?" As the leader, you need to meet briefly with individual team members to make sure they know exactly what they need to do to honor the commitments they made to the group.

This is where the performance contracting process comes in. The individuals need to know what they are expected to accomplish and in what time frame. What are the deliverables and when are they due? Each one needs to have a clear action plan that will accomplish these goals, and you need to be aware of the plan so that you don't end up second-guessing anyone later on.

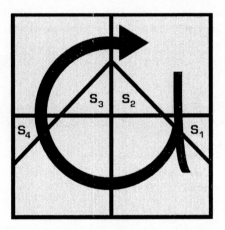

Use S_1 with individual team members to clarify roles and responsibilities and to start the performance contracting process.

Then use S_4 to empower individuals by delegating authority for the tasks they can handle on their own.

Figure 39 Phase 2: Individual Assignments

Each person also needs to be clear about the authority he or she has. What can I decide on my own? What can I just go ahead with? When do I need some input from you, the leader, or other key people, or the entire team? What decisions do you, as the leader, want to sign off on or make yourself?

And you and each team member need to be clear about critical checkpoints in the plan. Usually, there are a few key moments when timely communication is important. If these can be anticipated, it will be easier for you and your team members to manage your time efficiently.

The secret to being an effective leader in this *individual assignments* phase is finding the right balance between Styles 1 and 4. You need to do enough directing to clarify expectations so that there is no ambiguity about what the outcomes look like. And you also need to do enough delegating to empower people to handle their responsibilities. The performance contracting process enables you to do both—you are in charge of what gets done, and the team members are in charge of how. They are accountable for developing their own action plans, for asking for what they need from you in the way of support and decision making, and for anticipating critical points in the project plan.

You need to listen to members' plans and understand their needs. And in some instances, you may need to revise the proposal or insert an additional checkpoint. But the essence of this process is handing off responsibilities, and in most situations, if you have the right people on the team, Phase 2 is a quick check-in with each individual to clarify assignments and the authority team members have to handle them.

Secret 3

As shown in Figure 40, the work actually gets done in Phase 3. More time should be spent in Phase 3 than in any other phase. We call it the *work +*

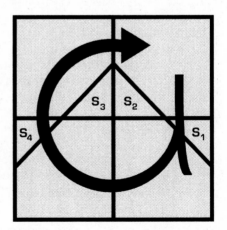

Use S_4 to delegate to the individual team members so they can apply their knowledge and skills to their responsibilities.

Use S_3 to develop individual team members when they need support to help them achieve the team's goals.

Figure 40 Phase 3: Work + Support

support phase to emphasize that when you let go, people usually need some type of support in handling their responsibilities.

After Phase 1, in which you got the group focused, and Phase 2, in which you clarified individual assignments, the prevailing need is to get out of the way and let your team members do what they are best at doing. They are the ones who have to get the job done on the playing field. They are being paid to handle significant tasks. You have to trust them and show them the respect you would want if you were in their position.

You also need to be available if and when members get stuck and need some input from you or some guidance about their work.

The secret to leading your team through Phase 3 is finding an appropriate balance of Styles 4 and 3. You have to do enough delegating to let people do their work and sufficient developing so that you stay informed and they get the support they require. This balance will vary from person to person and from assignment to assignment. Some individuals work best on their own; others need frequent check-ins to be sure they are on the right track. Some tasks present rather routine, familiar types of work. Others are new, unfamiliar, and very challenging.

Finding the right balance is an art. But knowing when to make your moves always comes down to two critical actions. First, you have to give people the space to do their work with your trust in them. Second, you need to be available to listen to your team members so they can use you as a sounding board and take advantage of your experience and your broader vision of the team's mission.

Secret 4

Phase 4, depicted in Figure 41, is probably the most overlooked aspect of building and sustaining high-performance teamwork. Once the individuals start to crank out the work in Phase 3, their focus is on their respective assignments, and they tend to lose their connection to the other people on the team. Even if they work closely with one or two other individuals, they pay attention to their own goals and deadlines and forget about the overall team mission.

If the individual initiatives are going to result in a solid team effort, the whole group needs to come together periodically for *team problem solving*. That involves bringing the group together to make sure the Performing stage is well coordinated. It also requires some managed leveling to keep the group energized.

To manage performance, team members need to take operational time-outs to keep one another informed about their progress and make one another aware of problems that are slowing them down or opportunities that are coming up. They need to work together to resolve the problems and organize for the opportunities. That means listening to the people who are on point

Use S_3 (distributed S_2) with the group to facilitate updates and coordinate team members' areas of responsibility.

Use S_2 to focus the group on continuous improvements by identifying problems and giving input to solutions.

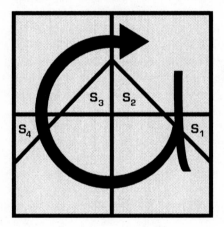

Figure 41 Phase 4: Team Problem Solving

for each responsibility, asking questions to help them think through the issues, and giving them suggestions or resources that can help them deliver results.

To manage the Leveling process, team members need to take developmental time-outs to revitalize the group. Sometimes that can be as simple as taking time to have some fun or to celebrate a success. At other times it may involve teambuilding activities, re-engineering processes, strategic planning, or other mechanisms for thinking continuously about alternatives to improve the way members are approaching their work.

Whether the time-outs are short or long, tactical or strategic, operational or developmental, they enable the team to capitalize on the synergy that results from group interactions. They are spontaneous and/or structured events that help team members connect with one another.

The secret to being successful with this team problem-solving phase is using the right balance of Styles 2 and 3. You should use Style 2 to structure the meetings, use time efficiently, and keep the meetings productive. In your areas of responsibility, you should also use the problem-solving style to give team members information about new developments and seek their input about any problems that you may be wrestling with.

Where team members have been empowered to handle various responsibilities, you need to use Style 3 to facilitate a discussion that links the distributed S2 process back to the team. With listening skills, you can structure the conversation by asking questions, encouraging openness, reflecting people's concerns, and summarizing key points. The goal is to have an open discussion in which those who are on point share their best thinking about critical decisions, get to hear other people's ideas, and can test the waters to see if a consensus exists.

If there is a consensus, the next step is making an action plan to implement the idea. If there is no consensus, the team member who is leading in that area of responsibility should still be empowered to make the decision. Your use of Style 3 with the group is an efficient way to manage the D2 approach to teamwork. The group doesn't sit around forever trying to get everyone's agreement. Team members give input to one another, but someone is always authorized to make the decisions.

In many organizations, Phase 4 gets addressed through quality circles, total quality management, or continuous-improvement teams. Many other buzzwords are used to rationalize the bringing together of groups of people to think about better ways of doing business. Unfortunately, too many of these initiatives are not fully integrated into the day-to-day interactions of intact work teams. Often, they take place outside the normal course of work activities, or they include a cross-section of people from different units who do not work together on a regular basis. Frequently, participants report that they had trouble getting focused and could not bring about meaningful changes.

For Phase 4 to work, team problem solving needs to be integrated into the normal flow of work and become a regular event that adds value to the team members' ability to accomplish their individual and collective goals. Successful self-directed work teams always build Phase 4 into their group norms. These teams create structures for sharing responsibility and can be successful only if the people who own the responsibilities have mechanisms for coordinating their efforts.

Core teams provide a similar structure for cross-functional units that are expected to use the strengths of their functional processes to accomplish a common mission. Again, Phase 4 is critical so that these people, who come from different parts of the organization and report to different managers, can maintain their focus and coordinate their efforts.

Whether you have a group of direct reports in a functional department, a new product team, a customer service team, a merger integration team, a task force, a committee, a quality team, a cross-functional team, or even a virtual team, you need to bring the whole group together periodically. And to do that successfully, you need to use a balance of Styles 2 and 3 to make team problem solving work.

HOW WELL DOES YOUR ORGANIZATION USE THE LEADER'S WINDOW?

All four phases of The Leader's Window are shown in Figure 42. This picture enables you to use the 1-2-D2-3-2-1 *group development* cycle while

PHASE 3
WORK +
SUPPORT

Use S_4 to delegate to the individual team members so they can apply their knowledge and skills to their responsibilities.

Use S_3 to develop individual team members when they need support to help them achieve the team's goals.

PHASE 4
TEAM PROBLEM SOLVING

Use S_3 (distributed S_2) with the group to facilitate updates and coordinate team members' areas of responsibility.

Use S_2 to focus the group on continuous improvements by identifying problems and giving input to solutions.

PHASE 1
TEAM
ORIENTATION

Start with S_1 to orient the group by explaining the team's mission and the members' roles on the team.

Then use S_2 to get the group's buy-in by involving them in identifying the best ways to work together.

PHASE 2
INDIVIDUAL ASSIGNMENTS

Use S_1 with individual team members to clarify roles and responsibilities and to start the performance contracting process.

Then use S_4 to empower individuals by delegating authority for the tasks they can handle on their own.

Figure 42 The Four Phases of The Leader's Window

simultaneously using the 1-4-3-2 *empowerment* cycle with individual team members. The Leader's Window is your guide to opening windows of opportunity at work. It is a road map for building high-performing teams. Most important, it shows you which windows need to be opened at what times so that you can become a highly effective leader.

With this picture in mind, take a minute to think about how it applies to you and your place of work. How do you see The Leader's Window being used in your organization? Unless your company has learned The L4 System, it is unlikely that The Leader's Window itself is being used, but most organizations do cover some of these four phases. Which phases are encouraged by your organization's culture? Which ones are done poorly or not at all?

When we put this question to groups of business leaders, there is usually a lively discussion about the missing pieces in their organizations. Most often, these leaders identify problems with Phase 1, *team orientation*. They talk about teams with unclear missions and lack of direction from above. Team objectives are not as clear as they could be, and limited time is spent on group discussions about what has to get done and how it will happen. As a result, people focus on their own assignments with little or no concern for the work of the overall team.

Phase 2, *individual assignments,* usually gets mixed reviews. In most organizations, the leaders say that they do a good job of giving out individual assignments. However, their team members often complain that the assignments they receive could be a lot clearer. The biggest concern about Phase 2 is not feeling truly empowered. Work is parceled out, but a true commitment of authority is often withheld and open conversations about the support people need rarely occur.

Phase 3, *work + support,* gets the best marks from most organizations. This is where the individual work gets accomplished, and most companies are pretty good at the first half of Phase 3—giving people lots of responsibility. It's the second half of Phase 3 that usually breaks down—providing them with support. Most organizational cultures strongly advocate the individual work ethic, but it is only the best leaders within those cultures who make themselves available to create developmental opportunities for their people.

Phase 4, *team problem solving,* gets overlooked in most settings. When Phase 1 is ignored, managers only deal with people as individuals and never consider Phase 4. In many teams that do go through a team orientation, people still get so busy and scattered that they won't stop to catch their breath. Even in organizations with institutional initiatives to use teams to improve quality, strengthen customer focus, or re-invent the way they do business, managers still say that little or no time is spent on continuous improvement in day-to-day operations.

Is your organization like these? Which phases do you do well? Which ones get overlooked?

PHASE 0

These discussions with managers about the phases that need the most attention have also taught us some new things. Several years after *The Leader's Window* was first published, we were working with the engineering department of a Fortune 500 company in the aerospace industry. Initially we were asked to train several hundred managers who had been given broad responsibility for designing and delivering precision components for jet engines. In their words, each of the leaders of these teams had "cradle to grave" accountability for their components.

Initially these leaders got training on techniques for analyzing technical problems and tools for streamlining inefficient processes. When we trained them to use The Leader's Window, they said it was the most practical training they had received because it focused on the real issue that consumed most of their time—people. They were like sponges, eager to learn and absorb how to organize a team, let the team members apply their knowledge and skills, and hold people accountable for delivering results.

They also taught us an important lesson. These "cradle to grave" team leaders were operating in a matrix where none of their team members reported to them—they all worked for heads of various functional departments. Since they were totally dependent on skill sets that they didn't own, they said The Leader's Window was a perfect tool for them. It showed them how to bring together team members from multiple parts of the functional organization, get them focused on the team's priorities and their roles in accomplishing them, and create structures for staying on top of the progress being made by individuals and by the team.

However, in one of the early training sessions, one of these engineers came up to the front with a hand-drawn transparency of the matrix and explained to us that there was a serious flaw (an engineering term) in our system. He said, "We don't have the luxury of starting with Phase 1. We have to start with Phase 0. Before we can bring our teams together, we have to talk with potential team members to see if they are interested and then talk to their bosses to get them assigned to our teams."

He was right. In their system they had to beg, borrow, and steal human resources before they could even think about Phase 1. So we thanked him and used his drawing in every subsequent training session.

We now explain Phase 0 as a parallel on the team level to what we had learned so many years before about leading P0 situations with individuals. In chapter 9, we said that P0 situations require HR strategies—training, reassignment, and/or selection of new players. We also said that to build a high-performing team, you have to select the right people, assign the right people to the right tasks, and give them adequate training. But these actions only put them on the playing field. You then have to use all the styles on an ongoing basis to ensure that all team members perform to their full potential.

We now understand that when you are putting together a new team, especially one where all the people don't report to you, P0 is not an individual concern; it is a team issue. Not every team starts with Phase 0, but a lot more do now than ever before. And in the wake of the rapidly growing economy of the 1990s, when the "war for talent" put renewed emphasis on attracting, developing, and retaining talent, it is an increasingly relevant issue for the new millennium.

As companies downsized in the early 1990s, the outsourcing phenomenon created a need to partner with people outside the organization. Globalization has spawned mergers, acquisitions, and strategic alliances that also necessitate partnering across previously well-guarded borders. Rapid changes in technology have pulled droves of systems architects and computer programmers from consulting firms into teams with corporate IT people. Studies of customers, competitors, vendors, and suppliers have sometimes created all sorts of teams that blend consultant methodologies and broad perspective with insider knowledge and deep understanding. Now we even have venture capitalists and e-commerce incubators nurturing dot-coms and helping the brick and mortars transform themselves into brick and clicks. There is some Phase 0 activity with all of these—lining up the players from inside and outside the organization who have the skills, resources, and motivation to be part of your team.

DOES ANYONE DO IT RIGHT?

Once we understood that Phase 0 existed and was critical to the success of today's teams, we also realized that there were many examples of this expanded Leader's Window right in front of our eyes. Think of athletic teams on the professional or even collegiate level. They offer a good view of the Window in action.

What do they do in the off-season? They recruit talent to replace the skills they have lost, enhance the skills that are coming back, and put pressure on the returning players to keep developing their skills so they can retain a position on the team. That's Phase 0.

What do they do in training camp? They introduce the new players to the returning squad, find out what each player has the skills to do, and get the group to bond. They also develop plays and game plans that identify specific responsibilities for each player under a variety of circumstances. That's Phase 1, forming and focusing the group.

Before the first game, the coach speaks to each player to make sure he or she understands what the team is counting on him or her to do—a personal pep talk about pride, commitment, personal accomplishment, and the success of the team. That's Phase 2, the individual assignments that each player will have to deliver on the playing field.

The season begins and the team takes the field. The players know their roles and specific assignments to carry out, but the coaches can't go onto the field with them. The coaches can offer encouragement, support, and even intense pressure to get the players to live up to their potential. But the individuals have to dig deep within themselves to do their part for the team. That's Phase 3, work and the support to go with it. And on occasion, a player will be pulled to the sideline or put on the bench for some problem solving about his or her role—those moments when all the support in the world isn't enough and you have to go to the end of the 1-4-3-2 cycle.

But most of the problem solving is done as a team. There are time-outs to stop the clock and regroup, chalk talks and pep talks at halftime, postmortems at the end of the game, and videotapes at the next practice. These group times can lead to new strategies, new tactics, new ways for players to be in sync with each other, or new players being added to the team. All of these are Phase 4 activities, mechanisms for looking at what's working and what's not and then making adjustments to improve performance.

Professional orchestras engage in similar activities in the same sequence. They audition new talent and sometimes recruit people with particular skills—Phase 0.

Early rehearsals are opportunities for players to learn who the other musicians are and what they can contribute, as well as to size up the types of music this particular group will be able to perform—the first half of Phase 1, forming the group. Later rehearsals focus on specific pieces with detailed instructions for each instrument and some specialized parts for key individuals—focusing, the second half of Phase 1.

The conductor will often speak privately to certain leaders about their roles in inspiring their sections to perform—Phase 2.

When the curtain goes up, the conductor sets the pace, provides feedback throughout the performance, and encourages each player to perform at the highest level. But ultimately, every individual has to put hands and/or mouth to instrument and reach inside to do what only he or she can do—Phase 3.

Some concerts have an intermission during which adjustments can be made, but most of the reevaluation comes in the next set of rehearsals, after the critics have spoken, sometimes with tapes so the group can hear what the audience heard and grow from their experience. The rehearse-perform-review-rehearse cycle continues until new auditions start—Phase 4.

Knowing how to look through The Leader's Window makes it easy to see this pattern. There are countless examples, from the sports world to the music world, from theater groups to political groups, from the financial services industry to the high-tech industry. In these final pages, you will read a few more stories of real leaders, some with the ability to see clearly, others who could have benefited from a clearer view of what makes teams work.

THE BEST COACHES IN THE BUSINESS

Bill Parcells is widely regarded as one of the best coaches professional football has seen. He turned around the New York Giants and took them to two Super Bowl championships. He turned around the New England Patriots and took them to the Super Bowl. And he turned around the New York Jets and took them to the AFC championship game. Just before he retired from football, Parcells (2000) wrote an article for the *Harvard Business Review* about what it takes to lead the highest-pressure teams in the world. What he learned from the school of very hard knocks is Window Wisdom at its finest.

Phase 1

After almost being fired following his first season, Parcells came to the conclusion that "to lead, you've got to be a leader." What did he do? He says, "On the first day of training camp, I laid it on the line: I told everyone that losing would no longer be tolerated. Players who were contributing to the team's weak performance would be given a chance to change, and if they didn't change, they'd be gone. It was a tough message, but I balanced it with a more positive one. I told them what I think a team is all about: achievement. Sure, they could make a lot of money in football and they could buy a lot of nice things, but the only permanent value of work lies in achievement, and that comes only with relentless effort and commitment" (Parcells 2000).

He outlined his values and his vision, put out a challenge to the entire group, and made it clear that there would be upside and downside consequences for the team and each team member. That was Phase 1—no ifs, ands, or buts about it.

Phase 2

Parcells's next move was right out of the book. He says, "After I talked with them as a group and established my credibility as a leader, I began talking with them personally. I've found that holding frank, one-on-one conversations with every member of the organization is essential to success. It allows me to ask each member for his support in helping the team achieve its goals, and it allows me to explain exactly what I expect from him."

What's his reason for doing this? He says, "Leaders can do everything right with their teams and still fail if they don't deliver their messages to each member as an individual" (ibid.).

Phase 3

When the whistle blows, coaches have to step aside and let the team go out and play. They have to use Style 4 whether they want to or not, although some are better at letting go than others. In that regard, Bill Walton has an interesting comparison of John Wooden and Bobby Knight. "While Wooden fostered hope, Knight represents the death of hope, the stifling control freak. Look at his coaching style: 'Get the ball, and look over here at me, and I'll tell you what to do. I'll put you in a position where you can win by one or two points, because it's my strategy in the end.' Wooden gave you the freedom to perform. He was the conductor of a free-form symphony. He always said, 'Don't look over here at the sideline. I've already done my job. When the game starts, it's about you guys having fun playing a game and doing your best' " (Walton 2000).

Joe Torre, who coached the New York Yankees to three consecutive World Series championships, has the same attitude. "Always, Torre was inclined to trust his players, unwilling to smother his clubhouse with rigid rules and loud language. 'Even in the midst of great adversity over the years, the only thing that has been constant has been his confidence in us,' Bernie Williams said" (Wojnarowski 2000).

Good coaches also balance their confidence in their players with a personal interest in each team member's ability and motivation to perform. Developing people means helping them perform to the best of their potential. In professional sports, where the salaries are astronomical and the egos are bigger yet, that is no easy task. Many people think of developing as the soft stuff, but Parcells's version is tough love.

He says, "As a coach, I've always tried to turn up the heat under my people, to constantly push them to perform at a high level. Creating pressure in an organization requires confrontation, and it can get very intense, very emotional. Confrontation does not mean putting someone down. When you criticize members of the team, you need to put it in a positive context. I've often said to a player, 'I don't think you're performing up to your potential, you can do better.' I also made it clear that my goals were his goals: 'It's in your best interest that you succeed, and it's in my best interest that you succeed. We really want the same thing' " (Parcells 2000).

Phil Jackson, the most successful coach in the NBA, has a similar reputation for tough love. "In practices he treats players respectfully, but he can get loud if someone isn't living up to his standards. Slack off and Jackson, who is 6'8" tall, beam-shouldered and deep-voiced, can be intimidating, 'He's definite about things,' says his longtime assistant coach Tex Winters. 'He doesn't let things slip. He's not afraid to go face to face with Kobe or Shaq or anybody' " (Farley 2000).

Jackson's players also value his support. "Bryant credits Jackson with helping him to become 'more aware' of what's happening on the basketball court. 'It sounds like a minor thing,' says Bryant, 'but it's very big when you're playing at this level to really be aware of everything around you.' Jackson's positive attitude has also helped O'Neal's confidence. 'This is a team that needed discipline badly, and I knew Phil could bring it,' said O'Neal, who threatened to leave after the '98–'99 season if the team didn't sign Jackson" (ibid.).

In most organizations, this Style 3 approach would get you a reputation as an in-your-face dominator, but in the world of Phil Jackson and Bill Parcells, those conversations can be very motivating. Parcells said that when he saw players who had retired, they often thanked him for how passionately he believed in them. His straight talk helped them believe in themselves.

In our experience with 360-degree feedback and executive coaching, we hear similar responses from managers to whom we deliver some very tough messages. These conversations are quiet, relaxed, very open, and extremely honest, and our role is 90 percent listening. What these sessions have in common with the NFL version of development is that we look people in the eye, give them straight talk about their strengths and weaknesses, and help them look inside their heads and hearts to decide for themselves what changes they want to make. Then we help them go back onto their playing fields to achieve their own standards of success.

Phase 4

In sports, Phase 4 happens in the huddle, on the sideline, in the locker room, and at practice. It can involve minor adjustments, changes in strategy, changing team members' roles and responsibilities, replacing injured players, and upgrading the talent pool. Those are all tactics.

Anyone can call a time-out, but the ultimate goal of Phase 4 is, in Parcells's words, "building a culture of success. To win games, you need to believe as a team that you have the ability to win games. That is, confidence is born only of demonstrated ability. That may sound like a catch-22, but it's important to remember that even small successes can be extremely powerful in helping people believe in themselves" (Parcells 2000).

He goes on to say, "When we start acting in ways that fulfill these goals, I make sure everybody knows about it. I accentuate the positive at every possible opportunity, and at the same time I emphasize the next goal that we need to fulfill. If we have a particularly good practice, then I call the team together and say, 'We got something done today; we executed real well. I'm very pleased with your work, but here's what I want to do tomorrow. . . .' When you set small, visible goals, and people achieve them, they start to get it into their heads that they can succeed" (ibid.).

Phase 0

In the sports world, as soon as the season is over, coaches start recruiting for the next one. Even during the season, they are on the lookout for new talent. Constantly recruiting new talent is the hallmark of every winning franchise, and Parcells was as good as anyone at spotting the keepers.

We talked about the free-agent economy in chapter 10 because the mind-set that challenges big league coaches has found its way into the mainstream workplace. Even Parcells has seen the changes. Bemoaning the fact that he used to have the luxury of developing players, he says, "Today, you no longer have the time to develop your talent in the old way. When I started, coaches reworked maybe 8% or 10% of their teams every year. Now it's sometimes as high as 30%."

He then says, "You have to be extremely careful about the new people you bring on. You can do some serious damage with a few bad choices." And he concludes, "It's not always the one who has the best reputation or even the most outstanding set of talents. It's usually the one who understands what it will take to succeed and is committed to making the effort" (ibid.).

Managers often ask us which is more important, ability or motivation, and we always say both. If you don't have the skills, you can't play, and if you don't have the motivation you won't apply the skills you have. Parcells's experience is interesting in that even in a profession dominated by highly specialized skills and on-the-field experience, motivation is extremely important. A lesson for all of us is that as we look for the skills we need, we also have to look for people with drive. Or as Parcells puts it, "I'm convinced that if you get people onto your team who share the same goals and the same passion, and if you push them to achieve at the highest level, you're going to come out on top" (ibid.).

A WOMAN WITH A CLEAR VIEW

Another example of a highly successful executive is Carly Fiorina. Since 1999, she has been president and CEO of Hewlett-Packard, and the highest-profile and most talked-about businesswoman in the country. At HP and in her previous position as CEO of Lucent, this extremely effective leader has demonstrated an elegant mastery of the four phases of The Leader's Window. While we have not had the pleasure of seeing her apply the phases to one team, the business press is full of stories about her mastery of the principles. Here are some examples of how, in taking charge of and reinventing her new company, she has brought the phases of The Leader's Window to life.

Phase 1

After being appointed to her CEO post, Fiorina wasted no time articulating a vision for the company and the mission of her executive team. At a company event in June 2000, she told employees that her vision was to remake HP into "a winning e-company with a shining soul" (Burrows 1999).

She has since gone on to restructure and reorganize the company in dramatic ways—at times shaking up her senior staff, some of whom have chosen to leave. But she has utilized her impressive problem-solving and influencing skills to win the loyalty of many. For example, two of HP's major divisions, the laser printer and inkjet printer divisions, together contributed almost two-thirds of the company's profits. Aware of customer frustrations over the fact that they could not swap inkjet printers and laser printers, Fiorina made the bold move of dismantling the two divisions and merging them. The

VPs leading those divisions, Neal Martini and Vyomesh Joshi, suddenly found themselves with diminished autonomy and authority over sales, marketing, and manufacturing.

While a lesser leader would have found herself searching for new executives to run the newly formed division, Fiorina used her Style 2, problem-solving, skills to involve these key players in the transition. The result was that both Martini and Joshi retained senior positions in the merged printer division and, in the fall of 2000, HP introduced a fully compatible line of inkjet and laser printers.

Phase 2

Fiorina has also demonstrated an uncanny ability to unleash the talents of her staff in concrete and focused ways. Consider the case of Ann Livermore, a senior lieutenant of Fiorina's who formerly ran the server division. Upon learning of a widely reported customer complaint about the difficulty of doing business with HP when it came to large purchases, Fiorina set her sights on the problem.

Key customers were complaining that they were frustrated with the need to deal separately with different divisions. Fiorina charged Livermore with the formidable task of consolidating dealings with the company's top hundred customers and turned her loose. One customer, e-tailing giant Amazon.com, had used twenty of HP's top-of-the-line servers to run its site the previous Christmas. Building on that success, Livermore—with Fiorina backing her all the way—approached Amazon with a proposal to supply the company's entire infrastructure. The result of Livermore's barrier busting was a contract with Amazon to provide the company not only all of its server needs, but printers and personal computers as well, a deal that was ultimately worth hundreds of millions of dollars.

Phase 3

The day after announcing the Amazon deal, Fiorina crowned Livermore "Amazon Ann, warrior woman" at a company meeting attended by hundreds of employees. This simple move gave Livermore some well-deserved recognition for a job well done—and encouragement to maintain her commitment to extraordinary customer service. This is but one example of Fiorina's capacity to give people the freedom to execute and to support them when they perform.

In many ways, Fiorina's approach on the individual level is a blueprint for the effective execution of Phase 3. "Our people are very proud and smart," she said in an interview just after taking the reins at HP. "So, first, you reinforce the things that work, and then you appeal to their brains and address what doesn't"(Burrows 1999). And consider this observation of her high-support approach from her days at Lucent. "As a leader, she has a personal touch that inspires intense loyalty . . . When Lucent was spun off from AT&T in early 1996, Fiorina stayed up all night with Comptroller Jim Lusk and other employees to make sure the prospectus for the stock offering was perfect. And it's not just business: When the wife of a senior Lucent executive fell ill recently, Fiorina helped make sure he got medical advice, doctors, and emotional support. 'I think the world of Carly. She's a great leader,' says Nina Aversano, president of North America for Lucent's global service-provider business" (ibid.).

Phase 4

Fiorina has also demonstrated her capacity to be a team problem solver and troubleshooter of the highest order. Consider the case of HP's basic research division, HP Laboratories. At the time of Fiorina's arrival, the lab was experiencing morale problems due to a rash of funding cuts. In her typical "high-touch" fashion, she began visiting the lab herself to see what the problems were. During one visit she met with the researchers for a product called Cool Town, a Web technology that enables various devices to communicate with one another.

She soon learned that one of the key researchers on the project, Stan Williams, an expert in nano-technology, the science of manipulating atomic structures, was planning to move his team out of HP to another test and measurement company because of the lack of support he was getting. Fiorina moved quickly to secure funding for the project and reassert HP's commitment to the research. The result was that Williams and his team stayed on, HP is building a new multi-million-dollar nano-fabrication facility, and morale throughout HP's research community is way up.

A WINDOW ON THE HIGH-TECH WORLD

Not every Window master is as well known as Carly Fiorina, but we have seen some good ones in our work. Barry Carden, a Charter Oak director, tells the story of a highly successful executive, Ed, who at the time we worked with him was a senior vice president at a high-tech Fortune 500 company. Since then, he has advanced to other positions of greater responsibility. As you read this case, you will understand why. In his own way, without knowing about The Leader's Window, Ed successfully led his team through its four phases as he took over a major operating division that needed to implement broad-based changes.

Phase 1

According to Carden, Ed started out by calling together his direct reports for an initial team meeting. In essence, what he said at the start of that meeting was, "Here's who I am, this is how I like to operate, and here's what you need to know about my style in order to have a good working relationship with me." He then went on to say, "Here's my value system and my vision. I need to change this culture. For this business to win, we've got to start doing business a very different way."

In the context of that organization, it was clear to everyone in the room that Ed was saying that in order to turn the business around, he was going to have to be very directive in the early stages of the changes.

Once he made it clear where he stood with the group and what his expectations were, he began scanning the group for their input. He was orchestrating the Focusing stage of group development by making himself an expert in what they knew and getting their buy-in at the same time. To both motivate his team and get their involvement, he would say things like, "This is where we need to go; there is no doubt about it. And what I need is for you guys to help set the strategies in place that will get us there."

Phase 2

As soon as he felt that his team was "onboard," Ed shifted his focus to clarifying goals for individual performance. He started saying to people, "These are the goals you will be accountable for and the behaviors you need to exhibit. I'm going to measure your success based on those behaviors—and I'm going to give you ongoing performance feedback on how you're doing." He went on to say, "In fact, I'm going to tie 51 percent of your salary at the end of the year to your ability to accomplish these objectives."

Following this meeting, Ed worked with each individual member of the team to establish the specific measures of success. He didn't want to leave any room for guesswork or confusion about what he needed each person to accomplish. In these one-on-one discussions, not only was he able to make his expectations concrete, but he also found out more about his new reports, what they were confident they could handle on their own, and when they anticipated needing some input from him. In essence, without ever calling it performance contracting, Ed applied the PC process perfectly.

Phase 3

As soon as he saw that individuals on his team were clear about their roles and were ready to run with the ball, Ed was very good at getting out of the way. Knowing that everyone was clear about the team's mission and his or her role in accomplishing that mission, he was comfortable delegating full authority to his team.

Once everyone was off and running, he continued to delegate to individuals but always modeled the type of leadership style he wanted them to use with their people by offering ongoing feedback and support when they needed it. Says Carden, "He was constantly communicating with his people on an informal basis, saying things like, 'Here's what you're doing that's helping the business and here's what you're doing that's hindering it.' And once a month he would sit down with each of them to review their goals. He gave people a strong sense that they belonged and always let them know where they stood."

Phase 4

As time passed and individual members were fulfilling their respective roles, the work of the team as a whole became increasingly complex. It was at this critical point that Ed managed to harness the power of the group—and the individuals—without giving up control. Remember, he had oriented the team in Phase 1 by empowering each member with different team responsibilities, thus creating distributed leadership within the team. Now, in Phase 4, he brought everyone back together to coordinate their respective efforts.

Speaking about this phase, Carden said, "He was able to maintain control and a sense of accountability with the team by bringing rthe team together for open communication among the otherwise free-wheeling individuals.

"He was also able to manage the size of the team as it grew to twenty members. Using team problem solving, he decided (with lots of input) to charge three subgroups with the authority to make decisions on behalf of the total team. To expedite this, the entire team met until they signed off on each subgroup's authority. Then each subgroup would go off with its designated leader, make its decisions, and bring them back to the team to keep the other subgroups updated and identify new problems that were surfacing."

By paying attention to both the needs of the group and the capabilities of the individuals on his team, Ed was able to maximize his individual and collective resources. As Carden put it, "He was truly remarkable at getting people to really feel empowered and get beyond the bureaucracy that previously hindered the organization."

What you've just read in the above case illustrates the secrets of The Leader's Window perfectly. This leader started out with a clear articulation of his vision and operating style. Then, by soliciting input from his team regarding strategy, he gained the buy-in that turned his personal vision into a collectively owned team mission. That was Phase 1, team orientation.

Next the leader focused on individual roles and responsibilities, set parameters for individual success, and gave team members huge responsibilities. That was Phase 2, individual assignments.

Then he got out of their way and gave them ongoing feedback as to how they were doing. He also gave them guidance whenever they needed it. That was Phase 3, work + support.

Finally, he capitalized on the collective resources of the group by creating a forum for mutual support. Later he revitalized the team by reorganizing it into subgroups charged with authority over various aspects of the team's work. That was the ultimate Phase 4. Not only did he bring the group together for team problem solving, but he also shifted meaningful responsibilities to the team at the same time.

A WINDOW ON COMMUNICATIONS

Tony Daloisio, another Charter Oak director, tells a success story in which all the right things happened. A major telecommunications company had identified the need to shift its new product development group to create a faster, more efficient process in an area that was growing too fast to tolerate a traditional organizational hierarchy.

"Bill, the senior vice president in charge of network services" says Daloisio, "realized that, over time, the company had created a functional organization with very strong fiefdoms within the various segments of the division. As more products were being developed and customers realized the potential for even more possibilities, marketing requests surged to the point where the organization could no longer respond as swiftly and effectively as it needed to in order to retain its market share.

"When you think about this problem in terms of organization alignment, the environment was putting competitive pressure on this department. New developments by competitors and extremely tight time frames for getting products to market had made their functional structure outmoded. The change required some sort of restructuring. The challenge was to reorganize in a way that would work. And that meant focusing on the culture of the overall organization as well as the departmental norms, which could be impacted by Bill's leadership."

The process began with our helping Bill realize that his use of leadership styles, which was in line with the culture of the organization, fell into a 1-4 profile. He would give his instructions to each of his respective charges and then delegate responsibility for implementation to each of them. When that assignment was completed, he would give them new directions. Essentially, the whole flow of work was centered around his position.

While this seemed to work well for him as a one-to-one leader, he realized that the individuals he was giving duties to were not communicating cross-functionally with the other people on the team. The result was a much slower and less efficient product development cycle than was needed. Somehow team members needed to know more about what everyone else was doing, and the work needed to be better coordinated.

The culture and the structure of the division both had to be addressed. Unless this leadership pattern changed, there was not much point in reorganizing the team. So, to help Bill manage this change successfully, Daloisio worked with him to implement the four phases of The Leader's Window.

Phase 1

Bill's first step was to call a meeting of his executive team. He pointed out that the product development cycle, with its six stages of design, piloting, redesign, test marketing, redesign, and marketing, needed to be streamlined in order to more effectively meet market demands. He invited input from his team, asking for their suggestions on how they thought the process could be improved.

In addition to providing a great deal of input, the meeting generated a lot of excitement over the prospect of creating new ways of operating. Everyone was excited about being listened to by people in other areas, some perhaps for the first time. They were even more enthusiastic about the possibility of having input into one another's areas.

And, most important, since everyone participated in redesigning the product development cycle, everyone felt ownership over the cross-functional teams that were created to improve the workflow.

This was Phase 1, team orientation. In this case, it was not enough for the leader to set the group members off on a new mission and get their ideas about how to make it happen. It required giving people a chance to understand one another's perspectives. This gave everyone an idea of what the problem looked like from Bill's vantage point. It also enabled people to start feeling as if they were part of one big team instead of several small units.

Phase 2

Next, Bill met with each of the individual members of his executive team and focused on how the new configuration would affect each of their roles and responsibilities. Once everyone was clear about expectations, Bill directed each executive to go off on his or her own to do what needed to be done.

This was Phase 2, individual assignments, and it didn't take the executives long. They were already good at Phase 2.

Phase 3

Since he knew that he was asking his executives to operate in a different way, Bill did not leave them alone, as was his usual habit. "He knew he was asking his people to think and operate differently," says Daloisio, "so he was careful not to create conditions in which they felt overwhelmed. He knew he had to make some fundamental changes in his leadership approach if he expected his people to make changes with the people below them. Instead of riding herd over every aspect of every product's development, he offloaded responsibility and authority for overall development, and his job became more of a counselor or coach."

In Phase 3, work + support, the biggest change was on the part of the leader. He let his team have more control than he ever had before, but, instead of just disappearing, as many leaders do when they first let go, he still met with his team members on a regular basis. The difference was that now he was helping them figure out their challenges instead of parceling out assignments and directing their work.

Phase 4

Group meetings, which prior to the change had rarely been held, and were at the worst one-way communications from Bill and at the best report-and-update sessions by various executives, took on quite a different form. Cross-functional project teams were set up to break down the functional barriers that had previously proliferated throughout the organization, and coordinators were assigned for each of the project teams. Meetings consisted of brief presentations by various project team coordinators and often lengthy problem-solving sessions in which Bill and other executives offered support and guidance to the project teams.

Phase 4, team problem solving, was absolutely critical to making these structural changes really work. Without it, the new cross-functional teams would still have had a short-term positive impact; however, if the leaders of these teams had not built communication links, the new teams would have become as isolated as the old ones.

The overall result of the problem-solving process was a dramatic increase in cross-functional communication and dramatic improvements in the product development and delivery cycles. The short-term, quick-fix solution would have been to have some cross-functional meetings or maybe even put together a couple of cross-functional teams. The long-term benefit came from involving people in a structured and organized way that led to shared responsibility for the process and the ultimate outcomes. Using The Leader's Window is what made that happen.

A VIRTUAL WINDOW ON TEAMWORK

What is a virtual team? A group of people who need to work together to achieve results while working in remote locations. A virtual team may be spread throughout a building, or across a campus, a country, a continent, or the globe. It can involve people from multiple departments, customers, suppliers, vendors, consultants, and even competitors. What virtual teams have in common is that their members spend little time, if any, in face-to-face communication in one location.

This type of team isn't new. Field forces of independent salespeople working their own product lines and territories have operated in a virtual environment for years. So have many executive teams, in which all the leaders spend 99 percent of their time on their own businesses and pay attention to other businesses or the overall company only when they have to.

What is new is that these teams have become more widespread. As the business world has grown increasingly complex with globalization, outsourcing, mergers, acquisitions, joint ventures, and spin-offs, the need to partner across previous boundaries has grown exponentially. Simultaneously, our ability to communicate via conference calls, videoconferences, voice mail, e-mail, networked computers, and the Internet has made it much easier to create bridges across traditional organizational borders. Consequently, more managers need to know how to make these long-distance teams work.

In this era of virtual everything, team myth #8 is already forming around the virtual concept. Calling a team *virtual* implies that the team materializes in some ethereal realm and results magically appear. The reality is that they take a lot of work.

We have always known that some teams have more need for the group phases (1 and 4), while others have a greater need for the individual phases (2 and 3). Some, such as a product development team or a consulting team, need a lot of coordination and precision hand-offs. Like a basketball or football team, they need to plan, practice, play, and take time-outs as a group. Other teams, such as a sales force, a call center team, or a team of HR generalists in different units, work very independently. Like a golf team or a track-and-field team, all they do as a group is offer each other encouragement and see how their numbers add up at the end of the day.

The Individual Phases

Most virtual teams are of the track-and-field variety, with a strong need for Phases 2 and 3 but limited need for Phases 1 and 4. The case in chapter 10 about Henry, the "performance contract guy" with nineteen direct reports working on three continents, is a perfect example. The way he formulated performance contracts, gave his managers the freedom to implement them, was available for coaching, measured results, gave feedback, and provided recognition was a perfect match for his far-flung team. These Phase 2 and Phase 3 activities were exactly what his highly independent managers needed.

The Group Phases

Henry's team spent a little time on Phase 1. When he took over the division, Henry brought all of the team members together to meet him, learn about each other's issues, and get aligned around specific priorities. He also used that time to initiate the PC process to take the planning to a deeper level.

Henry also spent some time on Phase 4. He brought all of his managers together twice a year to look at their results, discuss initiatives that cut across their locations and businesses, identify better ways to work together, and build relationships with one another. These events didn't last long, but they enabled members to stay connected to one another.

Henry also did some Phase 4 with subgroups. You may recall that one of the things Henry liked about the PC process was that managers often discovered that they had the same goals and could help each other achieve them. When this occurred, Henry would make sure that those managers stayed in contact with each other throughout the year—via e-mail, voice mail, or videoconference—to keep abreast of ways they could help each other. Henry's role in these meetings was to facilitate the conversation so that his managers could do most of the talking, a good use of Style 3 to orchestrate the D2 process.

Henry didn't totally ignore the group phases; he just didn't dwell on them. They served a purpose, not unlike an annual sales conference or a quarterly meeting of a senior leadership team. They kept people linked to organizational goals and one another without distracting from their ability to run their separate organizations.

PASS THE VIRTUAL WINDOW CLEANER, PLEASE

Virtual teams like Henry's have been around for a long time and are relatively manageable. Those that require more coordination—the football variety—are more challenging. These teams need all four phases, and since they generally don't have the luxury of coming together frequently, they have to find other ways to deal with Phases 1 and 4.

Charter Oak director Jonathan Spiegel has helped a variety of organizations build virtual teams. He observes, "The needs of the group are similar to those of more traditional teams; however, each stage of development takes longer. Virtual teams can't reach the Performing stage unless they form and focus, and many teams can't do that unless they meet face-to-face and develop some level of relationship with each other."

We recently experienced this dynamic with a team that had three locations: New York, California, and Germany. Members had a strong need to collaborate with one another and some serious cultural issues to resolve before they could get on the same page.

Phase 1, Unfinished

The Forming half of Phase 1 started smoothly but remotely—the team's initial meetings occurred via videoconference. The head of the team, Alfred, a senior VP based in New York, was clear with everyone about the team's purpose: to launch a software system for global human-resource management. He also did a good job of making sure all the team members knew why they had been asked to join the team and understood the broad roles they would play.

Problems started in the Focusing aspect of Phase 1. Instead of clarifying the goals of each subteam, defining specific responsibilities for each team member, and making decisions about how to make the team function smoothly, Alfred addressed only lines of authority. Knowing that the virtual nature of the team could create coordination problems, he assigned a site coordinator for each of the three locations. This person's job was to ensure that there was accurate flow of information among the three sites. Joann was site coordinator for New York, Klaus was site coordinator for Germany, and Andy was site coordinator for California. The problem was that all the team members did not agree with this delineation of responsibilities, and Alfred didn't invite any discussion about the assignments. In hindsight, it was not surprising that conflicts began to emerge almost immediately.

Phase 2, Never Done

To compound the lack of focusing in Phase 1, Alfred didn't deal with Phase 2, either. He assumed that each of the coordinators knew what it meant to maintain communication, and he left them on their own to do so. What he failed to realize was that each of the three coordinators began to see him- or herself as project team leader and behaved as such.

Phase 3, Not Pretty

Klaus, who had the most technical depth, started making decisions that would take the project in a particular direction. Joann, whose office was across the hall from several important players at world headquarters, was the most politically savvy, and she began making conflicting decisions for the project. Andy simply watched as these conflicting decisions traveled electronically around the globe.

These conflicts and power struggles were the result of the team's failure to resolve ambiguities about goals and roles in Phase 1. The team had Alfred's mission instead of a shared one, and it had a hierarchy instead of clarity about how the work would be organized. These problems were exacerbated by Alfred's failure to discuss expectations with each site coordinator.

An additional complication for this team was the virtual team myth that technology holds all the answers. In the absence of a clear operating plan, the team members relied heavily on teamwork software designed to organize the team's information. In their three separate locations, they believed that since they were conscientiously completing their information-sharing templates, they were effectively organized for success. The reality was that they were doing work, but it wasn't focused or productive.

The final straw was that there were disconnects driven by cultural norms that came to light only after we had the benefit of sitting in on conference calls in all three locations and could observe the group dynamics from the perspective of each location. In New York City, team members would begin meetings by engaging in small talk to build informal relationships and by comparing notes about what they were hearing from firm headquarters about their project before tackling the agenda. The reaction in Hamburg was frustration regarding the Americans' failure to get down to business and inability to forgo socializing and what they saw as gossiping instead of getting the work done. The response in San Francisco was laid-back puzzlement about the power struggle between New York and Hamburg.

After several electronic ping-pong communications that left Andy increasingly frustrated and his California team increasingly hamstrung, Andy contacted Alfred and asked him to intervene on behalf of the team. He told Alfred that Joann and Klaus—and their various loyalists—were becoming increasingly at odds with each other and sabotaging everyone's work. It was at that point that Alfred asked us to help.

Phase 4, Help!

Our first step was to talk to the team members to get their perspective on what was going on. As we went to each location, we could also observe the breakdowns among the three sites. It was clear to us that this team had no chance of succeeding. To Alfred's credit, he was willing to call a time-out for some serious Phase 4 work.

When all three virtual subgroups convened on neutral territory to talk out their problems eyeball to eyeball, one of the first issues they addressed was the cultural disconnects. In hindsight, the team members had not dealt with this dimension of forming, but once the dynamic was named, it was easy to resolve.

Then they spent some time talking about the political nature of the project and the need to balance making prudent technical decisions with providing their various stakeholders with user-friendly tools. Klaus and his people learned some things about the firm's dynamics that made them more sensitive to the needs of Joann and her group. Joann's camp learned some things about the limitations of some of the more popular software packages that some people at headquarters were lobbying for. In the end, each side developed an understanding of the other's perspective and an increased appreciation for the formidable challenges that lay ahead for them together—as one team.

After that, it was easy to address the myth that the software would do all the work for them. It was painfully clear to all that the people issues were paramount. Then the team was able to clarify specific deliverables and time frames for each location, identify all the roles and responsibilities that were needed to coordinate across the three sites, establish milestones and checkpoints for monitoring progress, and create norms for keeping the team's dynamics on track.

Phase 2, At Last

Since Alfred had never done Phase 2, we advised him to spend time with Joann, Klaus, and Andy separately to clarify expectations with each of them. In these one-on-ones he made it clear that Klaus was the technical guru and that Joann would have primary responsibility for the rollout of the new infra-structure. He also asked Andy to monitor the team's progress and empow-ered him to call a time-out whenever it was needed.

Phase 3, Rolling

After these meetings, things got better, and a lot of productive work started to happen as the team began piloting the new system. As time went on and the high-stakes global rollout was about to happen, tensions once again increased. Joann began to complain that Klaus was making decisions that would be unpopular in key offices around the world, and Klaus began to complain that Joann was slowing the rollout by second-guessing his technical decisions.

Phase 4, A Quick Fix

This time, they called time out immediately. The team had a videoconference, named what was happening, identified what had to happen so the team could succeed, and clarified who owned each critical decision and the roles others would play in the process. After an hour of Phase 4, they were back on track.

Had Alfred brought the team members together in Phase 1 to really get to know each other and start building the relationships that are so crucial to suc-cessful teams, they might not have wasted the first six months. They could have clarified operating norms, decision-making processes, and protocols for com-municating. The members could have avoided some of the conflicts fueled by cultural and style differences, as well as disconnects about who was ultimately accountable for what. They could have focused their individual efforts pro-ductively and achieved the high level of performance they eventually got to.

But the reality is that this is a perfect example of how The Leader's Window most often works. It is extremely rare for any team to cover every-thing at the outset. Even the ones that do a very thorough job of forming and focusing can't anticipate everything that will come up. And if they tried to, the work might never get started. While this virtual team had other complications to deal with, it was fairly typical in the way it got down to work quickly. What made this team unusually successful was its willingness to take a Phase 4 time-out and refocus when it was clear that it was having problems.

A DOT-COM THAT GOT IT RIGHT

eZiba.com is an Internet and catalogue retailer of artisan-made goods from around the world with its headquarters nestled in North Adams, Mas-sachusetts, an area often referred to as "Silicon Village." Unlike so many Web-based retailers, eZiba was meeting with great success. This was one dot-com that had a very clear window on the e-commerce world, and it provides a good example for any business that wants to make The Leader's Window work.

Phase 0, Executive Search

When eZiba grew to such a size that it needed experienced leadership, founders Amber Chand, Deborah Jackson, and Dick Sabot painstakingly searched for the right person to assume the position of CEO for their gem of a company. When they found Bill Miller, previously FAO Schwartz's EVP of Catalogues, Marketing, and FAO.com, they knew he was the one. Besides having the right credentials, he knew how to build a strong executive leadership team and how to lead eZiba.com forward onto the uncertain, challenging road ahead, or, more appropriately, into the ambiguous virtual space to be conquered.

Phase 1

When Bill first arrived, he spent a lot of time listening and learning about eZiba. But it didn't take him long to clearly articulate the direction he wanted to take the company. Prior to Bill's arrival, the highly spirited founders, along with their launch team, perceived the company as an Internet/technology company. Bill brought the senior team together to challenge this view and set the record straight by identifying his vision of eZiba as a retail company that happens to be powered by the Internet as a channel to sell merchandise. He said, "We are here to sell product, not to be an innovator in technology. The Internet empowers us to do our job; it does not define us."

This new focus required some changes in strategies, roles, and the way business was done. So Bill created a new organizational chart, identified his leadership team, and clarified the scope of their responsibilities. As one might imagine, there was some resentment and pushback regarding Bill's focus as some members of this highly entrepreneurial launch team resonated more with the identity of innovative technology than with retail. However, Bill brought his team together on numerous occasions to get them focused by encouraging dialogue, questions, and open debate.

Bill also used some Style 1 and Style 2 at a companywide meeting. He expressed his vision and the shift in strategy while encouraging questions and dialogue from his larger team. He also set in motion a CEO FAQ (frequently asked questions) virtual forum where eZiba employees could ask questions and express concerns via e-mail, and responses would be sent out to the whole community. This served as a way to get buy-in to strategic initiatives that affected the entire organization.

Phase 2

After meeting with his new leadership team and the whole organization, Bill met with the individuals from his team to further clarify their new roles and responsibilities as well as his expectations. He began the performance contracting process by clarifying expectations and goals. He also used this time to better understand his team members' needs, learning about their strengths as well as the areas where they might need more direction and guidance.

A few months later performance reviews were due, and Bill used those meetings as an opportunity for further discussions about current performance, desired results, long- and short-term goals, and what he could do to provide support.

Phase 3

Here's where Bill really shined. He knew how to empower his team members. He delegated well and backed up his people with support as much as possible. When mistakes were made, he framed them as learning opportunities, encouraging thoughtful review followed by the clear message "let's move on." His team members described Bill as follows: "Bill enables others to act. He makes his team members feel important and accountable. He is a great listener and he engages in dialogue without preconceived ideas. He leads with heart."

The chairman of eZiba's board, Dick Sabot, compared Bill to Phil Jackson. He said, "While talking to the general manager of the Chicago Bulls, Phil once asked the question, 'What do you think motivates people at the core?' The GM replied, 'I think it's fear and greed.' Phil disagreed. 'I think what motivates people is love and pride.' I think Bill Miller is like Phil Jackson; he leads eZiba with love and pride. He is attuned with the times and understands the leadership style people need in a culture like eZiba. He instills pride, leads by example, and is trusting of the knowledge of others and empowers others because he trusts them."

The work that Bill did in Phases 1 and 2 combined with his skill in Phase 3 made his transition into eZiba very smooth. During the first six months, his team gradually shifted gears. His leadership team was committed, the employees were doing everything as expected, and the new direction was starting to take shape.

Success drives the need for change. With a number of new players on the team, including Bill, major shifts in roles and responsibilities were taking place on the leadership level as well as trickling down throughout the organization. eZiba had grown to more than sixty employees and opened an office in New York and a warehouse in Pennsylvania. All these factors added to the complexity of the organization and required the institution of more policies and defined processes. Additionally, the downward shift in the economic climate for dotcoms presented this team with extraordinary challenges.

Phase 4

Although Bill had provided opportunities for his team to come together in Phase 1, he wasn't satisfied: As far as he could tell, there was no visible resistance to the new direction, but he had a lingering suspicion that everyone wasn't 100 percent onboard; the demands of the business hadn't allowed for enough time to do the work that the team needed to do; and the challenges were so steep that he knew he had to do more. Bill knew that if he was patient, people would eventually come around, but patience isn't a virtue in the dot-com world.

Bill understood that it would take some dedicated time to move his team to the level he wanted. Although time is difficult to spare in the fast-paced realm of a start-up, Bill was willing to invest the resources necessary to build a high-performing team—an unusual phenomenon for a dot-com. He brought in Cathy Crosky, a Charter Oak consultant, to provide some guidance and facilitate a two-day off-site meeting for his executive leadership team.

Bill wanted the meeting to provide an opportunity to clarify the team's mission, establish strong working relationships to coordinate the high level of interdependency necessary at that stage of eZiba's growth, clarify operating principles, generate agreements about specific actions, and enlist total commitment from his team. Bill had great confidence in the talents of his executives and described them as thoroughbreds, each doing a good job of running his or her own race. His concern was that "they need to run the same race in order for eZiba to win." That was his Phase 4 objective.

The hard work of the team during the two-day off-site meeting paid off and was a turning point for eZiba. The results of the eZiba leadership team's collective effort enabled them to refocus by gaining clarity about the team's mission and engaging in a thorough process for learning how to best work together. It also precipitated some additional work in Phase 2 by alerting Bill to the fact that he needed to provide more Style 1 clarification about new roles and performance expectations.

Phase 2, Round 2

After the off-site meeting, Bill revisited the performance contracting process with several of his team members who needed further role definition and clarity about expectations and deliverables. As a result of the work the team had just completed, these conversations were much more complete than when Bill had first arrived. It helped that he was clearer about what the organization needed and the executives were clearer about their roles in making the business successful. Equally important was the trust that they had developed during the Phase 4 work. The result was much more open dialogue about what these executives could accomplish on their own and what they needed in the way of support.

Phase 3, More 3

At this point, Bill was interested in finding out if there was anything more he could be doing to increase his effectiveness as a leader, so he completed the L4 Self questionnaire and asked his team members to fill out L4 Others about him. Even though one of Bill's clear strengths was Style 3 and he used it frequently with his team, the feedback indicated that his people wanted more. Since Bill had a highly competent team, he was surprised—if anything, he had expected them to want more independence, not less.

When he talked with his team members, they said they wanted more focused one-on-one time with Bill to think out loud about what they were doing. Some wanted his advice, others wanted to make sure their thinking was aligned with his, and some just wanted a sounding board.

Why did these highly capable executives want more Style 3? They said that the e-nature of eZiba plus the charting of new territory created a continuous state of ambiguity and change. They told him that their performance bar would always be extremely high, and they valued his insights about how to reach for the stars.

The nature of a new start-up such as eZiba is that there is so much to do that one-on-one meetings don't happen as frequently as many team members need, and many of them get postponed. Everyone understood that reality, but Bill agreed to be more available, and his executive team committed to letting him know when they needed him.

Phase 4

One other change after the off-site meeting was that Bill brought his team together on a weekly basis for updates, information sharing, and group problem solving as well as coordinating work. He encouraged his team to put problems and opportunities on the table to keep the team focused on improving the present while creating the future. Bill also used these times to praise his team's efforts and celebrate their successes.

In the past, people used to skip team meetings if they had anything else on their agenda that they felt was more important, but after the team realized the value of face-to-face communication, these times were labeled as "sacred" and considered essential for the team and company to get the results they needed.

The team members also scheduled two follow-up sessions to review the agreements they had made, evaluate progress, and make sure they were working together as a team.

As a company, eZiba takes pride in the "Rare Finds" component of their business, where they source rare and valuable treasures from around the globe. We think they did a great job in finding Bill Miller, another rare treasure.

NOW IT'S YOUR TURN

So that's it. Now you know the four secrets, and The Leader's Window is yours to put into action—in person or online. It might sound easy, but it's not. It takes a lot of practice to get it all to work the way it's supposed to. Just remember that practice makes perfect. If we have learned anything about leadership, it is that experimentation is a hallmark of the very best. Trial and error is the way the hardest lessons are usually learned.

One way to focus your leadership experimentation is to measure your ability to do what good leaders do. In the beginning of this book, we gave you a short questionnaire about the styles you tend to use. As we said in chapter 7, if you would like to find out how others perceive you, the companion questionnaire, The L4 Other, is available in hard copy or online. It gives you feedback about the styles you actually use and the ones you ideally need to use to help your people perform to the best of their potential.

On the next page is another questionnaire that we use with our clients to help them implement the L4 System. The Leader's Window Baseline Measure asks eight simple questions about how well you lead teams—one question for each step of The Leader's Window.

Immediately after learning the system, program participants are asked to complete this questionnaire. Knowing that perception is reality, we also collect feedback from their direct reports and their managers and, in some cases, their peers so that they can compare what they think they do to what they really do. We also collect suggestions about specific actions they should take to increase their effectiveness.

Approximately a month after learning the system, the participants get a report that shows which phases of the Window are going well and which ones need some attention. That helps them make plans with their managers about their own development needs as a team leader. It also helps them talk with their team members about ways to strengthen their team's performance. After twelve months, we come back with the same eight questions in the Leader's Window Follow-up Measure to give them ongoing feedback about how they are doing.

You can start that process for yourself right now. Just take a few minutes to think about a team you lead and rate yourself. If you want to compare your self-assessment to others' perceptions, it's easy to do. Just show them these eight questions, ask them how they would rate you, and ask for suggestions about ways you can improve.

Or, if you want to maintain confidentiality, we would be happy to do a study for you. Just send us an e-mail at cocg@cocg.com or go to our website at www.cocg.com and click the "send us a message" button. We will send you back an e-mail with a link to our Internet Assessment Site, where you can register your feedback givers. When you do that, each of them will get an e-mail

LEADER'S WINDOW BASELINE MEASURE

Directions: Circle the number that reflects how good you are at each step of leading a team.

Scale: 5 = excellent, 4 = very good, 3 = good, 2 = fair, 1 = poor

1.1 Bringing team members together, explaining the team's mission, and clarifying team members' roles

 5 4 3 2 1

1.2 Getting team members' buy-in by involving them in organizing the work, defining responsibilities, and identifying the best ways to work together

 5 4 3 2 1

2.1 Meeting with individual team members to confirm the goals they are accountable for and clarify their action plans for achieving them

 5 4 3 2 1

2.2 Giving individuals authority for the tasks they can handle on their own and identifying the areas where they will need support

 5 4 3 2 1

3.1 Letting go—getting out of team members' way so they can apply their knowledge and skills to accomplishing team goals

 5 4 3 2 1

3.2 Being available to provide the support that individuals need; helping team members solve problems in their areas of responsibility

 5 4 3 2 1

4.1 Bringing the team together for updates, problem solving, and opportunity identification; facilitating input to each other's decisions

 5 4 3 2 1

4.2 Inviting input to your decisions, being decisive about ways to continuously improve performance, and adding talent to strengthen the team

 5 4 3 2 1

with a link to a confidential questionnaire that they take online. When all the questionnaires are completed, we will send you a confidential report.

Whether you do just a self-assessment or collect feedback, do it yourself or have us do it for you, the value of this exercise is to identify which phases of the Window you need to strengthen. Armed with this information, start the experimentation. Make an action plan that will guide you to try some of the ideas you've been thinking about as you read this book. Then see what happens.

Reading a book is easy compared to making the ideas work. So give yourself permission to experiment and learn from your mistakes. We all make them.

And if you get stuck, don't forget to lead upward or outward or in any direction you can—so that you can get the support you need to keep yourself on the cutting edge of your own window of leadership.

CHARTER OAK CONSULTING GROUP

We wish you good luck with your leadership efforts, and may all your windows be open with the right people in the right places at the right times!

Our firm, the Charter Oak Consulting Group, specializes in leadership, teamwork, and organizational effectiveness and provides consulting, training, and assessments in all three practices. Please let us know if we can help you put The Leader's Window into action.

Charter Oak Consulting Group, Inc.
Mill Crossing Office Park
1224 Mill Street
East Berlin, Connecticut 06023
(800) 741-7788
www.cocg.com

Epilogue

We'd like to leave you with a short summary of the most important points about working with individuals and group dynamics in ways that lead to high-performing teams. These are the keys for making The Leader's Window work for you.

TEAM = INDIVIDUALS + GROUP DYNAMICS

Teamwork doesn't mean sending each individual team member onto the playing field to do his or her own thing. Neither does it mean bringing everyone together for endless discussions to try to achieve total consensus on every decision. Instead, it requires working with each individual in unique ways that are right for that person relative to the tasks he or she has to accomplish. It also requires orchestrating the group dynamics that develop when those individuals come together as a team.

Figure 43 Team = Individuals + Group Dynamics

THE FOUR KEYS TO WORKING
WITH INDIVIDUALS

1. Use all four leadership styles on a regular basis. When you use them, integrate your actions so that your communication and recognition strategies are consistent with the decision-making methods you need to use.

2. Remember Leadership by Anticipation:

• Try to avoid the 1-4-1 frustration cycle.

• Use the 1-4-3-2 empowerment cycle to surround your delegating with the up-front directing, ongoing developing, and timely problem solving that lead to true empowerment.

• Use the 1-2-3-4 development cycle to give team members increasing amounts of responsibility without feeling overwhelmed.

• Use the 4-3-2-1 intervention cycle to gradually reinvolve yourself as performance drops or pressures mount.

3. Match your main style to each team member's performance potential (ability + motivation) on a task-specific basis.

4. Use the performance contracting process to implement 1-4-3-2 with each team member.

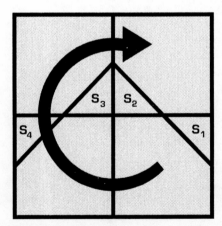

Figure 44 The 1-4-3-2 Empowerment Cycle

THE FOUR KEYS TO LEADING
GROUP DYNAMICS

1. Use Styles 1, 2, and 3 to lead the group dynamics that surface when your team members come together. Don't use Style 4, delegating, with the group, because if it's everyone's responsibility, it's no one's responsibility. If you can't be there, delegate to an individual and ask him or her to lead the whole group or a subgroup.

2. Let a D2, distributed leadership, mindset guide you to organize the team's work into manageable responsibilities for which individual team members are accountable.

3. Stay focused on the group development cycle to help members move through the stages in a way that leads to the greatest level of productivity.

4. Remember to shift your style of leadership to match the stage of group development the team is in by using

- Style 1, directing, to launch the team in Stage 1, Forming

- Style 2, problem solving, to organize the team in Stage 2, Focusing

- Style 3, developing, to give individuals responsibility with team support and to coordinate the team's work in Stage 3, Performing

- The intervention cycle, moving from developing to problem solving to directing as required, to manage refocusing and re-forming in Stage 4, Leveling

Figure 45 Performing: Distributed Style 2

THE FOUR PHASES OF
THE LEADER'S WINDOW

Move through the four phases of The Leader's Window to simultaneously lead individuals and the group dynamics:

1. *Phase 1—team orientation.* Use Style 1, directing, to orient the group by explaining the team's mission and members' roles. Use Style 2, problem solving, to get the group's buy-in and identify the best ways of working.

2. *Phase 2—individual assignments.* Use Style 1, directing, with individuals to clarify roles and begin performance contracting. Empower individuals with Style 4, delegating, to assign authority for tasks they can handle on their own.

3. *Phase 3—work + support.* Continue Style 4, delegating, by allowing team members to apply their knowledge and skills. Use Style 3, developing, to support individuals whenever they need help achieving team goals.

4. *Phase 4—team problem solving.* Use Style 3, developing, to facilitate a distributed responsibility approach by supporting team members in their leadership responsibilities. Use Style 2, problem solving, to focus the group on continuous improvement by identifying problems and getting input to your decisions.

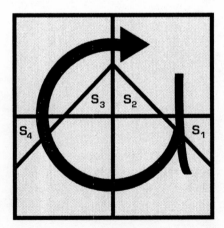

Figure 46 The Leader's Window

References

ACKNOWLEDGMENTS

Bales, R. F. "Task Roles and Social Roles in Problem-Solving Groups." In *Readings in Social Psychology,* 3rd ed., edited by N. Maccoby et al. New York: Holt, Rinehart & Winston, 1958.

Blake, Robert R., and Mouton, Jane S. *The Managerial Grid.* Houston, Tex.: Gulf, 1964.

Fiedler, Fred E. *A Theory of Leadership Effectiveness.* New York: McGraw Hill, 1967.

Hersey, Paul, and Blanchard, Kenneth. *Management of Organizational Behavior: Utilizing Human Resources,* 4th ed. New York: Prentice Hall, 1982.

Lewin, K., Lippett, R. and White, R. "Leader Behavior and Member Reaction in Three Social Climates." In *Group Dynamics: Research and Theory,* 2nd ed., edited by D. Cartwright and A. Zader. Evanston, Ill: Row, Peterson, 1960.

Likert, Rensis. *New Patterns of Management.* New York: McGraw Hill, 1961.

Reddin, William J. "The 3-D Management Style Theory." *Training and Development Journal,* April 1967, 8–17.

Stogdill, R. M., and Coons, Alvin E., eds. *Leader Behavior: Its Description and Measurement.* Research Monograph No. 88. Columbus: Bureau of Business Research, The Ohio State University, 1957.

Tannenbaum, Robert, and Schmidt, Warren H. "How to Choose a Leadership Pattern." *Harvard Business Review,* March–April 1958, 95–102.

INTRODUCTION

Bennis, Warren, and Nanus, Burt. *Leaders: The Strategies for Taking Charge.* New York: Harper & Row, 1985.

Blanchard, Kenneth, and Johnson, Spender. *The One-Minute Manager.* New York: William Morrow, 1981.

Covey, Stephen R. *Principle-Centered Leadership.* New York: Summit Books, 1990.

Depree, Max. *Leadership Is an Art.* New York: Dell, 1989.

Goleman, Daniel. *Working with Emotional Intelligence.* New York: Bantam, 1998.

———. *Emotional Intelligence: Why It Can Matter More Than IQ.* New York: Bantam, 1994.

Peters, Thomas J., and Waterman, Robert H. *In Search of Excellence: Lessons from America's Best-Run Companies.* New York: Harper & Row, 1982.

Senge, Peter M. *The Dance of Change.* New York: Doubleday, 1999.

———. *The Fifth Discipline Fieldbook.* New York: Doubleday, 1994.

———. *The Fifth Discipline: The Art and Practice of the Learning Organization.* New York: Doubleday, 1990.

Taylor, Frederick Winslow. *The Principles of Scientific Management.* New York: W. W. Norton, 1911.

Wheatly, Margaret J. *Leadership and the New Science.* San Francisco: Berrett-Koehler, 1992.

CHAPTER 3

Allman, T. D. *Miami: City of the Future.* New York: Atlantic Monthly Press, 1987.

Croce, Paul Jerome. "A Clean and Separate Place: Walt Disney in Person and Production." *Journal of Popular Culture* 25 (winter 1991), 91–103.

"The Forbes 400: The Jean Pool." *Forbes,* October 1999, 302–303.

Gibney, Frank, Jr. "Iacocca Gets New Wheels." *Time,* 1 February 1999, 36–37.

Greenberg, Herb. "Will Out of Style Etailers Soon Be Fashionable Again?" *Fortune,* 10 January 2000, 214–16.

Hume, Scott. "Jack Greenberg's New Populism." *Restaurants and Institutions,* 1 July 1999, 10.

Labich, Kenneth. "The Seven Keys to Business Leadership." *Fortune,* 24 October 1988, 58–66.

Lee, Louise. "Gaping Holes at the Gap." *Business Week,* 24 April 2000, 54–55.

Mitchell, Russell. "Inside the Gap." *Business Week,* 9 March 1992, 58–64.

Moser, Penny. "The McDonald's Mystique." *Fortune,* 4 July 1988, 113–14.

Nordland, Rod. "Saddam's Long Shadow." *Newsweek.* 31 July 2000, 32.

Ola, Per, and D'Aulaire, Emily. "Sixty Billion Burgers and Counting." *Reader's Digest,* September 1987, 39–44.

Serwer, Andy. "The New Richest Man in the World." *Fortune,* 13 November 2000, 98–124.

CHAPTER 4

Blake, Robert R., and Mouton, Jane S. *The Managerial Grid.* Houston, Tex.: Gulf, 1964.

Dearlove, Des. *Business the Bill Gates Way.* New York: Amacom, 1999.

Gates, Bill. "Reorganization: A Necessary Art." *Executive Excellence,* December 2000, 3–8.

Gillespie, Marcia Ann. "Winfrey Takes All." *Ms.,* November 1988, 50–54.

Gimein, Mark. "Smart Is Not Enough." *Fortune,* 22 January 2001, 125–33.

Goodman, Fred. "The Companies They Keep . . . [Madonna and Oprah Winfrey]." *Working Woman,* December 1991, 52–57.

Janis, Irving L. *Victims of Groupthink*. Boston: Houghton Mifflin, 1967.
Labich, Kenneth. "The Seven Keys to Business Leadership." *Fortune*, 24 October 1988, 58–66.
Schendler, Brent. "Damn the Torpedoes! Full Speed Ahead." *Fortune,* 10 July 2000, 68–71.
Schifrin, Matthew, with Newcomb, Peter. "A Brain for Sin, and a Bod for Business." *Forbes*, 1 October 1990, 162–66.
Simison, Robert. "For Ford CEO Vasser, Damage Control Is the New Job One." *Wall Street Journal,* 11 September 2000, cover story.
"Yitzhak Rabin and Yasir Arafat." *Time,* 3 January 1994, 40–49.

CHAPTER 5

Alter, Jonathan. "How He Would Govern." *Newsweek*, 20 July 1992, 40–42.
Banham, Russ. "The Deal of the Decade." *Reactions*, August 1998, 12–20.
Brooks, Steve. "Warren's Whim." *Restaurant Business*, 1 March 1998, 32–40.
"Clinton: The Company He Keeps." *New York Times*, 13 September 1992.
Cone, John. "How Dell Does It." *Training and Development,* June 2000, 58–70.
Dell, Michael. *Direct from Dell*. New York: HarperCollins, 1999.
Fisher, Anne B. "Buffett's School of Management." *Fortune*, 14 June 1993, 116–18.
Gelb, Leslie H. "Is Clinton Tough Enough?" *New York Times*, 8 November 1992, Op. Ed. section.
Huey, John. "America's Most Successful Merchant." *Fortune*, 23 September 1991, 46–59.
Loomis, Carol J. "The Inside Story of Warren Buffet." *Fortune*, 11 April 1988, 26–34.
Stewart, Thomas A. "GE Keeps Those Ideas Coming." *Fortune*, 12 August 1991, 41–49.
Walton, Sam. "Sam Walton in His Own Words." *Fortune*, 29 June 1992, 98–106.
Will, George. "'Peace Psychosis' in the Mideast." *Newsweek,* 8 January, 2001, 64.

CHAPTER 6

Bailey, Steve. "Loser of the Decade." *Boston Globe,* 15 December 1999, Business section.
Briones, Maricris G. "A Funny Thing Happened on Turner's Way to Building a Network: A TV Revolution." *Marketing News*, 29 March 1999, E2–E12.
Bryant, Adam. "The Making of a Media Giant." *Newsweek,* 20 September 1999, 34–36.
Carney, James. "Why Bush Doesn't Like Homework." *Time,* 15 November 1999, 46–50.
Henry, William A. III. "History As It Happens." *Time,* 6 January 1992, 24–31.
Kao, John J. *Managing Creativity*. New Jersey: Prentice Hall, 1991.
Landler, Mark, with Smith, Geoffrey. "The MTV Tycoon: Sumner Redstone Is Turning Vicacom into the Hottest Global TV Network." *Business Week*, 21 September 1992, 56–62.
Meeks, Fleming. "The Sneaker Game." *Forbes*, 22 October 1990, 114–15.
"Merger Brief: One Mouse, Many Windows." *The Economist,* 19 August 2000, 60–67.

Spector, Robert. *Amazon.com: Get Big Fast*. New York: HarperCollins, 2000.

Tedeschi, Mark. "Can Fireman Put Out the Fires at Reebok?" *Sporting Goods Business*, 4 January 2000, 10–12.

Veverka , Mark. "Plugged In: Is It Amazon.com? or obfuscation.com?" *Barron's*, 25 September 2000, 58–62.

CHAPTER 8

Hersey, Paul, and Blanchard, Kenneth. *Management of Organizational Behavior*, 4th ed. New York: Prentice Hall, 1982.

CHAPTER 11

Hirsh, Sandra Krebs, and Kummerow, Jean M. *Introduction to Type® in Organizations*, 3rd ed. Mountain View, Calif.: CPP, Inc., 1998.

CHAPTER 13

Burrows, Peter. "HP's Carly Fiorina: The Boss." *Business Week*, 2 August 1999, 67–72.

Dumaine, Brian. "Who Needs a Boss." *Fortune*, 7 May 1990, 52–60.

Farley, Christopher John. "The Philospher Coach." *Time*, 20 March 2000, 61–62.

Orsburn, Jack, Moran, Linda, Musselwhite, Ed, and Zenger, John. *Self-Directed Work Teams*. New York: Business One/Irwin, 1991.

Parcells, Bill. "The Tough Work of Turning Around a Team." *Harvard Business Review*. November–December 2000, 179–184.

Walton, Bill. "Basketball's Tarnished Knight." *Time*, 29 May 2000, 96.

Wojnarowski, Adrian. "Torre Proves Nice Guys Finish First." *The Record Online*, 13 October 2000 (www.bergen.com/wojnarowski/wojspx13200010131.html).

Index